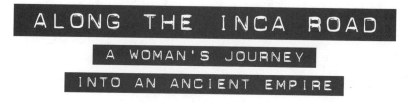

ALONG THE INCA ROAD

A WOMAN'S JOURNEY
INTO AN ANCIENT EMPIRE

Karin Muller

ADVENTURE PRESS

NATIONAL GEOGRAPHIC
WASHINGTON, D. C.

Published by the National Geographic Society
1145 17th Street N.W., Washington, D.C. 20036

First Printing, September 2000

Interior Design by Kathleen Cole.
Printed in U.S.A.

CONTENTS

CHAPTER 1

THE THIN RED LINE

T he map has been my undoing. Whenever it comes time to move I climb on my bed and stand on tiptoe to peel it off the ceiling. I carefully trim the edges, thickened with layers of yellowing tape, and fold it away. For a while I even forget about it. Then one day, when I'm sitting in my new place surrounded by piles of kitchenware and camping gear, I open a box and there it is. I think about slipping it inside my old toxicology textbook— somewhere I won't find it for years. Then I go get some more tape, stand on my bed, and tack it back up. Just one more time.

Twelve years ago I sat down on a whim and drew 21 historical highways onto that map—the Silk Road, the Salt Trail, the Burma Road, the Ho Chi Minh Trail....I used a thin red marker of indelible ink, and some of it bled through onto the table underneath. At the time I was annoyed that I would have to live with the consequences of such a foolish act.

Ever since then I've lain in my bed at night and let my thoughts wander along those roads. My eyes always gravitate to one line that runs down the spine of the Andes, along the world's second-highest mountain range. It starts on the border of Colombia, just south of the point where Central America peels away from its squat motherland like the spout of a teapot. The road curves in a great quarter-moon arc to the south and east, through Ecuador and Peru. To the west it is flanked by the barren coastline, in places so dry that the idea of water falling from the sky is the stuff of myth and fairytales. To the east lies the dark and impenetrable Amazon, sending endless octopus arms snaking up the Andean mountainside until they wither in the thin air and fierce cold. My red line wanders through the wrinkles of those snowcapped peaks until it reaches the sacred blue waters, the birthplace of ancient civilizations. Lake Titicaca—the very name sounds like the beating of exotic drums. From there it drops arrowlike toward the bottom of the world, through Bolivia, Argentina, and Chile. The Inca Road. I search for hidden valleys and forgotten villages in the shadow of its mountains until I fall asleep.

And I dream.

I dream of vicuñas flowing like liquid gold across the Andean plains, their hooves pounding the frozen earth as they flee the human chain tightening across their flanks. They are the Golden Fleece of the Andes, and their gossamer wool is the finest on Earth. In Inca times it was sent in yearly tribute to Cuzco, where the sacred sun virgins spun it into exquisite garments to be worn by the emperor for a single day, and then ritually burned.

I dream of the *caballito*, reed boats that still ply the coastal waters of northern Peru. They are rightfully named "little horses" for the way they prance through the surf. Their bows curve gracefully into long, tapering points, a shape that hasn't changed in 1,500 years.

ALONG THE INCA ROAD

COLOMBIA

Quito • • Otavalo
ECUADOR + *Cotopaxi* 19,347 ft
Riobamba • • Latacunga
Ingapirca • • Achupallas
Guayaquil • • Cuenca
Tumbes • • Nambija
Caxas • • Huancabamba
Piura • • Chachapoyas
Cochabamba • • Leymebamba
Huanchaco • • Cajamarca
Chan Chan • • Trujillo

PERU

Barranca • • Vilcabamba
Lima ★ • Machu Picchu
□ • Ollantaytambo
□ • Cuzco
Nazca • • Picotani
Puerto Inca • *Lake Titicaca*
□ • Puno • Island of the Sun
★ • La Paz
Oruro • • Cochabamba
Copacabana • ★ Sucre

BOLIVIA

Uyuni •

SOUTH

BRAZIL

AMERICA

ARGENTINA

Santiago ★

CHILE

★ Present-day country capital

□ Inca ruins

— Inca road

0   miles   800
0   kilometers   1200

Present-day country boundaries shown.

I wake up. I'm on a business trip, too exhausted to remember what state I'm in or the color of my latest rental car. I can still taste the thin mountain air, feel the spongy moss beneath my feet. This place I'm in, with its beige walls and anonymous flower-print furniture, isn't real. I struggle to find my way back into the landscape of my dreams, and fail.

One day I wander into a travel store. I know I shouldn't. I know exactly where it will lead. But I can't stop myself. It's like falling in love.

I tell the man behind the counter that I'm looking for a laminated map of South America and dry-erase pens. They have only plain paper. Secretly I'm relieved. I take it home. I use indelible ink. I stand on tiptoe, tear down my world map, and put the Andes in its place. And then I lie down and look up. There's a secret beating fierce and hot inside my chest. It's hard to breathe.

I'm going.

The weeks that follow are only half real. I sit through meetings. I shuffle papers around my desk. The moment I get home, I move into overdrive. I stay up late at night, researching the Inca Road, polishing my Spanish, and sweating off months of candy machines and late-night coffee. I write out several feet of cue cards with Quechua vocabulary words and tape them to my refrigerator, the living room mirror, and across from the toilet. I stuff them into Ziplock bags and hang them over the side when I do laps in the community swimming pool. My bicycle takes up residence in my living room.

Daily chores fall by the wayside. The milk runs out first, then the vegetables and meat and cheese. I plow through my supply of canned stews and smoked oysters. For three days I eat nothing but rice, olive oil, and onion soup mix. I wander into the kitchen at

2:00 a.m, stare at empty shelves, and I drive to the grocery store. I stand in the checkout line practicing my Quechua glottal stops. Everyone thinks I have hiccups. On the way home I'm so starved for vegetables that I rummage through my shopping bags and pull out a head of broccoli. I nibble around its edges. Several lights later I realize that I'm gnawing on the stem. The next car over is a BMW. The driver is staring at me. Every muscle in his face tells me that he thinks I'm crazy. I don't care. I have a dream.

I put away the groceries and stagger off to sleep. In the morning I find shampoo in my freezer and hot dogs in my desk drawer.

My checklists get longer, the days get shorter, and a mountain of gear begins to accumulate on the living room floor. Sunscreen and syringes, iodine tablets, batteries, clothing to suit all climates from blistering desert to the snowcapped peaks of the world's second-highest mountain range. I gradually pack away my normal life—power of attorney to my mother, a will, and good-bye e-mail lists. Christmas gifts properly wrapped for yet another holiday spent away from home.

Everyone knows that something's up. Friends come to visit and find my refrigerator full of film. My housemates discover the frizzy balls of what were once pantyhose, until they shared the dryer with my Velcro-laced expedition bags. I inadvertently pack away my Chapstick and show up at work with lipstick on.

I read several inches of Inca books each week. I discover *The Conquest of the Incas.* The bedroom walls around me dissolve into an epic story that spans a continent. The place-names that connect that long-lost Inca Road suddenly spring to life. Cuzco, where an obscure tribe successfully repelled a neighboring war party and began its long journey down a road that would one day make it the most powerful empire in the Southern Hemisphere. Quito, where the reigning Inca ruler died unexpectedly, leaving behind two sons who coveted an empire that had room for only one king. Five bloody years later the civil war finally ended with the victory of the battle-hardened northern son. Tumbes, where a motley band of 160 Spaniards arrived and set off to conquer a land of ten million. Cajamarca, where the newly crowned Inca emperor was enjoying a victory bath, not knowing that within 24 hours he would be a Spanish captive, his warriors dead, his empire in ruins. For nine months the Inca Road became a river of gold and silver as the world's greatest ransom flowed from the four corners of the empire to buy the freedom of their god-king. The ransom paid, he was tried, sentenced, and....

The phone rings. It's National Geographic. "You got the grant," a disembodied voice says.

"Me?"

"Yours was one of the most popular proposals." *Why me? Didn't they check my résumé? I'm not qualified for this.* "Television should be calling you this afternoon...." *You've mixed me up with someone else.* The National Geographic grant had been a long shot, my application wedged in between those from fields as diverse as anthropology, mountaineering, ecology, archaeology. I wonder what category they put me in. Vagabond, probably.

"When is your team leaving for Ecuador?" the voice is asking.

Team? It's just me, on a shoestring. Leaving whenever.

"September first," I say firmly. "We'll be ready."

The Society's television division assigns a part-time cameraman to help me document the trip. His name is John Armstrong. He speaks Spanish, seems amenable to hitchhiking, and looks like he can carry a small elephant up a steep mountain pass. He's 46, gray-haired, and vegetarian. No meat. No cheese. No eggs. No milk. He wants a detailed itinerary of where we'll be each day. So does National Geographic. Suddenly my thin red line isn't enough anymore.

The heart and soul of my journey is an exploration into the unknown. Six unscheduled months to take advantage of every opportunity that comes my way—to spend time with farmers plowing their fields and to cross the high plains with a llama caravan. To participate in festivals and attend weddings, births, and sacred ceremonies.

National Geographic is intrigued by the idea, and scared to death. "What will you be doing on day 17?" someone asks. "I have no idea," I answer honestly. They panic. I go home and rewrite my proposal, replacing every "might" with "will." Do I know the family whose wedding I propose to be at on page two? "Of course." I lie, knowing that somewhere along 3,000 miles of villages and mountain paths I am sure to see births and deaths and everything in between.

In vain I try to explain the concept of a "hero's journey"—not the modern Indiana Jones of Hollywood fame, but the protagonists of ancient mythology the world over, from the Chinese to the Iroquois. These heroes are often the most ordinary folk. Some have to be tricked into undertaking their journey. Others go willingly. They are not the strongest nor the bravest, nor even the most deserving. But they all share one trait: They are traveling into the unknown. It is an internal journey as much as a movement through a foreign landscape—a personal odyssey through uncharted territory. They will encounter dragons—real and imagined, within and without—find shelter among strangers, and falter, fearful, then move on. They will all, at some point, have to reach beyond themselves. In the end they return with new knowledge—of themselves, of the world, of the act of journeying itself—to share with those who stayed behind. It is this final step that turns them into heroes. "Anyone," I say, "can be a hero. You don't need to travel halfway around the world. Starting a new job is a heroic act, or having a child...."

"You're not pregnant, are you?" National Geographic asks.

But in the end, they take a chance and let me go.

I settle into the plane seat and close my eyes. When I next wake up, my other life—the real one—will finally begin.

CHAPTER 2

TO THE NORTHERNMOST
REACHES OF THE EMPIRE

FIELD NOTES: The doctor sat me down and whacked me on the head with a guinea pig until the poor thing died, then tore it open to figure out what diseases I had.

That thin red line I'd drawn on my map had been somewhat simplistic. In reality there was not one Inca Road but many. The most famous one—the High Road—ran down the spine of the Andes from northern Ecuador 3,000 miles south into Argentina and Chile. A second road kept pace with it along the coast. In between there were hundreds of connectors, feeders, highways, and byways. The result was a 15,000-mile network that crisscrossed the Inca empire like a spiderweb, allowing its rulers to conquer new territory, administer their people, and collect tribute. The Inca Road was the nervous system that kept the kingdom running smoothly. And in the end, it was also the conduit that allowed a virus—a small group of Spanish conquerors—to penetrate into the heart of the vast nation and cut off its head.

I planned to use the High Road as the backbone of my journey south to Chile. From time to time I would leave this *Capac Ngan*—Beautiful Road—to venture along its feeders in search of remnants of an empire conquered 500 years ago. My expedition would begin in Otavalo, at the northernmost reaches of the Inca Empire.

Otavalo was once a major settlement along the Inca Road. It was here, a hundred years before the conquistadores arrived, that the voracious Inca war machine was finally fought to a standstill—for a while—by the equally fierce and utterly desperate Otavalo Indians. The landscape still resonates with traces of their bloody struggle: *Yawar Cocha,* the Lake of Blood, where the Inca once dumped the corpses of seven thousand defeated warriors, turning the waters red. And in the people themselves. The Otavalo Indians are as unwilling to bend to modern influences as they had been to their Inca conquerors. Not for them the ragged T-shirts and housefront cafes that cater to the burgeoning tourist trade. Here and there among Otavalo's drab streets I caught bright flashes of color, as elusive as butterflies. The Otavalo Indians were even more beautiful than their intricate weavings and carved bamboo flutes. The women wore long black dresses with frilly white blouses and loop upon loop of golden beads around their necks. They held their shoulders proudly and took tiny steps, but bargained fiercely and laughed long and merrily among themselves. They looked like the offspring of ferocious desert warriors and elegant Spanish courtiers in fancy dress.

Modern-day Otavalo was disappointingly unexotic—gray, boxlike buildings huddled up against grayer streets and a dusty central square lined with tourist cafes. It only gradually revealed its true nature in subtle anomalies—old women selling hard-boiled eggs from handwoven baskets, Andean corn with marble-size kernels, and vulcanizing shops on every corner. Here and there the sidewalk looked slightly gnawed, as though the city's rats were sometimes desperate enough to eat cement.

It was half a day before I raised my eyes above the second floor and saw the Andes. They towered. They loomed. In an instant they reduced Otavalo to an inconsequential speck in the shadow of those soaring peaks.

I had arrived.

Late in the afternoon I stumbled across a crowd gathered four layers deep around a reedy, melodramatic voice. The normally reserved Indian women were standing up on tiptoe, craning their necks to see. I wormed my way inside. A long-haired man in baggy pants was describing with great enthusiasm and realistic pantomime the local illnesses that his magic pills could cure. "Do you have gas?" he asked an older Indian paying rapt attention from the front row. "Are your farts in Otavalo heard and— *piueeew!*—carried on the wind all the way to Quito?" The audience roared while the old man nodded solemnly. "Do you eat and eat"—he guzzled like a pig at a trough—"but have no energy to work?" His shoulders slumped forward and he shuffled half a step before falling to his knees. "Do you have trouble urinating? Diarrhea and vomiting?" His list went on, each symptom more graphic than the last. When he had run through his list of human ailments, he whipped out a notebook and passed around repulsively realistic photographs of diseased body parts. His coup de grâce was a vivid drawing of an intestinal tract that looked like it had been dragged behind a truck.

The problem diagnosed ("Fear not, I won't abandon you in your moment of need!"), he set about providing the cure. He mixed up fresh lemon juice, strained it through his teeth, and added honey ("not sugar, which dissolves the liver!") and a few drops of food coloring ("stand back!"). The lumpy mixture turned fire-engine red and brought a communal gasp to the audience's lips. With great solemnity he reached into his sleeve and withdrew a thick piece of aloe. He peeled it slowly, offering a nonstop litany of health cures and tips. "Avoid calcium! It weakens bones and causes oh-stee-oh-poroh-size. Do you know what that is? Bone cancer!"

When he had a handful of the sticky aloe pulp he immediately slathered half of it into his filthy hair. "A wondrous shampoo! Overnight your baldness will disappear! And if you desire it, a heavy mustache will grow where there was the merest wisp before!"

He squeezed the rest of the aloe until it oozed through his fingers into the bloodred pitcher. And finally, the magic ingredient that gave his concoction its wondrous potency—"natural medicine pills from distant Quito." With exquisite care he opened up two capsules— "Do NOT eat the wrappers! VERY poisonous!"—and tossed them over his shoulder in disgust. The gray powder cascaded into the brew. He stirred, then stood stock still. The silence was deafening.

"Who will be first?" he thundered, holding up the pitcher like an offering to the gods. There was instant pandemonium as a hundred bodies strained forward, hands grasping at the air. He reached into the audience and drew out two squealing, squirming women, pulling them to the table like contestants in a game show. Each received a dirty glass of clotted liquid. They drank. The crowd waited breathlessly. The women smiled, their lips stained bloodred. Shouts and cheers. He doled out the drink in dribs and drabs, saying, "I am a poor man with but one set of clothes—BUT it is my burden in life to cure the weak, the sick, the helpless...." The pitcher was almost empty. "A lemon, an aloe leaf, and THIS," he'd timed it perfectly. The magical pills appeared. His spiel accelerated. They cost two thousand sucres— 40 cents—each in Quito. He was willing to part with a package of eight pills AND the recipe for how to mix them AND a book on illnesses and their miraculous cures for the bargain price of ten thousand sucres—about $2.00. An apparent loss of at least $1.20 per sale, but no one was doing the math. They surged forward to snatch up his packages. For a man who couldn't calculate a profit, he was lightning fast at making change. More than 50 customers shuffled off, carefully mouthing the recipe displayed on the front of the pamphlet. The lemon sellers in the marketplace were in for a surprise.

I returned to my room and waited uncomfortably for a knock on the door. The thought of meeting Dr. Juan Domingo Jaramillo was about as appealing as going on a blind date. He was the friend of a friend of a friend, recommended to me as an expert in Otavalo's history, a man who would know *exactly* what we needed. I had visions of three days of being ferried around from one important person to another, listening to endless speeches and learning exactly nothing.

I couldn't have been more wrong. Juan burst into my hotel room looking like he'd just crossed India in a third-class train. His shirttail flapped out of ragged jeans. He had the round cheeks of a chipmunk, an irrepressible grin, and at least a week's worth of whiskers. "At your disposal," he said, grabbing my hand in both of his and kissing me on the cheeks. I liked him immediately.

"If you're just beginning your journey," he told me over a cup of coffee, "then you might want to get a shaman's blessing or maybe consult a seer who can tell you about your coming trip."

An intriguing idea. But where, exactly, did one find a shaman-for-hire?

He hesitated. "Taitaichuro is a *yachac*—a healer—known throughout Ecuador. But first," he added, choosing his words carefully, "you might want to do a *cuy* cleansing?"

Cuy was Quechua for guinea pig. "How," I asked suspiciously, "do you cleanse someone with a furry rodent?"

"You'll see," he said, his eyes twinkling.

The healing center had both a Western doctor—who sat alone in his modern examination room and did paperwork—and a guinea-pig healer, whose clientele lined the walls and stairs and entryway in stoic silence as they waited their turn.

The cuy doctor, Dr. Alvarez, was Juan's exact opposite—tall and severe, with a thin face and solemn, lecturing voice. He planted me firmly in a chair, reached into a sack, and hauled out a guinea pig. It wriggled unhappily. So did I. "How about," I said quickly, "we let someone else go first?" Juan laughed, and Dr. Alvarez obligingly called the next in line.

I relinquished my chair to an old Indian woman who sat head down, as though staring at her own gravestone. The doctor began beating her on the back with a guinea pig, moving to her arms, her legs, and head. The tiny animal made wet slapping sounds and squeaked miserably like a bicycle in need of oil. After several minutes the doctor abruptly stopped and held the guinea pig over a bucket of water. A razor blade materialized and the animal was slit from chin to tail, its skin pulled off like a glove. The doctor examined the musculature, then split open the abdomen and fingered the internal organs.

"You have bad lungs," he told the woman solemnly. "You cough in the mornings with phlegm. Your limbs are stiff with arthritis—your knees—sometimes it hurts to walk early in the day." She was 69. "Your heart gives you an occasional pain." She suffered headaches, especially when the weather was due to change. Her bladder was inflamed, causing her to urinate frequently. She nodded after every comment and the doctor smiled, pleased with his patient's corroboration in front of an audience. He dropped the carcass into the bucket and pronounced the cure—a drink of lemon juice, honey, and a therapeutic massage. Then, to my astonishment, the woman stood up, stripped down to her panties, and climbed onto the massage table.

She was pummeled and kneaded and pretzeled into a variety of shapes. The doctor lectured while he worked. "The gift of cuy healing is hereditary—both my uncles and my grandfather were blessed with extra sight. I myself studied in a hospital by watching them cut open humans to prove to myself that the diagrams are correct." A Schering Plough poster of the human body hung on one wall. "I am a skeptical man. But I saw many similarities between guinea pigs and humans.

"There are other ways of curing," he added. "Tobacco, alcohol"—he pointed at a dusty pile of dried leaves in the corner—"and herbs."

"Do you ever send anyone over to the Western doctor?"

"Sometimes there are certain illnesses of the body that we cannot cure. I tell them...." He paused. "Usually they do not go."

"Why guinea pigs?"

He nudged the carcass in the bucket. "Cuys," he said, "can propagate within 15 minutes of giving birth. They are the fastest breeders in the world." I watched the skinned body floating in the bloody water. Somehow that didn't make me feel any better. Still, it was a marked improvement over the old Inca habit of slaughtering llamas—up to ten thousand at a time—to propitiate the gods and divine the future from their steaming intestines. Back then there wasn't much to choose from between a guinea pig and the deerlike indigenous camelids. Most of the livestock that now dotted the Andean landscape—chickens, sheep, horses, donkeys, pigs, dogs, cats, rabbits, cows, and mules—were by-products of the Spanish conquest.

The old woman dutifully swallowed a concoction of lemon juice and honey, climbed back into her clothes, and shuffled off.

Then it was my turn.

The guinea pig—small and brown—slapped rhythmically against my back, my arms, and legs. It urinated into my lap and squeaked pathetically in time with the thwacks. The doctor knocked it against my head a dozen times, enough to give us both a headache. I started squeaking too.

The razor blade appeared. "Wait!" I said involuntarily. "Couldn't you just look at it from the outside? Check its vital signs?" The doctor laughed and dropped it to the ground, where it lay stiff and still. "Already dead," he said. He was right. "It has absorbed all of your ailments into its own body."

He hadn't handled it that roughly. Had it died of fear?

He slit it open with his razor blade. There was a large growth on the guinea pig's left shoulder blade. "What's that?" I asked.

He waved his hand in dismissal. "Sometimes the cuys already have ailments of their own."

I waited for the diagnosis. I'd be a much more difficult patient than his usual clientele—not only did I know my own body, but I hadn't been raised in the harsh Andean highlands. The usual ills— arthritis, bronchitis, and parasites—didn't necessarily apply.

"Your heart is strong," he said, fingering the marble-size lump of flesh. A bit of stomach, weakish lungs—what I needed was a massage, and all would be well. The carcass dropped into the bucket with a splash.

"I'm fine," I said quickly. Juan burst into peals of laughter. The doctor handed me a sheet only slightly larger than a handkerchief and told me to strip.

I was briskly prodded and poked, my limbs twisted, my vertebrae cracked, and finally ushered out the door smelling faintly of olive oil and puckered up with the aftertaste of lemon juice. Properly cleansed and ready to be ritually blessed, it was time to visit Taitaichuro, one of Otavalo's spiritual healers.

Despite a Ph.D. in psychology, Juan believed deeply in the shamanic arts. *Curanderismo*, he told me, was as much a part of Andean life as science is to the Western world. Curanderos did not claim to replace modern medicine—they simply cured a different set of ills. They treated ailments produced by supernatural causes—bad winds, restless spirits, and enchantments. Some of these occurred naturally and others were cast by *maleros*, corrupt healers who secretly practiced the evil arts. Curanderos also dealt with Sicknesses of God—like loss of reason—that originated in the Christian world. Most important, curanderos did not work for money but rather to do good.

We pulled up to a trash-strewn yard beside a pockmarked barn on the outskirts of town. Taitaichuro was a tiny Indian with Oriental features and the shuffling gait of someone who was too proud to use a cane.

"I am the greatest healer in Ecuador!" he called out by way of greeting. "I can call down the sun and the moon and the spirits"— he snapped his fingers—"the way you call a dog. I can tell the future to the number of your children." He paused for effect. "Last year I did a public healing in front of 2,000 people and was paid one million sucres for it"—about $200. "You"—he pointed an arthritic finger at me—"will pay me twice that much." He stomped away.

Two million sucres. Four hundred dollars for an hour-long ceremony. I was appalled.

"He can be difficult," Juan whispered to me with his unflappable grin.

A tenth that much, he added, was about the going rate.

Northern Ecuador's Greatest Healer finished urinating in his garden, hitched up his pants, and turned back to us. I bargained respectfully. The price fell in fits and starts to $100 and stuck there. Taitaichuro ordered us into his house.

The basement was a dirt-floored storage area littered with farming tools and chicken droppings. A central table was piled high with carved skeletons, rotting rose petals, and other bits of sorcerer's debris. Behind it hung a tin sun and moon, a crucified image of Christ, two leopard skins, and several enlarged photos of the healer in full ceremonial regalia. Taitaichuro stood in front of his own images and raised his arms like a prophet speaking to his flock.

Eventually we negotiated down to $60 plus money for props. The ceremony would happen two days hence. Taitaichuro ushered us outside and carefully locked the barn door behind us in case we should decide to steal some of his candle stubs.

"He is *metalica*," Juan said thoughtfully as we drove home. "He thinks only of money—a healer shouldn't be that way." Hard words from such a gentle man. "And he is involved in politics." Apparently Taitaichuro had quite a hold on the local Indians— enough so that the Catholic Church was paying him to put a hex on anyone who dared to leave the flock. "Not good," Juan said again and stared at the road with troubled eyes.

That night Juan showed up at my damp and dreary hostel with that all too familiar twinkle in his eye and another adventure up his sleeve. "You'll see," he said.

Twenty minutes later we arrived at a low-slung building perched on a lonely hilltop far outside of town. It was ringed with rusty pickups like flotsam thrown up on the tide. Empty beer bottles and bloody feathers littered the parking lot. Evil-looking men slouched around the ticket gate.

Inside, a red-carpeted pit was surrounded by concentric rows of raised seats. All the chairs were nailed down so that the spectators could neither inch forward nor throw them into the ring. Several hundred men muttered to each other and fingered brick-like wads of bills. A clock swung slowly back and forth over the arena. It was a cockfight.

"They have to be exactly the same weight to fight," Juan said, hurrying us over to the scales. A grizzled man caressed the head of his rooster as though it were a newborn baby. The bird looked nothing like those cotton-ball chickens that grace the cover of egg cartons and fast-food billboards. These were war machines— long, sinewy necks, tight wings, swordfish bodies, and iridescent tails that pulsated with aggressive energy. It was only from the belly down that they bore some vague resemblance to their barnyard cousins. Their undersides were plucked clean, exposing the naked, goose-bumped flesh of supermarket broilers.

"This is a very large tournament. Birds from Peru, Ecuador, Colombia—even Argentina—are here to fight!" Juan said. A bell rang and the men shuffled silently to their chairs. Juan's brother had season tickets, and he led me to a coveted ringside seat. I was the only woman in the room.

The pit cleared of all but two referees, a caller, and the birds' handlers. They fingered their roosters lovingly and stroked their feathers straight while Juan whispered the rules into my ear.

"They're betting," he said, indicating the audience with his chin. Gradually I began to see the subtle, stock-market movements. A finger raised and crooked, a quick sharp nod, a wiggled pinky. "The highest bets are drug money," Juan whispered. "Up to five million sucres." My nose began to itch. I sat on my hands.

The two birds in the pit had each staked out a few square yards of turf and were patrolling up and down. They pecked at the ground in pretend nonchalance, though their eyes followed each other like the crosshairs of a gunsight. They lobbed occasional insults back and forth, while being careful not to overstep the invisible line into the other's territory.

The men had other plans. They scooped their animals up and thrust them at each other, slicing and parrying as though the birds were merely swords and it was the men themselves who had come to fight. Locked eyeball-to-eyeball, the roosters' territorial instincts took over. Feathered ruffs arched forward like lions' manes.

The clock was set. The cocks released. They exploded at each other like loaded cannons, leaping upward at the last second with powerful sweeps of their wings to swing their naked thighs in a high arc and bury their claws in each other's breasts. The crowd fell silent, every man leaning forward on his elbows like a wolf evaluating prey.

It was over quickly. One cock fell face down, flapping spasmodically. His handler grabbed him by the feet and walked away without a trace of the tenderness I had seen a few minutes ago. Blood ran from the rooster's mouth. The red carpet suddenly made sense.

Another fight was about to start. "Ecuador is black, Peru is white," Juan said. Sharp objects protruded from the backs of their legs. "Razor blades?" I asked.

Juan shook his head. He nudged his brother, who opened a velvet case and produced a wicked-looking tortoiseshell spike. "Razors are for cocks who don't know how to fight. With this"— he rested an index finger very lightly on the point of the spike— "the cock must know to jump and pierce the heart or head." He tapped his temple.

"Why tortoiseshell?"

"It's lighter and doesn't do as much damage as iron. The fight lasts longer."

The slowly swinging clock read seven minutes. Both Ecuador and Peru were visibly tiring, the dark stains spreading across their chests where they had plucked each other's feathers out. They gathered their energy and waded back into the fight, like tired athletes determined not to quit. A round of applause rippled through the crowd. Bets doubled, then doubled again.

At twelve minutes they were so exhausted that they could do little more than lean against each other and pant. Just before the buzzer rang, one made a half-hearted leap; there was a flash of claws and Ecuador lay still, a wet spot widening around him on the carpet. Men poured into the ring and huge rolls of bills changed hands. Nobody counted their money.

"How do you teach a rooster to use an artificial spike like that?" I asked, fascinated in spite of myself.

"You can't teach them," Juan's brother said. "The knowledge is hereditary—but it is passed on only through the hen. A winning cock costs up to $20,000, but a hen can go for triple that. Her eggs know how to fight."

An hour later the pit began to smell like death and the men of sour sweat. We left before the next round started, walking across the carpet that had become wet and spongy with blood. I wondered about tomorrow's ceremony with Taitaichuro. How many more feathered and furry creatures would have to die before my journey officially began?

Northern Ecuador's Greatest Healer was late. We spent the morning kicking trash around his yard while John, my cameraman, tried to figure out how to get his six-foot-two-inch frame into the three-foot outhouse.

Taitaichuro shuffled up, unlocked the storage room, and immediately began to chant. "Wait!" I said, searching the shelves for candle stubs while trying not to step in the piles of dried excrement that littered the floor. Taitaichuro immediately demanded more money for the delay. *If he can really charge $200 for an hour-long ceremony,* I thought sourly, *why can't he afford electricity?*

At last I had two dozen candles shedding some light among the clutter on the table. Taitaichuro grabbed a filthy cup, half filled it with corn whiskey, drank, refilled it, and passed it to me. He chanted, rang a bell, and tossed a handful of rose petals on my head. He drank again. He took a mouthful of cologne and spat it in my ear. He drank again. This time the cologne went straight into my eye, feeling like one of those tortoiseshell spikes. Taitaichuro lit a cigarette, took a deep pull, and exhaled in my face, called down the gods, and drank again. He grabbed an egg and waved it around my head, then called to his young son in Quechua. The boy appeared shortly with a handful of leafy greens. Taitaichuro reached under my shirt and rubbed the plant over my back, my front, my arms, and face. Realization lagged several seconds behind reality—it was stinging nettle. My back and stomach began to burn. A fire crept up my neck. Whatever friendly thoughts I'd harbored toward this man were quickly evaporating. He blew another puff of smoke into my face. "Done," he said and stalked out. The entire ceremony had lasted less than ten minutes.

I caught up with him and asked for the agreed-upon hour. He demanded more money. I reminded him of his promise to take us up to the sacred tree behind his house.

The yachac agreed, disagreeably, to climb the hill. He called his daughter and stomped off.

"Why," I asked, once we had again caught up, "aren't you wearing your ceremonial robes?" He still had on his shiny nylon jacket with a football team insignia embroidered on the back.

"I can't change," he said. "I'm in a trance." He was silent for a moment, then offered to go back and put on his robes if we doubled his fee.

We slogged up the hill, the yachac periodically stopping to call out his own name and drunkenly slap the ground. Once we reached the sacred tree, he had his daughter dig a hole at its base and drop in small bags of quinoa, wheat, and rice. "To feed Mother Earth, to return to her the sustenance...," he chanted briefly in Spanish and Quechua. "Done," he said and dismissed us both with a wave of his hand.

Juan was quiet as we got into his car to drive home. "Did you see the human skull on the table?" he asked once we were well on our way. I hadn't thought anything of it. My mother has several such oddities scattered about the house from her medical school days.

"There was a photograph of a boy in one of the eye sockets," Juan continued in a subdued voice. "It's the curse of death. Black magic. He is a *malero*." Taitaichuro, he insisted, was using the evil arts to call down the gods in deadly vengeance against the hapless boy. He was silent for a moment, then a look of profound relief crossed his face. "Thank God you gave him a big tip."

CHAPTER 3

THE PEOPLE'S WAR

FIELD NOTES: ...and found myself in the middle of a full-scale riot. I kept getting great photographs of hundreds of people streaming by only to find myself standing in no-man's-land between the gas-wielding police and the rock-throwing rioters.

Curse or coincidence, we ran into trouble the very next day. Juan gave us a ride to the bus stop for the first leg of our journey south to Quito. A huge crowd surged toward us just as we reached the main highway. The air was heavy with oily clouds of soot and smoke from burning tires.

"The strike," Juan said as we watched a dozen Otavalo Indians drag out large stones to block off the road. The government, he explained, had slashed subsidies on basic commodities like gasoline. Prices shot up fivefold overnight. The indigenous people called a one-day protest strike. Juan was both skeptical and worried.

"These guys," he said, pointing at the young men waving flags and shouting slogans into megaphones, "are just politicians causing trouble. The real indigenous people are too poor to take a day off from their fields to rally in the streets. But if they ever do unite.... The Indians grow all the food in Ecuador. Once they stop working they can starve the government out."

Juan helped us cross the lines on foot and left us to catch a ride on the other side. In three short days he had become a friend and protector, his ready laugh and gentle ways an inspiration for our long journey south. Perhaps he, not Taitaichuro, was the omen we had come to see.

The Indians had set up roadblocks at intervals along the Pan American Highway, effectively cutting transport along the length of the country. Truck and bus companies responded by positioning their vehicles between the blockades. When a bus reached a strike point the passengers simply got off, walked across the lines, and waited for another bus on the other end.

I flagged down a ride with a friendly driver heading back to Quito. No, he didn't own his truck, nor did he have to pay for gasoline. Yes, he felt very bad for the strikers since they were too poor to handle such high prices. He was certain that the government was not going to reverse its policies and that the strike would eventually peter out as sheer hunger forced the protesters to return to their work. As much as he wanted to support their strike, he had a wife and three children to feed and couldn't afford to take any days off. He drove from Imbabura to Quito every day and caught a bus to see his family in distant Guayaquil on the weekends. The rising price of gas had dashed his dream of buying his own truck and therefore earning enough to be home each night to put his children to bed—and maybe even one day send them to college.

I thought back to my own university where, surrounded by ivy-draped colonnades and perfectly manicured lawns, I had written papers on the need for shock treatment in the financial policies of developing countries. How easily those words had flowed from pen to paper. I was ashamed.

The next morning John, my cameraman, left to spend three weeks working on another job. He got out just in time—the strike had spread to Quito and dire warnings were being broadcast hourly over the local radio.

The tense atmosphere seemed at odds with Quito's quiet, cobblestone streets, red-tiled roofs, and whitewashed colonial churches. Quito took its name from its pre-Inca inhabitants, the peaceful Quitu people. Their descendants were conquered by the Inca in the 1400s. Although it lay only a few kilometers from the Equator, Quito's altitude—nearly 3,000 meters—gave it such a pleasant climate that the last two Inca rulers chose to settle here rather than return to their court in Cuzco. Quito quickly became a major Inca city and hub along the Inca Road—so important that when the Spaniards arrived, the Inca general Ruminyahui chose to raze it to the ground rather than allow it to fall into enemy hands. What little was left quickly disappeared amid the subsequent war and reconstruction. Modern Quito traces its history back to colonial times.

By 9:00 a.m. I was on the streets, joining a stream of protesters marching toward the old city and the presidential palace. Side roads were plugged with burning tires, leaving only one main channel for the parading strikers. Well-dressed men chanted slogans into megaphones at every corner, urging the crowd forward on a wave of earsplitting sound. The marchers themselves seemed almost to be on holiday, dancing and banging pots and pans. Children proudly carried flags and several students had dressed up as slaves and chained themselves together. A young woman in a skeleton costume gyrated seductively, arms weaving as she slunk down the street. No one seemed the slightest bit concerned—or even aware of—the possibility of a police confrontation. We stormed noisily past several clusters of armed military watching silently from the sidewalk. I got an eerie feeling of imminent disaster.

The streets narrowed as we approached the city's old quarter. I slipped out in front of the marchers and sat down directly in their path to film their approach. I sensed, more than saw, a change in their behavior. The chanting slowed, stumbled, caught again, then died out. Everyone was staring over my head. I turned to face a line of police with heavy plastic shields, their hands on belts of tear gas canisters. They stood, boots planted wide, a solid flesh-and-bullet barricade across the street.

The marchers milled awkwardly, like horses suddenly realizing they've galloped into a corral. Even the organizers seemed shaken, their megaphones drooping as they reassessed their choice of weapon against the sinister tear-gas canisters on the other side.

Then, unexpectedly, the crowd turned as a unit and marched down a side street, the spring was back in their step, their chants redoubled as they passed by the row of grim-faced olive green. I stayed behind to film the police. A few minutes later I heard the first round of tear gas explode. I started running.

I felt the gas long before I saw it—an acid burn that enveloped my face and neck like a swarm of angry bees. By the time I'd turned the corner and saw the police line two blocks away, my throat had constricted and my tonsils felt as though I'd swallowed broken glass. Gone were the kids banging pots and pans, the slinky woman in the skeleton suit. All I could see were knots of young men in gangster bandannas, their arms windmilling as they threw fist-size rocks that ricocheted off cars and skittered along the sidewalk. The police ducked behind doorways, shields up and masks down, scuttling out every once in a while to lob a volley of tear gas from widemouthed guns. I ran forward to join the front-line troops and trained my camera along a uniformed arm as it took aim at the rock-throwing kids. With my eye to the viewfinder I couldn't see to either side, so I reached out and rested my hand lightly on the shoulder of the man in front of me. He spun around. The gas mask made him look alien and insectlike. His gun was still smoking—I was in trouble. He tore off his mask without a word and seized my hand. He turned it inexorably and planted it firmly on my camera. "Hold onto that with both hands," he said. "There are many thieves out today. They will steal it from you." He turned back to the confrontation.

The "People," as the youths called themselves, had splintered into several groups. The locus of fighting moved erratically through ten square blocks of Ecuador's lovely old city. I stumbled down a backstreet, coughing and rubbing swollen eyes after getting caught in the backwash of a particularly heavy round of gas. The tears were running down my face and I could barely see. A hand clamped onto my arm and I was literally jerked into a small, dark room.

"Here, inhale this," the owner said, pushing my head down over a can that smoldered with the remains of a smoky fire. I breathed in once, twice, again. The burning in my throat subsided. "Mel!" I heard a woman call. "Bring coke!" A glass of soda appeared and the owner's wife clucked sympathetically while I drank it down. She reached behind the counter and pulled out a tub of salt, then poured the bulk of it into a plastic bag and handed it to me. "Rub this along the inside of your mouth," she said, tapping her own gums with her finger. I did. The pain miraculously disappeared. The owner handed me a scrap of cloth. "Over your mouth," he said.

"Should I wet it?" I asked.

"No! That only makes it worse." He drew a map for me in case I needed to find my way back to his store, patted me on the shoulder, and stood outside to see me off.

The morning passed in a bewildering array of marching troops, their boots beating an ominous tattoo along the empty streets.... Of milky clouds blossoming in the distance and the suffocating feel of having stumbled into yet another unseen wall of gas. Of running—always running—to get to the front lines and then turning to catch up with the mob that was stampeding away. Of people leaning out of upper-story windows and fires built in front of all the stores. Of calm, eerie quiet—not a car in sight, no children's laughter, market noises, nothing—except the distant, muted thump of widemouthed guns. "Cuidado!" meant that stones would soon be raining down on our heads and "corre!" that tear gas was already flying in a lazy, white-tailed arc to land a few feet away.

I was shuffling down the street, running a hand along one wall to keep track of the sidewalk while I waited for the tears to wash out my eyes, when I ran smack into a group of young men. One of them immediately pulled open his jacket, put an arm around my shoulder, and buried my head against his chest. He held me there, the jacket canopied around my head, while he waited for the gas to dissipate. Normally I would have assumed the worst and fought my way free, but this time the thought never even occurred to me. I leaned against a stranger, tears dripping down his chest, feeling absolutely safe, until his arms loosened and I was once again blinking in the sun. I said "thank you," he grinned, and I walked away.

I had lost the locus of the fight. I wandered aimlessly around, hoping to run back into the battle on the right side. I turned the corner, heard a dozen people shout "corre!" and saw a crowd of two hundred people bearing down on me. I whipped out my camera. Terrific footage, I thought proudly as the wave engulfed me and then passed. Suddenly the crowd became a trickle and I was alone, looking through my viewfinder at an approaching line of police, their gas guns popping like grenade launchers. I turned and ran. Too late. A hissing canister landed directly at my feet.

This time my eyes were swollen completely shut as I stumbled away, struggling against the unseen hand that clenched around my windpipe, squeezing relentlessly. "Over here!" I heard a child shout. Three little girls, the oldest about ten, ran over to me, grabbed my hand, and pulled me into the entryway of a run-down house. "Paper!" the girl demanded, then ran to get matches. In no time at all they had built a smoky blaze on the floor of their home. I leaned over it, inhaling deeply. The little girls stood watching me in an unblinking row, crying in sympathy.

Years of television news had shown me what to expect in a riot—drama, violence, and the occasional barbaric act or two. Nobody had prepared me for what I'd really find: bystanders offering me salt, a place to hide, a smoky fire whenever I was in need. Far from getting angry when I wiggled my way among their ranks, the police just kept a paternal eye on me. One had even apologized for not being able to lend me a gas mask—there were not enough to go around, he said, and even his men had to share. Amid the armored cars and falling stones stood three little girls with blackened hands, weeping tears for me.

There was one side to the struggle that I had yet to see. I asked the girls to point me to where the "People" were throwing stones. They left their youngest sibling to sweep up the ashes of the fire and cheerfully directed me to the heart of the confrontation.

I slipped down a side alley and stepped boldly out into the street. Hundreds of men were screaming obscenities and hurling stones at the line of plastic-shielded police. Someone caught sight of me. I was instantly surrounded by masked men with angry eyes and hands full of broken concrete. "What are you doing here?" an anonymous voice demanded in Spanish.

"I want to hear your side."

A bandit in a red bandanna stepped forward. His eyes were dark slits above the dirty cloth. "Be careful," he said, "or someone will steal your camera. I'll stay by you."

A shout went up. We all scattered as an armored vehicle roared through the police lines, heading straight for where we stood. It parted the ragtag army like the bow of a ship, but the young men turned in its wake and hurled their rocks against the metal plates in a gesture of frustrated futility. The police shot several volleys of tear gas and everyone darted away like roaches suddenly exposed to light.

We regrouped around a side-street fire. I passed out the salt the store owner had given me. Several men started breaking up the sidewalk for more ammunition while others kept a lookout for the armored car. David was facing off against Goliath. Outside of fairy tales, the little guy almost never wins. I wondered how this was going to end.

Badly, it seemed. A crowd suddenly converged on a man in the middle of the street. I caught a glimpse of bloodstained clothing among the crush of bodies. "The police beat him up," someone muttered. He was in bad shape—his nose torn and hanging from his face, a deep cut in his upper lip, and blood pouring from a gash in his scalp.

He pulled off his shirt and held it to his face, shaking his head vehemently at suggestions that he go to the hospital. He was sure that he would be turned away as an indigent, or arrested as a rabble-rouser.

"I'll take him," I said.

The crowd waved down a taxi and we piled in. The driver got on his radio, asking for a clear path through the fighting to the nearest hospital. Twice we were overwhelmed by gangs and narrowly avoided being stoned before we had a chance to explain ourselves. At last we pulled up at a private clinic where a plastic surgeon set to work repairing his face.

The young man was from the coastal city of Guayaquil. A recent spate of plant closings had cost him his job. With nothing better to do, he had drifted to Quito to take part in the strike. Far from being the victim of a police beating, he had been set upon by his fellow pueblo fighters, who had torn a gold chain from his neck and relieved him of his wallet and an expensive watch. Rising prices were just the lightning rod that drew out his anger at the system itself—the lack of jobs, his own poverty, and bleak prospects. I sat beside him on the examination table and felt his fury at the doctor who was skillfully stitching up his nose. I heard him rage at me, despite his hand tightly gripping mine.

I slipped out once I knew he was all right, but had no desire to return to the riot. I had seen something far more devastating than tear gas and falling rocks: the angry face of poverty on a gentle people—a people who had reached out to help a stranger through a day of violence and despair.

CHAPTER 4

MAMA NEGRA'S GROOM

FIELD NOTES: They painted my face with suet and tar and put me in a harness to carry the 200-pound pig.

I had come to South America armed with a backpack and a GPS, prepared to hike the entire length of the ancient Inca Road over mountains, across raging rivers, and along the desolate Andean plateau. I'd spent months scouring the 16th-century accounts of Spanish soldiers and priests for information on the great highway. They had marveled at its size and the engineering feat it represented. "Such magnificent roads can be seen nowhere else in Christendom," one conceded. Some even thought that it had been built by gods, not men. It must have been an extraordinary sight—paved with flagstones, bordered by fruit trees, and lined with aqueducts. It both awed and terrified the Spanish troops, for they thought—correctly—that it represented the greatness of the empire they were up against.

But after 500 years of war and reconstruction, there was precious little of the Inca Road left to be found, and Ecuador was a particularly frustrating place to look. The country was dominated by two volcanic mountain ranges with a valley in between. Inca architects had built their road right up the center of this valley. Twentieth-century engineers, acknowledging the good sense of their predecessors, had in many places used the Inca Road as a foundation for the Pan American Highway. Although every major city down the center of Ecuador lay on the Inca Road, few could boast any visible reminders of their Inca heritage.

But there was one place where the ancient road had managed to evade an asphalt overcoat. Two hundred miles to the south there lay an arduous, four-day trek over the mountains to the magnificent Inca ruins of Ingapirca. I packed my bags and hopped a bus with the stench of burning tires still clinging to my clothes. As we labored out of Quito, the cityscape fell away and rural Ecuador began.

Llamas. Somewhere in ancient history a giraffe had fallen in love with a sheep and produced these fluffy, long-necked beasts. It was their extravagant eyelashes that gave them away, and their habit of swiveling their heads like periscopes.

Earth. Fresh-tilled fields so richly brown that you could feel the potatoes fattening beneath their skin. Children with brown eyes in brown faces and brown legs that perfectly matched the ground beneath their feet. They were the offspring of Mother Earth, still rooted to the land. Women as round as avocados and as sharp as chilies sat and spun fleece into yet another layer for their voluminous, handmade skirts.

Mountains. Ecuador was living up to its nickname, the Avenue of the Volcanoes. Snow-covered peaks rolled past us in endless, whitecapped waves as we threaded our way down its narrow central valley. The Illingas. Ruminyahui. The perfect cone of Cotopaxi, orange-tinted in the early morning light. It was the highest active volcano in the world, and deadly. In 1742 it erupted and utterly destroyed the nearby town of Latacunga. The survivors picked up the pieces and rebuilt their homes as best they could. Twenty-six years later Cotopaxi boiled over for the second time. The people had named their city Llacta Cunani—Land of my Choice—for good reason. Its long-suffering inhabitants dug in their heels and began sorting through the rubble. Then in 1877 Cotopaxi erupted yet again.

We were just entering Latacunga when our bus ran smack into a huge crowd of midgets with pointy heads, wearing feathery white costumes and wings. I didn't ask what was going on until my backpack was already lying on the curb. "It's the Festival of Mama Negra!" a toothless man shouted happily, and thrust a glass of homemade whiskey into my hand. I drank. I excused myself to haul my bags into the nearest guest house and dashed back out to join the festivities. The entire town, it seemed, was celebrating in the streets. It was a parade, a free-for-all, a raucous riot of competing bands. Lovely young women in embroidered skirts and matching scarves wove in and out in looping circles like courting cranes. Each troop was preceded by its own marching band, which made a point of playing music that was nothing like the group that came before or after it. And finally, Mama Negra herself, wearing a thick black mask and bouncing a baby puppet in her arms.

Slithering in and out among the dancers were the witches, sporting pinstriped masks and carrying deer horns and heavy spangled shields upon their backs. Whenever they spied an unsuspecting bystander, they pulled him out and danced circles around him, chanting incantations to the mountain gods, Mother Earth, and a host of other native deities. When they were done, they spat a mouthful of corn whiskey over their victim, then sashayed off to find another sorry soul in dire need of ritual cleansing.

I gravitated toward a group of young men with faces painted charcoal black and dressed in orange cloaks. They each took turns harnessing themselves to a wooden pyramid upon which perched a full-grown roasted pig. The entire structure was so heavy that two children had to follow the pig-carrier with a table so that he could set down his load every few yards to rest. "How much does it weigh?" I shouted, pointing at the grinning pig.

"Two hundred pounds," the man replied. His blackened face was unnerving, but his bright red lipstick curled upward in a friendly smile. He offered me a ladle full of gummy brown liquid from the bucket he was carrying. It tasted like flour and honey and coated my throat with fur. That earned me a hat and cloak and an invitation to walk with them. The pig—the *chancho*, they called it—was draped in all manner of food and drink representing practically every sin that could be done in public—liquor, candy, roasted rabbits and guinea pigs, cigarettes and cigars. Whoever carried it was, symbolically, the groom of Mama Negra, and this was her wedding gift. The pig circled the town for two days in the blazing sun, weeping sticky tears of viscous fluid from all its cracks and cavities. I wasn't sure if I felt more sorry for the young men strapped into the harness or the ones who had to eat the pig itself when all was said and done.

"*Mesa!*" the man carrying the pig called out, and his two young nieces scurried forward with the table. He unbuckled the harness, soggy with sweat.

"Mind if I give it a try?" I asked.

He looked at my hopeful face, then at the pig, the pride of his coming family celebration. "First we have lunch," he said.

The woman slaving over a huge cauldron of soup didn't miss a beat when her clan of young men barged in with two foreigners in tow. Today was the festival, and their doors were open to all. She sat us down to more cups of liquid fur, then slapped two bowls of soup in front of us, each with a pig's hoof rolling around in an oil slick. John, my vegetarian cameraman, didn't touch his. I picked up my spoon and searched around the pig's dirty nails for something soft enough to eat. The soup itself was pure pig fat, at least an inch thick. I pushed it from side to side, hoping to break through to vegetables, water, anything but rancid globs of grease. At last, accepting the inevitable, I turned off my taste buds and dug in.

All around me tar-black faces spooned puddled fat between bloodred lips and smiled at me.

They were gardeners and metalsmiths, students and sailors. The youngest had not yet finished high school. The eldest was father to three strapping young men, all of whom would be taking their first turn in the harness during next year's festival. Everyone was connected, it seemed, by a spiderweb of blood—brothers, uncles, in-laws, nephews—all held together by the woman toiling over the pot of soup, feeding chickens, children, and menfolk with cheerful efficiency. She laughed off my admiration. "This is nothing," she told me. "Tomorrow there will be over a hundred people here to eat the pig."

"How long has your family been carrying the chancho?" I asked, trying desperately to ward off another ladle full of loathsome soup. She paused for a moment to think.

"Thirteen years," she said. "For faith." She indicated a picture of the Virgin Mary. The woman in the poster had an openhearted face that looked remarkably like her own. The entire family was devoutly Catholic and painfully poor, yet not a single cup of whisky or roasted guinea pig was begrudged the yearly celebration of the Virgin and each other.

"What does a black-masked Mama Negra have to do with the Catholic celebration of the Virgin?"

"Mama Negra led an uprising to free the slaves in the Spanish mines," she pointed at the nearby hills, "200 years ago."

"And the witches?"

"They cleanse people against the diseases that come with the rains," she said matter-of-factly. It didn't seem to bother her that pagan rituals were happening under the very noses of the Catholic saints. Syncretism. My dictionary defines it as "an attempted blending of irreconcilable principles of philosophy or religion." To me it meant prioritizing devotion over dogma and family over all.

Mix and match was an ingenious response to centuries of Christian proselytizing and priestly pressure. When the Spaniards first arrived in 1532 they encountered a people who worshiped the mountains, rocks, trees, thunder, the sun, and the Earth itself. There wasn't a single high pass throughout the land that didn't boast a solitary cairn of stones. Travelers painstakingly carried a pebble to the summit as an offering to the local Apu, or mountain god. Seers consulted the higher powers through the media of coca leaves or the entrails of slaughtered animals. The first sip of every glass of home-brewed beer was poured onto the ground for Mother Earth. Everyone—even small children—had natural power objects to keep them safe.

These were all signs of a people who lived in close-knit harmony with the land around them and nourished their relationship with the elements that could bring them a bountiful harvest or a bleak and hungry year. And well they should, for the Andean mountains were harsh taskmasters. It took not only steady toil but a fair amount of luck to wrest a living from the rocky soil and short seasons in the thin mountain air.

Then one day the Spaniards stepped ashore. Their greed was twofold—gold and souls—and they were prepared to go to any lengths to procure both. While the soldiers stripped the temples of their precious metals, the priests brandished their crosses against the mountain gods and Mother Earth. They outlawed the worship of all idols and burned the mummified remains of Inca rulers. They found and smashed the villagers' power objects, down to the most inconsequential pebble or a tuft of wool. They planted crosses on the stone cairns atop each mountain pass.

Slowly, the Indians began to absorb the religion of their new rulers. The two faiths had a lot in common. Feasts in honor of the sun god Inti became Catholic festivals, and effigies of the holy saints displaced the ancestral mummies that were once paraded around town. Tribute paid to the Inca empire became tithes to the new Catholic Church. The sacred houses of the sun virgins passed smoothly into nunneries of virgin sisters. Shamans who had once ingested food and corn beer for the souls of departed spirits became black-frocked priests transforming wafers and wine. For this reason there were no martyrs among the first priests to wander into the Andean hinterlands to spread word of the Christian God.

But ancestral ways do not disappear overnight, and the new religion did nothing to tame the ferocious Andean weather, which could change in minutes from warm and mild to deadly hail or blinding snow. Who dared to face the consequences of turning one's back on the local gods? The Indians solved their problem by simply incorporating the new Christian God and rituals into their pantheon of holy beings. They celebrated saints' days with all the enthusiasm and joyous faith that any priest could wish for. But if one thought to look behind the Christian statues being paraded through town, he would almost certainly find the tiny idols of the local gods, placed there in secret lest they feel left out.

The result was a marvelous mix of old and new, without apparent conflict. It was the Andean way.

When lunch was finished we sat in the courtyard while I was made over into Mama Negra's groom. The black face paint turned out to be a mixture of tar and pig fat. It smelled like roadkill, glued my hair to my forehead, and worked its way up the inside of my nose. Then came glitter, and finally I found myself making that foolish, fishlike mouth while a tar-faced man carefully applied lipstick to my lips.

The pig had been quietly gathering flies outside. They reluctantly dislodged themselves as we made our way into town to rejoin the backbone of the parade. If I had been plied with liquor before, it was a mere aperitif compared to what I was offered in full makeup and costume. At every corner another dose of fiery brew was forced down my throat while bystanders clapped and cheered. I pleaded headache, wobbly legs, incontinence—all to no avail. Refusing drinks on this day was a dire insult, and the usual trick of pouring half onto the ground as an offering to Mother Earth was apparently against the rules. I drank. I drank for the family who had taken away the one thing that branded me a foreigner—the color of my skin. I drank for the old woman who hugged me for simply joining in the festivities. I drank for the unsteady old man who offered me a gift he would dearly have liked to swallow himself.

By the time we passed my hotel, the pig fat had solidified into an indigestible ball in my stomach, sloshing around amidst at least a dozen different homemade brews. I felt like there was an alien inside of me, clawing to get out. I excused myself and dashed up to my room, leaving John to film the festival from the first floor.

"You threw up," he announced when I got back.

I was mortified. "How did you know?"

"You left your mike on," he said, and tapped his camera. "I recorded it on channel two."

It was almost dark by the time my turn came to carry the pig. They strapped me in. I leaned forward to roll the beast off the table and onto my back. Nothing happened. It was like being tethered to a telephone pole. I tried again. Several men reached out to steady tomorrow's feast. I lumbered off.

Then I discovered that Mama Negra's groom wasn't supposed to merely walk the wedding gift to her doorstep and lay it at her feet—he was supposed to dance with joy—to skip and tap and turn in sweeping arcs and figure eights. There was a bottleneck up ahead, just before the parade spilled into the central square. Our progress was glacial. I looped and swooped and marched in place, my burden carefully propped up by a protective scaffolding of fearful hands. At last someone called for the table. The sweat-stained straps fell away. A dozen women crowded around to pour celebratory drinks down my throat. Everyone flocked to join the parade as it disintegrated into the square. I danced as darkness fell and into the night beyond. I squared off with white-winged angels and tone-deaf trombone players. With Spanish bandoliers and lovely ladies with swaying skirts and graceful hips. And with the crowds, who welcomed me with claps and cheers. On this night there were no strangers, only friends.

...until I tottered home and crawled up the stairs. I wanted nothing more than to close my eyes and float away, but I was still enveloped by a cloud of mingled tar and rancid fat. I staggered into the bathroom to do battle with my face.

I scrubbed. I rubbed. I scraped and swore. I used three rolls of toilet paper—leaving nothing for morning—and barely made a dent. What little had come off was now spread across the sink, the faucet handles, and the mirror. In desperation I dove into the icy shower and used a scouring pad. When I emerged my face was a blotchy mix of raw-meat red and corpselike gray, with tarry remnants still gluing down my eyebrows and clogging the hairs inside my nose. At least my lips were back to their normal chapped and peeling pink.

The rest could wait till morning. I took two aspirin and toppled into bed.

CHAPTER 5

A LIFE OF GIVING

FIELD NOTES: How, exactly, does one stop two water buffalo who have decided to go home?

It was time to resume our journey south. The train would take us past the marching mountains to the tiny town of Achupallas. To the Inca Road.

We pulled slowly out of the station. I scampered along the roof, looking for a place to sit. Whenever I jumped across the open space between carriages, an instant scaffolding of brawny arms appeared to make sure I didn't fall between the tracks. I hunkered down beside a pile of rusty rebars and watched the countryside roll by. Although Ecuador's central valley encompasses only a fraction of the country's total landmass, it is home to almost half of its population. Tiny thatched huts lay scattered like haystacks among a patchwork of fields and paddocks. Here and there they gathered around a shiny white church, its rooftop cross thrusting skyward like a sword. It could have been Switzerland, with its backdrop of craggy snowcapped mountains and sharp, brittle air. The difference lay in the details. Every hut had a six-inch high barrier across the doorway, to keep the guinea pigs inside. Here and there a long-necked llama stood watch over a grazing flock of sheep. And beneath the earth, the true wealth of the Andes grew fat and round. Potatoes. An Andean farmer could identify nearly two hundred varieties by their color, texture, taste, and smell. They ranged from the coveted "caviar of life"—tiny and yellow and buttery sweet—to the unassuming *chunyo* that was single-handedly responsible for human survival in the mountains above 14,000 feet. Chunyo was laid out at night to freeze, then trampled to break down the cells and squeeze out moisture, then allowed to dry in the harsh, high-altitude sun. The result after many iterations was the original freeze-dried food—a potato flour that could last almost indefinitely and formed the base of virtually every Andean meal.

Modern-day shoppers think of potatoes as the poor man's vegetable, available at every supermarket in five-pound bags or sold for a dime apiece. But the first conquistadores were awed by this exotic New World crop. "It is like a truffle when cooked and soft inside," one chronicler exclaimed. Little did they know that the dirt-encrusted vegetable in their hands was the real treasure they had come to find. Today the world's annual harvest of potatoes far exceeds the value of all the gold and silver looted from the Inca Empire.

The newly conquered Inca lands had an extraordinary variety of fruits and vegetables to offer the world. Although Switzerland has laid claim to chocolate, Italy to tomatoes, and Hawaii to pineapples, in reality all three originated in South America. Beans, maize, sweet potatoes, yucca, tapioca, manioc, earth nuts, cashews, red peppers, cayenne, papaya, avocados, squash, and quinoa...more than half of the basic foods that feed the world today were born in the southern reaches of the New World.

Our train hauled itself wearily up one final pass and plunged straight down the western slope of the Andes, sawing back and forth across the mountain on a track barely wider than the narrow locomotive. Before my eyes the land began to change.

I had always thought of climate zones as something one could find painted in wide pastel swathes on country-size maps. Not in Ecuador. Its microclimates zipped in and out like hummingbirds. Voluptuous dark and fertile green turned wrinkly and gray in the time it took to peel an orange. Creeping jungle vines made cautious love to cacti. Thin tendrils of fog curled up in the mountain's crevices like watchful cats hiding from the predatory sunlight that hovered hungrily a yard away. I felt as though I was wandering through a natural history museum, past desert scenes and bristling tumbleweeds only to turn the corner and find myself surrounded by palm trees.

I lay down to take photos of the gorge below us and squirmed forward until my upper body was hanging over the edge of the train. Suddenly I felt a stranger's hands on my back and legs. I looked around to see a young man, part of an Ecuadorian family group nearby, looking sheepish but determined as he clung to my belt under the obvious direction of an older woman who might have been his grandmother. A ten-year-old boy sat on my legs and grinned cheekily at me.

I got off three quick shots before Granny lost patience and I was hauled back and deposited safely in the center of the family group. She was, it turned out, accompanying three generations of extended relatives on a weekend outing. They owned a small shop in Riobamba and had often seen towheaded foreigners piled atop the train like prairie dogs, and she wanted to know what on Earth was worth such a crazy act. Grandmother hated heights of any kind, but apparently blood was thicker than phobias because here she was, having a windy picnic in the exact center of the roof as the train switched back and forth down the steep mountainside. She tucked her arm companionably around my waist to keep me from doing anything foolish on what was otherwise a pleasant afternoon, and rocked us both to sleep.

By the time we reached Achupallas, the sun had mellowed into a shimmering golden ball that bathed the nearby peaks with a soothing orange glow at the head of the Inca trail. The tiny village was a gem of ancient, cobblestoned streets, where old women hurried home in the gathering dusk with bundles under their arms and scarves tucked tight around their chins. To get there we had traveled along two axes—Achupallas is 200 miles south of Quito as the condor flies and 400 years back in time.

It had once been a thriving Inca settlement along the Inca Road. The ancient aqueducts that powered the local mill were built before cement. Its grinding stones were carved by hands older than the childhood memories of the gray-haired elders who gathered daily in its corner store. The farming tools that lined the shelves were heavy, utilitarian, and sold without handles. People made their own.

Achupallas is far too small to have a hotel. We were directed to "a white man's house" near the edge of the square. I approached with great reluctance, sure that the poor fellow was thoroughly sick of having every grubby backpacker with vaguely matching skin tones knocking on his door.

A woman answered and pointed at what she called a "college" across the way. It was empty, she said, since the students had just gone home for a vacation break. We were welcome to use whichever room we pleased.

We were somewhere between discovering that our stove didn't work and trying to decipher all the buttons on my new Nikon when I heard a discreet knock on the door. A round face appeared, incongruously white. His features were as simple as a child's crayon drawing—thin spectacles on a button nose held up by the saw-toothed line of a mustache. The hands that dangled from his burly arms were big knuckled and brown, made for crushing clods of earth and carving wood.

His name was Anselmo. He was an Italian missionary and had spent the last ten years living and working in Achupallas and the surrounding countryside.

Anselmo's mission was the chief source of modern medicine for the area's destitute farmers and their families. He turned no one from his dinner table, and periodically solicited used clothes from Italy to hand out to those in need. He was also, he said, proudly, teaching the locals to eat horse meat.

"In Italy it's a delicacy, but here they think it isn't fit for humans. Last year we organized a roundup of the wild horses in the mountains and had a barbecue. Now they like it very much."

His biggest success was the college itself, a school for young boys to learn carpentry. "This," he said, pointing at the rough-hewn walls, "is the only hope that Achupallas has left." Most farmers don't own enough land to feed their families, let alone an extra plot to divide among their sons. As a result, practically the entire male population has migrated to Guayaquil to seek work in its assembly-line factories. The women were left to shoulder the burden of farming and tending the herds. "The men come home only for the spring plowing, to help with the bulls. And some don't come home at all." He spread his hands. His fingers were thick, the nails clean but broken. "They get used to the city life and leave their families behind."

That would explain the streets filled with old women. I looked around and counted 24 beds in our room. Ten years to save two dozen families. What would give someone the courage to dedicate his life to such a lonely cause?

"I left home when I was nine years old to work," Anselmo said. "We were a very poor family and there wasn't enough food for all of us. I started by picking apples. Later on I fixed phone lines." He shook his head and pressed his thumbs into his mustache. "If I hadn't come here, then I would surely be dead by now. Most of my friends in Italy are gone from drugs and I was heading that way too. Then one day I saw a bishop, preaching. I was so angry by what I heard that I walked up to him and said, 'all this stupid talk is not doing any good for the world.'" Anselmo paused and smiled, as though remembering a particularly good joke. "The bishop turned and asked me what good *I* intended to do." He spread his hands. His calluses had calluses. "I had no answer. We talked until I was ready to dedicate my life to Ecuador. He has since become like a father to me."

From drug addicted youth to protector of the poor. Those must have been powerful words.

Anselmo laughed. "I can give you his address in Peru if you want to go see him for yourself. But be careful"—he wagged a finger at me—"he is a dangerous man. You may find your life changed in unexpected ways."

He took his leave as quietly as he had come, but not before inviting us to see the campo—the cultivated countryside that spread across the valley and up the mountainside. A place where women spun wool off the backs of their fluffy charges and small knots of men poked smoky fires and downed moonshine out of dirty plastic cups.

Early the next morning we shouldered our packs and hiked with Anselmo down the road. Within minutes we had left the village behind and were walking through rolling pastureland.

"When we were first building the school," Anselmo said suddenly, "a terrible thing happened." He paused and rubbed his chin. "We were putting on the roof when my helper fell from the third floor and hit his head. We rushed him to Riobamba in the truck and then flew him to the best clinic in Quito. He was bleeding from the ears. They did a CAT scan and told me that surgery might be necessary. They wanted to know if I had money. 'Of course I do!' I said. They gave me a list of medicines and I ran out to buy them. When I came back he was worse. They told me that surgery would be a waste of my money. I got so angry with them. 'You think I don't have money?' I shouted. 'Here, let me show you!' When they wouldn't listen, I took the CAT scans to another clinic. 'Why are you showing these to us?' they asked me. 'You've already heard your answer from the best doctors in the country.'" Anselmo paused. "I felt so helpless. Until that moment I had thought that money was power—that you could cure anything, help anyone, if you had enough of it. I'd never had to sit and watch a friend die like that. That was the day I realized there was something in life that was stronger than I was."

I waited for him to start talking about God. He was, after all, a missionary. Nothing came. He walked on in silence.

They say the Andes go through four seasons every day. Spring bursts forth with the morning sun. A short summer is quickly followed by the afternoon of autumn, and woe to anyone caught on the high passes once twilight brings in the wintry cold of night. As we climbed higher, the midday sun disappeared and the temperature dropped 20 degrees in as many minutes. An avalanche of heavy clouds barreled down the mountainside. It instantly enveloped us in a clammy blanket, so thick that I could feel it swirling sluggishly around my legs.

At last we stumbled over freshly tilled earth at the edge of a field. Thirty feet away I could barely make out the ghostly image of two buffalo pulling a plow. Anselmo hailed the man behind the beasts as we clambered awkwardly over clumps of sticky dirt. Yes, he said, we could join them in their work. "Her?" he added with considerably less enthusiasm when I asked to be allowed to help. One of the men grabbed a basket of corn seeds and thrust it into my hands. I walked behind the farmer, dropping the seeds in the newly furrowed row and scheming over how I was going to get my hands on the plow. How hard could it be? Surely the docile beasts weren't about to take off and gallop home, dragging a metal-tipped anchor behind them.

I made my pitch. They said no. Anselmo muttered a quiet word or two. Without further ado, I was hustled over to the plow. I grasped the slippery, mud-smeared handle and wondered how to put the bulls in gear. I clicked. I clucked. I cursed. I brandished the leather whip over my head. They were unmoved. The man beside me kissed the air softly and they shuffled off. I trotted behind them, struggling to keep the heavy plow from tipping over sideways, digging in too deep, or skittering across the top of the earth. We reached the edge of the field and I glanced back over our path. It looked like an enormous vulture had hopped along, clawing the earth at irregular intervals. I reached down to pick up the plow and swing it in a 180-degree arc around the animals. It stuck to the ground as solidly as a fire hydrant. The head alone must have weighed 70 pounds. Huge clods of claylike dirt clung to the shaft, and the whole contraption was as slippery as a well-oiled pig. I heaved and hauled and jerked it around in a clumsy circle, then sat gasping while the plowman kissed the air, and we were off.

By the third furrow I wasn't even pretending that I could turn the animals myself. By the sixth furrow my right arm was at least three inches longer than my left, my pants were sagging with layered mud, and my lungs were sending urgent signals to my brain about a sudden, disturbing lack of oxygen. It was at that moment that the buffalo, sensing a lost soul on the business end of the reins, decided to go home.

They took off straight down the hill, the plow cutting a deep gash across the freshly tilled furrows. I suddenly realized that nowhere among my three feet of Quechua language cards had I learned the word for "STOP!"

"Therefore, the school...," Anselmo said quietly as I watched a young man head off the animals. "Women cannot do this work alone." He led the suddenly obedient buffalo back to their place and began plowing arrow-straight rows again.

The incessant drizzle had made the steep mountainside banana-peel slippery and as muddy as a buffalo wallow. John and I stumbled down it, muttering and cursing. Anselmo followed, falling as often as we did but picking himself up each time without a word. By now he'd walked for hours with us through the bitter rain and sleet. He hadn't complained once as his fingers turned blue with cold, so numb that he had trouble manipulating the zipper on his jacket. He had never for a moment lost his indefinable air of calm, as though he was impervious to all earthly discomforts. But then again, he must take great solace in his faith in God.

"No," he said slowly as we paused to rest. "I am still looking for God. I haven't found him yet. One day, perhaps...."

I was dumbstruck. If he wasn't looking forward to a reward in the next life—or counting up the souls he'd saved—then why on Earth was he here?

"My entire purpose in life," he said, looking across the valley to his tiny village. "Is to see my father again." He turned and smiled at me. "He always thought I was a bum—lazy and no good. All my life he told me that I would never amount to anything." He paused again. "He died before we reconciled."

"What will you say when you meet him?" He must have rehearsed those words a thousand times.

He nudged a clod of dirt with his boot. "I don't know. It will be enough that I just see him. He will understand."

We were invited to dinner and, more important, a place beside Anselmo's potbellied stove to dry our clothes and warm our sleet-stiffened bodies. His kitchen was, as usual, filled to bursting with villagers in urgent need. A huge pot of spaghetti simmered on the stove and a mop stood ready to chase down muddy boot prints. A little girl of three or four exploded around the corner and wrapped her arms around Anselmo's leg. His hand fluttered down of its own accord and rested gently on her head. "My daughter," he said, beaming at her proudly. "When I first came here I wanted to live in a simple farmer's house," he explained, "but with children it is not possible."

I had seen her playing with the village kids as we passed through town. Although she had her mother's translucent white skin, it had never occurred to me that she was not Ecuadorian. Somehow her body language was so color-blind that she had momentarily made me see the world through her eyes.

"After supper," Anselmo said, "we've organized a bingo game in the village square to raise money for undernourished children." I helped him lay the table for a hungry hoard. He stopped to answer yet another knock on the door, and stood listening with his entire body to a ragged old woman holding a sick child in her arms.

His example was contagious. I'd been racking my brain to come up with a gift to thank him for all he had done for us. Money, of course. He must be perpetually in need, with so many mouths to feed and medicines to buy. That alone wasn't enough somehow. At last I settled on the Schrade knife I carried on my belt. It was dirty but sharp, and had been with me through several long journeys. Anselmo was thrilled. He tested the blade with his thumb. His son, barely five years old, reached up to grab it. Anselmo crouched beside the boy and showed it to him, keeping the tiny fingers out of harm's way. "When you are old enough, I will give it to you," he said. A great many things must pass through Anselmo's hands, I thought. And then I knew why he didn't need a god to keep him going. His entire life had been an almost mythical journey—from child laborer, through homelessness and drugs and anger—bringing him to this forgotten corner of the world. Here he had found the answer he was seeking all along— that the act of giving is its own reward.

CHAPTER 6

THE CRASH

FIELD NOTES: "If I'm a hostage, then you're the least of my problems! Get off the damn horse!"

The next morning Anselmo introduced us to a local guide who agreed to accompany us along the Inca Road to Ingapirca. Gido lived in a tiny hovel on the edge of Achupallas with his wife, four children, several chickens, two dozen guinea pigs, and a cranky mule. He led a few trips a year across the desolate peaks and spent the rest of his days farming potatoes. He arrived at our doorstep with two mules, a saddle blanket that would double as a sleeping bag, some vegetables, and the stubby end of a candle. He told me that he often crossed the sleet-covered mountains with nothing more than what he wore on his back. I hired him on the spot.

Gido was small, with high cheekbones and that smooth, stretched skin that never seems to age. He kept to himself, seemingly content to walk with the mules and think his own thoughts. Under my persistent inquiries and a steady supply of candy bars, he gradually let go his loud, stiff answers and began to relax. He had, he told me, two daughters and two sons—the oldest 19, the youngest 9. The sons had just taken their first group of tourists to Ingapirca a month ago, and all had gone well. One of his daughters—following in her mother's footsteps—planned to go to university. I was surprised. Gido himself hadn't gone beyond fourth grade before dropping out to take over his family farm. I wondered how he'd acquired a college-educated wife.

"We met in Riobamba," he told me shyly. "She was studying accounting." He had won her heart, married her, and taken her back to Achupallas. I remembered his dirt-floored hut and the bedraggled chickens perched on the windowsills. It must have been a difficult transition for a young bride, even with the light of new love in her eyes.

But 22 years later they were still together, and Gido had resisted the road to Guayaquil and its deceptive wealth.

"Hey, Gido," I said. "Do you like horse meat?"

He laughed and wrinkled his nose, then shook his head like a dog that had gotten a bad smell. "No one does. But don't tell Señor Anselmo."

We climbed up and up along carved stone steps, past crumbling walls of fitted stone. The Inca Road! That thin red line that had wandered through my dreams night after night....Now it was under my feet, rugged and rocky and utterly real. Laid end to end it would have stretched more than halfway around the world. But it was more than just a means of getting from one place to another.

It was a symbol of the greatness of the Inca Empire itself. In creating such a stupendous engineering feat, the Inca hoped to intimidate neighboring tribes into submission, to conquer without war or bloodshed. Often it worked.

But the Inca were not always the lords of all they surveyed. South America's greatest empire began as just another nameless tribe in the Cuzco valley. Its first seven rulers did so little of note that no one knows if they were real or part of the creation myth. Then, in the early 15th century, a child was born who would one day reshape the destiny of an entire continent. His name was Pachakuti. The Earthshaker.

It was 1438—a time when the Andes was splintered into many small tribes, all at each other's throats. One of these, the Chanca, prepared to invade Cuzco and subjugate its inhabitants. The Inca emperor fled the city with his heir apparent, leaving his people at the mercy of the advancing Chanca army. Earthshaker refused to leave. He rallied Cuzco's citizens, wrapped himself in the skin of a puma, and led the counterattack. As legend has it, when the two armies were engaged in hand-to-hand combat, Earthshaker called out to the sun god for help. The very stones on the battlefield came to life as warriors, to help fight his enemy. Earthshaker emerged victorious. When his father and brother returned, the young warrior quickly deposed them both and claimed the royal throne.

In short order Earthshaker marched his armies up and down the spine of the Andes, from central Peru in the north to Lake Titicaca in the south. Eventually he grew tired of conquest and handed command of the army to his son so that he could turn his full attention to administering his newly created empire. This would be Pachakuti's greatest challenge. Anyone can conquer, but to rule a hundred tribes with different languages and customs in a land that spanned bone-dry deserts, snowcapped peaks, and the steamy Amazon, required far more than battlefield courage. Earthshaker came up with several ingenious strategies to help him succeed. He allowed his conquered subjects to continue worshiping their own gods, provided they acknowledged the supremacy of the Inca's sun god, Inti. He even offered the local idols a place in the sun god's temple in Cuzco—officially a sign of their privileged status, but in reality a ploy to ensure the good behavior of their people. If a tribe decided to rebel then their idols were brought out into Cuzco's main square and publicly flogged. Who would dare visit such indignity upon their own deities?

Earthshaker also had the sons of local rulers brought to Cuzco to be educated. The young men, thoroughly steeped in Inca customs and history, returned to rule their people, thus hastening the incorporation of the various tribes into the empire. And if a tribal group seemed unwilling to step quietly into the yoke of Inca rule, Earthshaker would uproot entire villages and send them hundreds of miles to areas that had already been pacified. Suddenly surrounded by staunch supporters of the empire, struggling to learn new farming techniques and new crops, the rebellious villages quickly buckled under.

But Earthshaker's apparently enlightened vision had a dark underside. Each year the Inca chose the most beautiful and highborn young girls from the conquered tribes, took them into the mountains, and sacrificed them to the gods. Villagers were ordered to wear their native dress, even to part their hair in the traditional manner, so that they would be easily recognized should they wander beyond their tribal territory. Marriages could not take place without the consent of the Inca's local deputy. Inca census takers kept careful records of everything from ponchos to plows; it was said that if a single pair of sandals disappeared from the side of a bed anywhere in the empire, the Supreme Inca would learn of it. Tribute was levied on all. One legend has it that when a tribe pleaded utter destitution, the supreme Inca ordered each of them to deliver a cup of lice. The consequences of breaking Inca laws were severe: stealing a few ears of corn from state-owned land was punishable by death. Occasionally a convicted criminal was dropped into a labyrinth built under the streets of Cuzco, lined with razor-sharp flint and filled with scorpions, poisonous snakes, and half-starved pumas.

But perhaps the greatest hardship the people had to endure was the memory of the conquest itself, for the Inca were ruthless to all who dared to oppose them. They slaughtered not only subjugated rulers but their wives and children and extended families, and razed their homes and salted their fields so that the land would never again grow a crop.

Nevertheless, if you paid your tribute in a timely manner, dressed as your father did, worked the sun god's fields, and built the Inca's roads, you were left largely alone to till your fields, raise your children, and worship your local gods. You knew that you would be taken care of in the event of a disastrous harvest and that no invading hordes would swoop down over the nearby hills to kill your sons and rape your daughters. It was a hard life, but one of peace.

And then, there came a war.

At last, the relentless stone steps subsided into a narrow, packed-earth trail. We had reached the *páramo*—the high-altitude grasslands covering a tenth of Ecuador's total landmass. It was spongy and wet, like peat moss. The plants had adapted to the harsh environment: they had waxy skins to protect them from the high levels of ultraviolet radiation, or fine, hairy down that acted as insulation against the bitter cold. Wind had made its home in the high páramo, and carved the land smooth. It howled through the mountain passes and raced across the rolling plains. It rattled like distant gunfire, growing louder....

The thudding gradually resolved itself into the deep drumming of helicopter blades. Two military helicopters cut low through a pass and flew directly over our heads. They circled twice, so close to the ground that even the short, spiky grass bent under the backwash of their rotor blades. One of them sank over a nearby hill. *But there's no place to land down there...*, I thought. There was a thud and bits of rotor blade exploded across the sky, followed by a rising plume of smoke. I started to run. I caught a glimpse of the burning helicopter, and olive-clad men clambering out of a shattered window in a bleak landscape that had been utterly devoid of life just a few seconds ago. It felt utterly unreal.

I stumbled down the steep slope to where the helicopter lay on its side in a small stream. The soldiers were too stunned to notice me. I dropped to my knees beside the injured pilot. He caught hold of my hand and hung on. The second helicopter landed and a stretcher arrived. The pilot was crying, yelling, making no sense. I spoke to him in Spanish, trying to calm him down. And suddenly it hit me—he was neither hysterical nor incoherent. He was speaking Portuguese. I scanned the lapels around me. Brazilian soldiers. In a military helicopter flying over Ecuador. What the hell had I stumbled into? Thank goodness John had the sense to keep a safe distance. I glanced up the trail.

There he was, hunkered down amid the spiky grass on the hillside above us, filming furiously.

Twenty minutes later the military men were finally settling down—passing around a bottle of rum and laughing a bit too loudly, no longer having to hide their shaking hands. I watched with rising dread as John stood up from his hiding place and made his way down the hill to get a better shot. He was too far away to see the soldiers' uniforms or hear them speak. They spotted him in seconds. Several soldiers converged on him, covering his lens with their hands and trying to take his camera away. Outnumbered and outgunned, he turned and fled. I heard an order given and watched a military policeman follow him up the hill in hot pursuit.

There wasn't a whole lot I could do. Or maybe there was. I sidled up to the man in charge.

"Your helicopter," I said in Spanish, "are you going to leave it here tonight?"

His eyes flickered over the broken machine lying on its side in a small stream.

"Someone has to stay behind to guard it," I pointed out. "It'll be vandalized by morning."

His glance silently acknowledged the villagers already gathering on the hillside above us.

"We've got room in our tent—and plenty of food. You're welcome to camp with us. It's going to rain. And it gets freezing up here at night...." I was babbling. I shut up.

Another long silence, and then he nodded slowly. "All right."

I nearly hugged him. We were welcome. Well, at least tolerated.

I dashed up the steep hillside after John, expecting to find him arguing with the Brazilian policeman a few feet along the trail. To my surprise, there was no one in sight. Impossible. I scanned the treeless plains. There—two miles away, a small beige blob, moving resolutely toward the horizon. I could just make out an equally determined green blob a hundred meters behind him. They looked like they weren't going to stop until they hit Peru.

I started to jog. It was all uphill, a surreal pursuit at 12,000 feet. Clumps of puckered grass sprouted over the bare hills like goose bumps, their spiky leaves shivering in the bitter wind. It was high-altitude cold, the kind that cuts through clothes like radiation and seeps into the marrow of your bones. Mist lay in the valleys like pools of milk. The world gradually contracted to encompass three microscopic beings in an immense expanse of dark and brittle gray.

Thirty minutes later, the two men were still just moving blips. In a couple of hours it would be dark. Our tent, warm clothes, and food were all back with Gido and the mules. It began to rain.

It took another hour before I was close enough to hail them. "For the love of God, STOP!" I shouted. Neither one looked back.

Then, unexpectedly, I rounded a hillock and ran smack into the military policeman. John was just over the next rise, mounted on a rangy stallion, ready to gallop off into the sunset.

"Make him come back," the MP insisted, grabbing my arm.

I explained our offer of a tent and dinner. "We're friends now," I said, embellishing a bit.

"Get him," the MP said, keeping a firm grip on my arm and pointing at John.

"JOHN!" I shouted. He was barely within earshot. "IT'S OKAY! YOU CAN COME BACK!"

There was a pause as the wind carried back his faint reply. "ARE YOU A HOSTAGE?"

"NO!" How could I convince him? I hugged the MP. His name was Braga. We high-fived. I tucked my arm into his and shouted, "WE'RE FRIENDS!"

"IF YOU'RE A HOSTAGE AND YOU'RE TRYING TO TRICK ME, THEN YOU'RE IN BIG TROUBLE!"

I had a sudden vision of my mother telling me how glad she was that for the first time in my life I'd be traveling with a man who would keep me safe.

"IF I'M A HOSTAGE, THEN YOU'RE THE LEAST OF MY PROBLEMS! GET OFF THE DAMN HORSE!"

He didn't budge. I tried to convince Braga that John had to return to his tent and dry clothes before darkness descended and the temperature dropped another 20 degrees. We both suspected that John would rather bed down on the bare hillside than submit to Brazilian military might. But, then, Braga didn't look like he was going anywhere either.

"WHAT THE HELL ARE BRAZILIAN SOLDIERS DOING IN ECUADOR?"

Good question. I'd forgotten to ask.

"MOMEP," Braga explained. They were part of a six-country peacekeeping mission guarding the border in Ecuador's ongoing war with Peru. I relayed the information back to John at the top of my voice. He didn't budge.

We bargained for half an hour. John wanted to know why Braga was chasing him. Braga wanted to know why John was running away. John demanded that Braga turn around and head back on his own. Braga insisted that John get off the horse and accompany us back to the helicopter. We were eventually saved by a stout Indian woman who leaped out of the bushes and flung herself at her stolen stallion. She snatched the reins and began berating John in high-pitched Quechua. The wrath of an angry village matriarch succeeded where the Brazilian military had failed. John meekly dismounted and handed back her horse. After a moment of tense silence we headed back single file.

We reached the crash site just in time to watch the last of the soldiers clamber into the second helicopter and fly away. The only men left behind were the captain and Braga, our MP. It was time to tell John about my offer to share our tent. It didn't go over very well.

The two soldiers set about arranging camp with military precision, directing me to put up the tent while they pulled out rations and covered up the gear. A bottle of corn whiskey appeared. The hot meal bound us together in an island of camaraderie against the bleak world around us. The curious mix of Spanish, Portuguese, and English began to make sense. We toasted friendship and eternal peace, and after several rounds Braga invited us home to meet his family in Brazil. John asked him to come to New York City to run the marathon next year. At last I crawled into our bulging three-man tent and tried to wiggle space between two unwashed soldiers, our mule driver, and John. I had wanted a journey into the unknown. I was getting more than I had bargained for.

The Brazilians were up at dawn. They packed up camp in a cheerful hurry, stopping only to wolf down a quick breakfast of army rations. They wanted us out of there before the second helicopter returned with reinforcements.

Gido whipped his animals into a trot as we left the scene of the crash and didn't stop until we were well out of sight. He had an Indian's distrust of the government, particularly the military, and foreign military most of all.

That night we camped in the shadow of the highest pass, and the next morning struggled over it. We stopped briefly at a tiny hut in a wide, flat valley where all the grass had been grazed down to the nub. This was the high pasture where the women brought their animals, sometimes for months at a time. The men stayed lower, at the main village, tending crops with the help of their older sons. The hut had doors so small that I had to bend almost double to fit inside.The walls were coal black and sticky from countless fires. The only bit of furniture in the two closet-size rooms was an adobe shelf, which must have served as a sleeping platform. Bits of fleece clung to the door frames like spiderwebs.

I could just make out the outline of the old Inca Road, raised slightly as it ran straight as an arrow across the valley below. Five hundred years and nothing had changed. We left the deserted hut to plod through the treeless páramo. We seemed a thousand miles away from cars or streetlights or telephones—even the helicopter crash was impossibly distant and unreal, like an alien spaceship descending out of the sky. Less real than the thought of ghostly Inca armies marching along the well-paved road.

That night we came upon an Inca way station. Several walls had been knocked down and its thatch roof had long since rotted away, but the remaining stonework had been cut to such perfection that a knife blade couldn't fit between the mortarless seams. It was hard to believe that the Inca had neither metal tools nor draft animals to help them create such works of art.

Nor did they have the wheel—a stunning revelation, given the size of the empire that they had to administer. Instead they developed a system of runners called *chasquis*: young men posted at intervals along the road, ever alert for the distant sound of a conch—the signal that another runner was on his way. Eventually the message bearer would appear, the two running side by side as information was breathlessly exchanged or a bag handed off, and the new runner bolted for the next station several miles away. By this means information could travel up to 250 miles a day, or from Quito in the north to Cuzco at the center of the empire in less than a week. It was an achievement that the modern postal service still can't match.

The way stations were built for more than just the chasqui runners. They fed and lodged all manner of government officials, army personnel, and occasionally even the Supreme Inca himself. They were kept well supplied with food, blankets, belt buckles, cooking pots, and any other items that might be required along the road. The largest ones had room enough for 8,000 llamas. They were an achievement almost as great as the road itself.

Ours was small and cozy. We pitched our tent in the shadow of its lichen-spotted walls. Sick from the altitude and exhaustion, I crawled into my sleeping bag and shivered myself warm. Outside the temperature had plummeted, stiffening the grass with frost.

"Gido!" I called.

"Yes!" His replies were still as sharp as a military salute.

"Come in and get warm."

"I'm okay."

I opened the fly and looked out. He was standing stock-still, his back to the wind and his hands thrust deep into his pockets. His hunched shoulders reminded me of a horse stuck out in the rain, resigned to the cold and discomfort, not even thinking to complain.

"Come in, Gido. It's freezing out!" I said again.

He shook his head. We had just spent three days together. I knew what he had given his daughter for her birthday and why he'd argued with his wife the week before. And yet there was still an indefinable distance between us, a barrier of race and color that seemed to carry the weight of centuries. All the way back, perhaps, to the conquerors.

The next morning Gido produced a small round disk about the size of a hockey puck. He proceeded to cut a stick of straight wood and, to my utter joy, presented me with a spindle. I tore through my possessions in search of the dirty white sheep's wool I had purchased in Achupallas. We squatted in the shelter of the ruins while Gido plucked a wisp of wool from my fleece and twisted it onto the shaft. I watched, entranced as the disk whirled and the fluffy white wool was transformed into perfectly spun thread.

"Where did you learn to spin so well?" I asked. "I thought it was woman's work."

"I don't know how!" he explained indignantly, his fingers skillfully separating the fibers. "I just used to watch my mother when I was young."

I was surprised by his expertise. In a land where gender governed practically every activity from birth to death, nothing was more sacred to women than spinning. It was a custom that dated back to Inca times. The Inca categorized people by age, class, and gender within an almost flawless administrative pyramid based on the decimal system. Every ten tribute payers reported to an overseer, who in turn reported to a man responsible for ten overseers, all the way up the ladder to the Supreme Inca himself.

Although "Inca" has come to mean anyone living under the umbrella of the empire, the Inca title originally referred only to the nobility, who further differentiated themselves by inserting large golden disks into their earlobes. In the early days of the empire, there were only two kinds of "Inca"—those who were direct descendants of the very first Inca, Manco Capac, and those who had no royal blood but traced their lineage back to the original tribe in Cuzco. As time went on the empire expanded faster than there were Inca nobles to occupy the top positions, so a third classification was created: "Inca by privilege." This was usually bestowed upon the leaders of newly conquered tribes, hastening their incorporation into the empire. The Supreme Inca kept his position pure through royal incest—a custom that began when the first Inca married his sister, Mama Ocla. He kept concubines to propagate his bloodline; Atahualpa was said to have had more than 5,000. Few knew what the Supreme Inca looked like, for his face was hidden by a veil—the son of the sun was too powerful to be seen by mere mortal eyes. Everything the Inca touched became sacred—from the remains of his meal to his fingernail parings— which were carefully gathered and destroyed to prevent them from being used in black magic.

But the courtly customs of the nobility mattered little to the average peasant tilling the land. Their lives were divided into discrete age groups, each with a name and an assigned task. A boy from one to three months old was a "sleeping child." Then he became a "child in swaddling clothes." At two years old he graduated from "child that moves on all fours" to "child easily frightened." At 12 he was a "gatherer of coca" and at 16 a "messenger." Between 20 and 40 he was a "warrior," then on to "middle-aged man" and finally, after 60, "old sleepyhead."

The legacy of the Inca system can be seen to this day. Women are in charge of animal husbandry and take care of the small children. Men farm the land. Women cook and sew; men gather firewood, carve tools, and build houses. More than anything, women spin and weave. There is even a word for an expert spinner in Quechua—*santuyuq*, "one who is possessed by the saint"—in this case Santa Rosa, patron saint of spinning. Little girls are taught to spin almost before they can walk; and young women weave intricate garments to showcase their skills and attract a mate. Women are almost never without their spindles—whether herding animals, walking to market, or tending children by the fire. In the Andes, you aren't a woman unless you can spin, and spin well.

I tried it. By good luck I already had some experience in spinning, though at home I used a tread wheel and only the finest merino fleece, free of burs and dung. Here the spindle seemed to have a life of its own, leaping out of my hands to knot the thread, which was woefully lumpy and overspun.

I climbed one of the walls of the way station and sat on the topmost stone, feeling for the center of the spindle as it turned beneath my fingers, carefully smoothing the gossamer fibers before they were drawn into thread. Breakfast lay forgotten. The mules grazed contentedly nearby. The early morning light was turning the edges of my puffy fleece to gold.

"Karin!"

John was ready to go. Gido too, though with characteristic patience he was waiting passively until I was done. Then I remembered—today, if all went well, we would hike the last nine kilometers down the mountainside to the ruins of Ingapirca.

The bleak highlands around us looked naked, like the back of a newly shorn sheep. This was a primordial landscape, uncultivable and untouched. As we dropped lower, we seemed to accelerate through the centuries, as though passing through a chronological landscape. The 16th century. Small farms sprang up, surrounded by stands of stately trees. The 17th century. A church, its simple white cross pressed starkly against the blue sky. The 18th century. Women in homespun tunics prodded sheep down country lanes. The 19th century. An adobe school. The 20th century, and we were suddenly staring at the corrugated rooftops of a modern town. It clung to the flanks of an ancient round-walled stone tower—Ingapirca.

We spent the night on lumpy bedsprings and rose in the hour before dawn to stumble through broken streets. Daybreak found us among the ruins, waiting breathlessly for the sun to crest the nearby mountaintops. The clouds flared orange. The highest peak melted into liquid white. A single ray cut like a laser to touch my hair, my face, and flow down my body. The stone around me glowed like purest gold. It seemed as though the sun god himself had put a spotlight on this, the last remaining tribute to him, before deigning to illuminate the iron-roofed town below.

I ran my fingers over the rounded Inca stonework. Every seam was beveled inward, giving the walls a natural texture while high-lighting the incredible engineering that went into their uniform shape and size. I thought back to that tiny mud hut high in the mountain pass behind us. How could a people clinging to life on the thin crust of a harsh world find the energy to build a place where each stone was cut to a perfect fit? Would I, if I had nothing more than a stone ax, a plumb line, and a dozen hungry mouths to feed, even begin to dream of palaces and temples to honor the gods? The answer lay south, in the heart of the empire, along the Inca Road.

CHAPTER 7

NTO THE DRAGON'S LAIR

FIELD NOTES: They drilled seven holes for an enormous blast and then lit the fuses. "How long?" I asked.

"More or less, two minutes," they told me.

"More, or less?" I asked.

Nambija. Those who knew the name sucked in their breath and shook their heads, telling me that it was a desperate place, utterly lawless, beyond the furthest edge of civilization. Reckless souls who went to seek their fortune there were rarely seen again. It lay in the southern Oriente—the steamy, rain-soaked eastern Andes. It was dangerous, filthy, and unforgiving, but it had one redeeming quality—gold. The guidebooks, when they mentioned Nambija at all, warned travelers to stay away.

Gold. The Inca called it the "sweat of the sun." Only the nobles were allowed to own it. They ate off it, drank out of it, lined the skulls of their defeated enemies with it. Golden disks adorned their clothes, their palanquins, their palaces and temples. Many of the houses in Cuzco were faced with gold, breathing life into the legend of El Dorado, the fabled city of gold. But despite their apparent love of the precious metal, the Inca didn't worship gold the way the Europeans did. In fact, the metal itself had no particular value until it was crafted into an aesthetically pleasing shape. The Inca Empire had no monetary system. The everyday economy was organized around a more mundane coinage—labor. Sweat was sellable. Gold belonged to the gods.

Little did the Inca know that the precious yellow metal would one day cause their empire to come crashing down.

I had read volumes on the 16th-century European quest for gold. I knew all the details of Pizarro's fateful journey to Peru. I could give a blow-by-blow account of his victory in battle over the Supreme Inca and the famous ransom that delivered tons of gold and silver into Spanish hands. I had traveled to museums to see the few golden llamas and other relics that escaped the Spanish furnaces. I had even heard breathless accounts from modern-day treasure hunters of a golden chain—so heavy that it took 200 men to carry it—still hidden somewhere in Peru's remote lakes and jungle ruins. Despite the detailed descriptions of the priceless Inca treasure, there was surprisingly little information on how the Inca mined their gold. One day a chance meeting with an Ecuadorian history professor led me to an obscure reference in a 17th-century government tract that mentioned an old Inca mining town—Nambija.

I boarded the bus to the Oriente with my fleece in hand, prepared to spend the next eight hours wrestling with my recalcitrant wool. As I made my way to the back, a wave of crinkled, smiling faces followed me as practically every passenger—men and women alike—turned to see what on Earth I was doing with an Andean spindle. I plucked halfheartedly at the fleece, ashamed to admit to strangers that I could spin no better than a four year old. An old woman sat down beside me and gestured for my fleece. The spindle sprang to life in her warped hands, the fibers magically realigning themselves. I was captivated by the mesmerizing, whirling disk. It sang like a cricket testing its wings.

Thinking she must be tiring of a task she did every day of her life, I offered to take it back. "Leave it!" she said in Quechua, slapping my hand away. An hour later she reached over the seat in front of her and passed the spindle forward. It landed on the lap of a carefully coifed woman in a polyester dress. Her hands were slender, her belt buckle the same shade of purple as her shiny shoes. The saints were obviously unfazed by her brightly painted fingernails, because she too had been blessed with the gift that made the spindle sing.

Gradually the fleece worked its way around the entire bus— young and old, sophisticated or country folk—and came back to me in the form of two neat balls of yarn. At this rate, I'd be able to knit my mother a sweater for Christmas without ever having to learn to spin.

Once we turned off the Pan American Highway, I asked permission to ride on top. The bus's unsprung wheels hammered the corrugated dirt road. It fought back with indignant clouds of dust. I took refuge under the stiff blue tarp that protected the cargo, burrowing in among the bags and boxes, sacks and buckets and drums of every kind. Curious, I prodded a lumpy round ball inside a plastic sack. Cabbages. The nearby can stank of gasoline. A thick yellow slab, trussed up in twine and oozing a noxious, gummy liquid must be cheese. I wormed deeper, peeking and peering and poking, until I came to a sack that writhed beneath my hand. I nearly shot through the tarp. I heard a squeak and felt soft, warm fur poke through the rough gunny sack. Guinea pigs, bound for market. They smelled like the gerbils I'd had as a child and moved gently under my fingers.

We were unloaded at the halfway town of Namirez along with a dozen crates of bread. Shiny, amphibious children flung themselves from a rickety bridge into the dun-colored water. They lived in a cluster of houses held together by rusty nails and yellowing political posters. The entire town sagged listlessly in the heavy, humid air. A rooster patrolled the main square, ready to face down both cars and feathered foes. It was an empty boast. The only wheels around belonged to an old minibus with open sides and unpadded wooden seats. It looked like it had long since settled in and staked out its turf. Chickens scratched the dusty ground. Children scratched at scabs along their arms and legs. Women fanned themselves while nursing babies and old men snoozed in rotting rattan chairs.

I sat. I got a drink of water. I dozed, openmouthed, like the old men. Several flies investigated my teeth. I got another drink to rinse off my tongue. I slept again. The bus—our ticket out of here—remained firmly in place. A little boy with a watermelon belly walked by, expertly rolling a large inner tube in endless circles with a stick. Everybody sat up to watch.

At last I felt the faint stirrings of activity, like the first exploratory breath of air over a wind-still pond. Cargo appeared, and someone actually clambered on board. We raced for seats. Several hours later we were underway.

The driver carefully nosed the bus through a filigree of braided vines that clutched at the wheels and trailed along the windshield. The rain forest crowded in on us like a primeval mob, a remnant of an ancient era when vegetation rioted and consumed the Earth. Butterflies drifted past on torpid air. The road climbed higher and higher in great anaconda loops until we broke free to an endless vista of frothy green jungle, shimmering in the heat. Then back down again, to where the leaves grew huge and heavy and smelled of the rich, dark, decomposing, life-giving earth.

The bus struggled along a single-track road that waterskied back and forth across a narrow river. The thick brown water slithered snake-like through the jungle. Along the way it swallowed a dozen long plastic pipes that ran along its bed, periodically draped over handmade wooden tripods and sluicing gates. Gold. We were getting close.

The bus abruptly disgorged everyone about a mile outside Nambija and then turned tail and dashed back to the relative safety of the highway. By the time we'd shouldered our gear, the other passengers had all but disappeared down a muddy footpath. Darkness was falling fast. The dimly winking lights were our only beacon in the seething, writhing, sea of jungle green.

We heard it long before we saw it—a distant drumming, low and evil, as steady as a massive, monstrous heartbeat. Unknowingly, our footsteps settled into that earthshaking beat. *Boom-boom-boom-boom.* It sounded like an army approaching, like the thud of a million feet. When we reached the edge of town, we saw it—the great crushers rolling round and round as they smashed chunks of rock to dust. The noise gathered itself like the wave approaching shore, getting steeper, sharper, harder-edged. For a moment we were at the very center of the rolling thunder, and then we edged past it and it gradually faded away. A second wave of machinery reared up to engulf us, then a third.

The town itself clung tenaciously to the hillside, each rickety shack thrusting away from the mountain on spindly legs. We found ourselves climbing endless steps, past gamblers tossing down their cards beside huge wads of worthless bills. Dim cafés were wrapped in the stench of boiling pig fat and the bloodied clientele of whiskey shops lay propped up on stools against the moldy walls. I asked for a hostel. The card game paused just long enough for someone to point a chin uphill. Two white faces provoked surprisingly little interest. Or perhaps Nambija just played its cards close to its chest.

The "hotel"—an arrow pointed at an open space occupied by a single, soiled outhouse—was closed, but across the street a café owner offered us a miner's room upstairs. It was barely the size of a walk-in closet, with a narrow wooden bench that served as a bed and high up on a dusty shelf, a pair of broken leather dancing shoes. The bathroom, I was told, was in the non-hotel across the street. Showers? Well, we could use the hose out in the cement courtyard when no one was looking.

I waited until long after normal people are safely tucked between their sheets and crept back outside. Farther down the mountain I could see puddled light where people labored, filling the machines, sifting through the ore, always moving to that relentless, pounding beat. Nambija must never go to sleep. Cautiously I began to strip. A young miner appeared out of nowhere, sucked a mouthful of water from the hose, and began brushing his teeth with the frayed end of a stick. A half-naked white woman in the middle of his courtyard seemed about as likely as my finding a gremlin reading the morning paper on my front lawn. He nodded a brief greeting, rinsed out his mouth, and went back to bed.

This was going to be an interesting place.

The next morning Sebastian was waiting outside our door. He was twelve years old going on forty, shrewd and unsmiling and already working as a *kargador*—a carrier—feeding the ravenous machines. For 14 hours at a time, he entered the mole-like tunnels that burrowed deep into the mountainside to hammer fist-size chunks from the walls—until he had freed a hundred pounds of ore. Then up and out, bent double under the sack. The tunnel walls were so narrow that at times he had to turn sideways to thread his cargo through, gripping a flashlight with his teeth. Daylight at last, but the journey was only half done. Down the uneven flight of stairs, slippery with mud even in the dry season: 423 steps (how often had he counted them?) before he reached the crushing mill. Each sack earned him 60 cents. Twelve times a day.

Sebastian offered to take us down into the mines for the price of three sacks of ore. At the last minute his 16-year-old sister, Cecilia, decided to come along. We waited for her to get ready while Sebastian sniggered under his breath. Apparently, a young man worked in the mine.... She returned wearing heavy earrings, makeup, and her best blouse.

The stairs were foul with the refuse of the hundred huts above us. I counted 250 steps before I gave up, grateful that I had nothing more than a camera around my neck. We crossed over the river that ran through town, stiff with garbage and viscous with the runoff of the endlessly grinding machines. Tangled plastic hoses ran up and down the mountainside like a writhing knot of worms disgorging filthy water into both sluice gates and café cooking pots. Children played among the corrugated metal shacks, their bare feet unthinkingly avoiding the splintered holes in balcony floors and rotting second-story steps. Everything was the color of pounded rock—the laundry hanging on knotted ropes, the mud-splattered houses, the people, and the sluggish pigs that rooted through the river debris. There wasn't a single bright spot to rest the eye amid the endless gray.

The cement steps were Nambija's central artery, the only solid structure on the slippery mountainside. The houses clung to it for balance. The entire town looked precarious, like a layered house of cards.

We crested the final step, waded through a field of garbage, and stood face-to-face with a black hole that disappeared into the mountainside. Muddy men in rubber boots scurried in and out like a stream of ants, some slumped under the weight of ore and others taking a last few breaths of air before plunging back inside. Sebastian took his place in line, his face suddenly devoid of life.

The passage was only wide enough for one. Fully loaded kargadors had the right-of-way. When we heard them coming, we scurried to the nearest alcove to let them pass, muscles straining, eyes fixed on the next bend and the fantasy of daylight. The journey down was only half an hour—according to my watch—but the absolute blackness smothered time and the minutes struggled by like insects caught in sticky sap.

Just when it seemed that all of life swam in the small pool of my headlight, the narrow tunnel opened out and we found ourselves at the edge of an immense cave the size of a cathedral. I doused my light. Blackness settled on me like a coat of tar. All around a hundred stars glowed dimly, each a single candle by which a miner worked his claim. For the first time I realized that the heavy thumping of machinery was gone; we were too deep in the bowels of the Earth to hear it. In its place there was the *tack-tack* of countless hammers hitting stone. It was an eerie, upside-down hell, the winking stars below and only suffocating rock above.

One miner lay sleeping on a tattered mat across the entrance to an alcove. He woke up as the unexpected light from John's camera cut across his face. Rather than throw rocks at us, as I would have done had I been torn from sleep by that blinding glare, he sat up and asked us if there was anything he could help us with. Nambija was not living up to its bleak reputation.

He was, he said, sleeping there to protect his claim. He pointed at a piece of wall that looked just like any other. He shared a 24-hour shift with his partner, and came out only to eat, wash, and haul his ore down to the machines.

"Do you think you'll strike it rich one day?" I asked.

He shrugged. "We're all just looking for a better life." But, he admitted, there was always that chance that the next hammer strike would reveal a vein of solid gold. Everyone, it seemed, had heard of someone who had gone from rags to riches in a single day. No one knew exactly who, but the possibility was there. His body leaned forward, reenergized by the thought.

He must be a newcomer. I wondered how long his naive enthusiasm would survive this living hell.

"I came here eight years ago," he said.

Eight years. Twelve sacks a day; 423 steps. Sleeping in a stifling hole and seeing sunlight through eyes slitted against the unaccustomed glare. And yet he spoke as though tomorrow might well be the day when he stubbed his toe on that precious nugget of gold.

"And if you do?"

"I'd leave here," he said without hesitation. He'd take his wife and three children—children who had been born amid the sludge and refuse, who knew no other home than the rickety huts of Nambija—and build a proper house far away. As he spoke, I saw the dream emerge as bright and dependable as the rising sun.

Abel shook himself awake and offered to take us through the mine. It was built on three levels, he told me, stacked one on top of the other. No one knew when some miner would break through and send thousands of tons of rock crashing down to bury everyone below.

We heard a distant boom, then another. "Dynamite," Abel said, apparently unconcerned. He pointed at the hoses that snaked through the narrow tunnels and plunged down into the digging pits—hoses that I had assumed provided surface ventilation for us all. He smiled and shook his head. They did indeed carry compressed air, but it was to power the jackhammers that drilled holes into which the miners stuffed homemade dynamite. The blasts echoed through the cavernous room every few minutes. The stones above our heads wiggled like loose teeth and several came tumbling down. No one wore helmets. There was no shoring anywhere in sight. How many men, I wondered, had lost their lives while hammering through tons of rock in search of that elusive dream?

He thought a moment. "Last month someone died from falling rock." He looked around and said simply. "A thousand souls dwell here."

We wandered from one room to another, down tunnels knee-deep in muddy water. My flashlight's beam swept briefly across miners heaving heavy sacks onto their backs, leaving in its wake a darkness even more suffocating for the moment of bright light.

At last Abel led us to a chamber where three men were drilling holes with a jackhammer. The dust swirled around us like a desert dervish, so dense that we could barely make out the candles flickering along one wall. The workmen looked like flour-coated ghouls. Conversation was impossible. We sat and watched them drill three, four, five holes. In the middle of the sixth, the jackhammer ground unexpectedly to a halt.

"No air," the operator said, wiping his face with his forearm. A mustache suddenly poked through the dust. The compressor might come on in a few minutes or not at all. Most likely the engine operators had quit for lunch.

"Who built the stairs and dug the tunnels?" I asked the foreman as we waited for the hoses to reinflate. He was paying by the hour for the hammer and wasn't about to leave for lunch. "The Company," he said. Apparently it had no other name, nor did it need one. It was Canadian. It had bought the rights to the mountain, dug the passageways, and built the town's basic infrastructure before running out of cash. Once it pulled out, the mine became a free-for-all, with every man working for himself. Those with money set up the crushers to extract the gold from the sweat-soaked ore. The town was convinced that the Company had plans to return and expel the miners from what they now considered to be their rightful claim. There was talk of setting up a cooperative to fight the hovering threat, but everybody was too busy digging gold to take the time to organize it.

At last the hoses stiffened and the sixth and seventh holes were duly drilled. A stick of dynamite was stuffed into each one, followed by a cork of sand wrapped in newspaper. The driller prepared to light the first fuse.

"How much time?" I asked.

"Two minutes, more or less," he said.

"More," I asked, "or less?"

He turned and shouted, *"Fuego!"* The cry was picked up and repeated in a human-powered echo throughout the mine. We all made a dash for the relative safety of a solid arch around the corner. The chamber emptied instantly—each miner disappearing into his own private nook or cranny to wait out the blasts.

"How many?" a voice called out.

"Seven!"

It was the first moment of silence since we got off the bus. What came after more than made up for it. The blast shook the walls we were leaning against. It felt like the center of a thunderhead. Four more detonations. A long pause, then another.

"Done?" someone shouted.

"One more!"

We scurried back under the arch just in time for the final blast. My ears were clogged with sound; I felt as though I were wearing a Russian hat with thick wool flaps. I leaned over the edge of the pit to see what the dynamite had done. Someone grabbed my arm and hauled me back.

"Wait. The fumes are poisonous," Abel said. Many an overeager miner had succumbed by dashing in too soon after the blast to lay first claim to the glitter of a golden vein. Eventually two men went down to burn off the remaining fumes with lighted newspapers. Only then did a half dozen miners swarm over the rubble like rats. They analyzed the blast with fierce concentration, turning stones this way and that in the beam of their flashlights. I looked as well, but the tiny flecks just didn't carry the romance of the solid gold vein I had been hoping for. My interest flagged. Nambija obviously wasn't the place for me.

Eventually Abel returned to his mat to catch a few more hours' sleep before it came his turn to wrestle rock from rock. He would accept no money to compensate him for his time—a guided tour was such an easy thing that it didn't count as work.

The journey to the surface was interminable—at every turn I expected to see a distant light that never came. When we at last emerged, I had to cover my eyes against the glare. I looked at my watch. Three hours.

Eight years.

Unimaginable.

Just below the mine entrance, a cable ran across the valley to a crusher on the other side. Two open metal baskets whizzed back and forth, carrying loads of ore. "Can I catch a ride?" I called up to the brakeman. When the next basket returned, the loader held it obligingly while I climbed in. "You're nuts," John said. The brakes let loose and in a moment I was flying across the valley, the whirring of the cable rising to a primal scream. I looked forward just in time to snatch my hand out of the path of the second basket as it whipped by. From several hundred feet up I couldn't see the trash clogging the river or the wobbly underpinnings of the squatter's shacks. Nambija looked suddenly quite picturesque, nestled in a bed of jungle green.

"You wouldn't get me in one of those," the toothless loader said by way of greeting when I reached the bottom. "Last month the cable broke. Guy was in the cart."

I looked up at the station high across the valley. John was already climbing in. "Can we stop the carts from here?" I asked.

He shook his head, pointing his cigarette at the brakeman across the valley. His hand was missing three fingers. I didn't ask.

"How often does the cable break?" I said, watching John's cart pull away. The wires vibrated into their high-pitched squeal.

"Few times a year."

John slowed, then sped up again, then finally came to a bone-jarring stop against the tire at the bottom. He grunted, then clambered out without a word.

Once we were back in our tiny miner's shack, I gathered up soap and clothes. Unwilling to strip in broad daylight, I dragged a bucket into the rotting outhouse. I stood on tiptoe amid the filth and looked around in growing frustration for a peg to hang my towel...and suddenly, it all made sense. Nails, hard hats, ventilation—none of those things mattered here. The town existed because of gold; it lived to service a single, all-consuming addiction. Nambija was like a living being—the machinery its throbbing heart and the mine its soul. Everyone came here with the same intention—to steal a piece of Nambija's treasure and escape with it, like the legendary heroes who crept into the dragon's lair in search of a glittering hoard of gold. Or like the Spanish who crossed oceans and faced down hostile empires for a stake of the precious yellow metal. Driving a nail into a wall to hang a towel or fixing broken floorboards to make a balcony a little safer—those chores must seem a waste of time where every waking minute held the power and the promise of discovering the dragon's mother lode.

And yet life went on. The women scrubbed their laundry on the courtyard's cement floor. You could buy everything from batteries to lightbulbs in the shops that lined the stairs. Children grew up playing among the ancient hulks of discarded machinery. Deep inside the bowels of the Earth, young couples courted and babies were eventually born. As I left the courtyard I caught a whiff of something utterly incongruous amid the odors of pig manure and burning trash—the scent of freshly baked bread. It drew me like a half-starved dog.

The café owner laughed at my hungry, hopeful face and waved me onto a stool. "Ten more minutes," she said, looking over her shoulder at a blackened stove. I sat. A drunk staggered over and jiggled his half-empty bottle. She shooed him away like a pesky fly. He turned to me, doffed his hat, and offered me a drink. Then he wobbled off and threw up on one of his compatriots who lay senseless in a pool of drying blood.

She introduced herself as Maria-Celeste, a name that seemed too feminine for her work-chapped hands. She had nine children and had built her tiny store with discarded plywood boards after her husband left her for another woman. Her oldest boys were in boarding school in Zamora, the nearest town of consequence. The middle girls studied here—one was writing in a scrappy notebook amid the sleeping drunks—and the youngest she kept with her at the store. She made ends meet by selling bowls of puddled pig stew and mopping up the blood and urine of her more inebriated clientele. She stood straight and proud, one hand on the shoulder of a three-year-old girl who leaned against her thigh. Yes, she knew where her husband lived and, no, she didn't want him back.

At last my laundry was clean and hanging on the balcony outside my room and my belly was stuffed with freshly baked bread. I headed down the stairs in search of one of those fire-breathing, rock-stomping crushers. Now that I knew exactly where the ore was harvested, I wanted to see how it was eaten, digested, and what came out the other side.

An old woman in voluminous skirts waved me into the corrugated shed before I even had a chance to phrase the question.

Five minutes later I was hard at work swirling buckets of pulverized stone.

The rocks had been dumped into oversize cement mixers with heavy metal rollers, along with water and a dab of mercury to help leach out the gold. Several earsplitting hours later, they had been ground to watery paste, which was then emptied into the bucket where my hands were busy stirring under the watchful eyes of the old woman. The lighter paste rose in suspension and was gradually siphoned off, leaving behind the rougher grit and gold. When only a handful remained at the bottom of the bucket, we poured it into a wok. The woman took over, carefully swirling the water around and around, drawing off the grit. Try as I might, I couldn't see a single flake of gold among the coarse grains. With just an inch of water in the wok, she slowly drew three fingers through the sand. Several shivery snakes of mercury appeared out of nowhere and wiggled to the bottom of the wok. She did it again, and a second, smaller bubble popped out to join the first. With exquisite care she floated the mercury to one side, caught it in an old rag, twisted the rag to wring it out, and held the flaky silver ball up to the light before dropping it quickly down the front of her bra.

"And then?" I asked.

It took a second hour's labor to earn the answer. The balls of mercury-gold were allowed to dry for a day and then taken up to the roof and placed inside a miniature oven. Each lump was heated with an acetylene torch to vaporize the mercury. As the little balls cooled, they were no longer silver but bright gold. Why go through all the trouble, I asked, of climbing up to burn it on the roof?

"Very poisonous," her husband said, indicating the mercury. He passed a hand in front of his eyes. "Dizziness, headache...." He pointed at the three-foot length of pipe that stuck straight up out of the oven. "Ventilation." In a place were hard hats were an unnecessary nuisance, I wondered how many people had died before they'd decided to weld on that pipe.

But the vapors didn't just disappear—there were dozens of ovens in Nambija, each regurgitating toxic fumes. And the consequences were more than just headaches. Tremors, numbness, impaired vision, and dementia, and eventually renal failure and death. Children were particularly vulnerable. The mercury-laden runoff from the crushing mills ran straight into the river—which doubled as a source of drinking water for the entire town.

Late that afternoon I sat on my rotting balcony and watched the setting sun light up the corrugated rooftops with a golden glow. Nambija was beautiful—and treacherous. Not because of its lawless ruffians, as the guidebooks warned—quite the contrary, even the drunks treated me with respect. It was the unshored mines, the homemade dynamite, and the free-for-all within the mine itself, just waiting for the inevitable collapse that would send another thousand souls to join those who already haunted that hellish place. And outside—splintered catwalks, parasite-infested water, mercury-laden air. Even "safe in bed" had little meaning here. Only a few years ago, after particularly heavy rains, the entire side of the mountain had sheared away, burying 800 sleeping villagers in a suffocating blanket of mud. Nearly half the town had died that night. When people told me about it, their faces drained of all expression, just like the workers waiting to go down into the mine. Always there was a shrug. "We built new houses on the mud. Sometimes bodies still pop up and we bury them." They had pointed out the place to me, but I couldn't see a single scar among the rough-hewn shacks. Disaster strikes. Life moves on. The gold remains.

After three days of freeze-dried food even John was ready to brave the stench of pig fat in search of something freshly vegetarian. We trotted down the stairs to investigate.

The first café sold only meat and rice. The second had never heard of such a thing as murder-free cuisine. At the third we hit pay dirt—a mouthwatering stew, rich with vegetables, lentils, and a thick brown broth. John questioned the owner in detail about the contents—was it made with beef or chicken stock? "Absolutely not," the woman said. When she served us, she used the same ladle that had been sitting in a cauldron of boiled chicken parts. "Contaminated," John said with disgust, and stalked out.

The next—and last—café was ruled by an intimidating matron swathed in layers of filthy aprons and brandishing a heavy metal spoon. I slid into a seat, prepared to eat whatever she had to offer. John was not.

She shuffled over to take our order. John waded into battle. Did she have anything vegetarian? No meat, not even broth. No chicken, pig, or beef. No eggs. No cheese.

"Fish?" she barked.

"Fish"—he spoke slowly, enunciating every word,—"is not a vegetable."

Yes, she said, she had yucca soup. I breathed a sigh of relief. By this time I was starving, and still mourning that lovely lentil stew. John wasn't ready to give in. He demanded a list of the soup's ingredients, then followed the woman into the kitchen to verify her answers for himself. At last he emerged. The woman, by now thoroughly annoyed, slapped our meals down on the filthy table, snorted twice, and stalked away.

Fried plantains, a bowl of rice, and a serving of shoe-leather beef for me. John was two-thirds through his soup when his spoon scraped bottom and dredged up what looked suspiciously like a piece of fish. I hunkered down in my seat. He ordered the woman out of her kitchen.

"What's this?" he asked, indicating the offending morsel with his spoon.

She glanced at it. "Yucca."

Several bones stuck out of it. John demanded a confession. The woman stood by her assessment. I kept a cowardly silence. Eventually she grabbed the bowl and stormed off into the kitchen. I sadly gave up my plans to ask for a second bowl, afraid of what I might get by association.

I did, however, leave her a substantial tip.

It was pitch-black by the time we headed back up the stairs. I dreaded another evening spent in that suffocating little miner's room, cleaning cameras and doing logs. We passed three young men who seemed sober, despite the time of night. "What is there to do around here on a Friday evening?" I asked. They looked at John, then at me, then at John. I knew exactly what they were thinking. Nambija was sorely lacking for women. A hard week's wages, a bottle of booze....

We followed them to a large warehouse whose thin plywood walls vibrated to the blaring beat inside. I entered warily. I had worked with prostitutes before, during my stint as a Peace Corps volunteer. I was more concerned about treading on their turf than for being the only white female face in an Ecuadorian frontier bar.

Several dozen pairs of eyes latched on to us like sniper sights as we made our way to a far corner of the room. Miners slumped over tables, their hardened hands curled around bottles of even harder liquor, their faces carrying the memories of knife fights and mining mishaps. Women sat among them, wearing too much makeup and too little clothing, looking every bit as hard-bitten as the men they were paid to serve. Two walls were lined with rooms the size of horse stalls, each with a number and a light above it. Every once in a while a woman would rise and disappear into a cubicle, followed by an unsmiling man. The door closed, the light went out, and less than five minutes later they were back, sitting among the rest. "How much?" I asked one of the three young men who had accompanied us. "Twenty-thousand sucres," he said with a leer. Four dollars.

Two prostitutes sat down with us and John bought them drinks. They lived in Zamora, some six hours away. On weeknights they plied their trade in the downtown strips and on weekends serviced the remoter towns. The price in the provinces was lower, but the turnover more than made up for it. One of the women was slender and elegant, with lovely long legs and narrow wrists, but her chubbier companion disappeared more often into the numbered rooms. The less favored prostitute ran a finger down her arm. "I am *morena*," she said. Dark-skinned—in a land that disdained its own indigenous features in favor of a more European look. She shrugged. The night was young. The more the men had to drink, the less choosy they became.

The fellow sitting next to me had drawn his own conclusions from my questions. He was leaning over me, his hand beginning to slither up my leg. I stood. John followed, reluctantly. The three young men chose their women and headed for the numbered rooms.

By my fourth day in Nambija, the throbbing machinery had become so much a part of life that I had to strain to hear it anymore. I wondered if people's hearts began to beat in sync with its pounding rhythm, like a town-size pacemaker.

I spent the morning asking around for any clues to nearby Inca ruins or remains. A shopkeeper pointed to a large hole in the rock wall across the valley. "They used to dig there," he said. "But the gold ran out." I didn't bother to go up and investigate. I knew the Inca hardly ever mined for gold, preferring to pan it from the rivers. But then, what did I expect to discover in a town that had learned to forget yesterday's disappointments and think only of the possibilities of each new day? The past had no place here, only the present. And the future.

On my way out of Nambija I stopped at the last crusher, strangely reluctant to carry on. That endless beat was like a parasite that had wormed its way into my chest and started thumping from the inside out. I sat and watched the army of young men dropping their loads of ore into the waiting bins. I'd been wrong about Nambija. It wasn't greed that drove the miners here. It was hope. Hope for a better life, for themselves or for their children, or just to leave a little better off than they had come.

CHAPTER 8

LAND MINES IN PARADISE

FIELD NOTES: "You want me to jump over THAT? You gotta be kidding."

Our bus was stopped half a dozen times by military checkpoints on our way back to the Pan American Highway. Our bags were searched and papers checked. We were close to the border of Peru. The tension was palpable. Soldiers kept both hands on their guns. No one smiled.

Ever since that fateful helicopter crash, I had been wondering about the war. Why on Earth would Ecuador, a country the size of Colorado, pick a fight with Peru, the size of Texas and California combined?

The answer lay in a conflict that could be traced all the way back to the bloody civil war between two Inca rulers—one based in Quito, Ecuador, and the other in Cuzco, Peru. Once the Spanish came and conquered, they seemingly put an end to native boundary disputes. The truce was short-lived. A group of conquerors settled Quito and, worried over potential incursions by other Spaniards from the south, almost immediately sent a mission to mark the border with Peru. A line was drawn that would reverberate through the centuries.

In 1802 the Spanish crown gave title over the region to Peru, taking it from the amalgamated state that included modern-day Colombia, Ecuador, and Venezuela. The subsequent wars of independence among the new nations resulted in even more border conflicts and produced confusing and often contradictory treaties. The disputes were really battles waged on paper, with maps and rulers and blank green spaces, for neither side had managed to settle this most inaccessible corner of the world.

Then rumors spread that the forbidding land of rumpled mountains, deep ravines, and impenetrable rain forest might hold a secret treasure—petroleum and gold. In 1941, Peru moved suddenly against Ecuador. The winner was a foregone conclusion: Peruvians outnumbered Ecuadorians four to one. If the fighting had continued, Ecuador might have been conquered outright. Both sides eventually agreed to arbitration. Unfortunately for Ecuador, World War II was underway and the United States desperately needed a unified Southern Hemisphere to oppose the Axis powers. More to the point, Peru's copper, rubber, and quinine were urgently required for the Allied war effort.

The resulting Rio de Janeiro protocol of 1942 signed almost half of Ecuador over to Peru. The treaty was based on the findings of a Brazilian arbiter who selected the Condor range as the new border because it was assumed to divide the waters between the Santiago and Zamora Rivers. Ecuador agreed—it had no choice—

but the treaty's immense unpopularity forced the government to look for a way out.

Five years later, the Cenepa River was discovered. This technically invalidated the geographical premise of the Rio de Janeiro protocol, since the Condor range no longer constituted the watershed divider. Ecuador had found an excuse. It declared the treaty void and both sides moved in troops.

Despite significant international pressure, Ecuador refused to back down. It was feeling increasingly beleaguered by its land-hungry neighbors. The prior 150 years had seen its territory whittled away to the point where it was now the smallest country in the Andes, a buffer nation between the region's two superpowers— Colombia and Peru. And as South America's most densely populated nation, Ecuador simply couldn't afford to lose any more land.

Those were the facts. Opinions were far more complicated. "Monkeys," the Peruvian taxi drivers called the Ecuadorians. "Chickens," the Ecuadorians snapped back, referring to the war Peru had lost to Chile. "The land is ours," Peru intoned with a collective shrug, secure in its military superiority. "They stole it!" Ecuador cried, and turned it into a national rallying cry. But beneath the bluster and the politics, there was great sadness. "We are brothers," a policeman told me. "We celebrate the same festivals, wear the same clothes, laugh at the same jokes. Why are brothers killing brothers? It is blasphemy."

A month-long undeclared war in 1995 took lives on both sides and ended in a stalemate. It was also responsible for the most horrific consequence of the struggle—the laying down of tens of thousands of land mines, by both parties, in an effort to keep the respective armies from crossing the cordillera and claiming more land.

But no one had taken the mountains—or perhaps the mountain gods—into account. The Cordillera was steep, dense, and impenetrable. When the rains came, the mud shifted and the mines moved, as though the land itself were trying to shrug away the explosives laid under its skin. Soon no one knew where their own mines lay, let alone the enemy's. All maps were useless. The Cordillera had become a death trap for man and animal alike. Misty mountains filled with singing birds and pink and purple orchids. An Eden, lost forever.

The Inca Road led south, across the border into Peru. If I was to follow it, I would need permission from the Ecuadorian military and an escort to the border. Perhaps they would even let me join them on patrol, to see for myself what all the fighting was about. I caught a bus for Quito and made an appointment with the Ecuadorian Ministry of Defense.

Colonel Borja was a compact man with a severely pressed uniform and childlike grin. He greeted me with a firm handshake, and in no time at all we were sipping sweet black coffee and poring over a large map. A supply plane flew to Macas—he pointed at an intriguingly empty spot on the map—once a week. We were welcome aboard if we didn't mind sharing space with onions and potatoes. We didn't mind at all.

So far so good. I took a breath. Could we, I asked carefully, accompany his troops on a de-mining patrol?

He hesitated, clucking with concern over our safety. Wouldn't we rather fly into the Amazon, canoe upriver, and visit one of the remote villages where the native men had six wives apiece?

Tempting, I said, but I had my heart set on a patrol. He picked up the phone and it was arranged. He paused for a moment, his hand still on the receiver. There was a de-mining base just outside of Quito where the young men drilled every morning to prepare for their time out in the field. Would I care to join them for a workout and a demonstration of their work?

"Of course," I said, and swallowed hard.

The next morning I hauled myself out of bed at seven and caught a taxi to the base. I already had two strikes against me—a case of giardiasis I'd picked up in Nambija, and Quito's altitude. At 9,300 feet, it is the world's second-highest capital. When I presented myself to the military commander, I was introduced to 20 strapping young men—all lungs on legs. Not one of them over 18 years old. Strike three. This was going to be a disaster.

After a quick set of warm-up exercises, we formed a tight group to jog around the base. *I can do this*, I thought, trying to ignore the acidic backwash of the breakfast I had forced down. The drill sergeant trotted next to me, leading everyone in a rousing song. The lyrics were a little disconcerting—"Engineers never die and if they die it's because they want to." I glanced over. The soldiers had yet to break a sweat. I tried to breathe and sing and run at the same time. The next 15 minutes took an hour to crawl by. The obstacle course appeared in the distance.

I can make it that far, I thought. We jogged past. A new song began. Everyone clapped in time to the words. I tried to breathe and sing and clap and run at the same time. Still not a drop of sweat among the troops. Damned if I was going to make everyone slow down for me.

At last, we reached the far end of the base and executed a tight U-turn. Now, if I could only make it back to the obstacle course. I stopped singing. There it was! I concentrated on looking good until we reached the gate. We jogged by. I stopped clapping. If they made us run all the way back to our starting point....

They did. Then, with nary a pause to catch breath, the men lined themselves up for wind sprints. When the whistle blew, everyone breezed by me as if I were a parked car. We lined up to do it again. This time they passed me so fast I felt like I was jogging backwards.

"Hey, Karin," John said as we reformed into a square to continue running. "I think that was the warm-up." I wished him dead. I was afraid he might be right. He was.

The morning passed in a blur of push-up platforms, pull-up bars, rope climbs, jumping jacks, jogging, and finally, the obstacle course. I got a quick look—lots of barbed wire to crawl under, walls to jump over and climb up—just the sort of thing I had loved doing as a child. A third of the way through, I looked up to see everyone lounging about the finish line, waiting for me. The drill sergeant stuck by my side like Velcro.

We formed back into a jogging square. What next? The pool! I couldn't run or climb or jump to save my life, but I could swim. I could swim so well that I was halfway through the first lap before I realized I was absolutely out of air. I prayed to be reincarnated as a sea turtle, a frigate bird—anything with larger lungs. I hoped fervently never to find myself in battle with the Ecuadorian military. I swore off candy bars and diet cola. The young men toweled themselves off and, whistling merrily, headed out to do their day's duty. I hauled myself on board the bus to town and crawled into bed.

The phone rang that afternoon. The flight to Macas was leaving the next morning. We were going on patrol.

We presented ourselves at the military runway early the following morning. While waiting for the supply plane to arrive, I pulled out a map and drew in the line of the 1942 disputed border through the vast green space of Ecuador's eastern Amazon. The result was disconcerting. Ecuador was suddenly tiny beside the mighty Peru. Perhaps the Ecuadorians were right to be afraid. It wasn't the first time that a conquering race had swept up the Andes to rape and pillage their neighbors to the north.

In the 1400s, southern Ecuador was a peaceful country in the hands of its native Indians. That ended when the Inca first appeared. For years the Cañari fought bitterly against their marauding neighbors, but in the end were overcome. The conquering Inca married a Cañari princess in Quito and fathered a son by her. The boy did likewise and in due time Atahualpa—Heroic Turkey—was born. From a very early age, Atahualpa accompanied his father into battle. By the time the old man was ready to retire from the field, Atahualpa was already a seasoned—and ruthless—fighter.

Then disaster struck. The reigning Inca contracted what was probably smallpox, a European disease that had ripped through Central America to engulf the Andes long before the first white-skinned foreigner set foot in Peru. The illness that carried him off also struck down his probable heir. The stage was set for strife.

The task of choosing a successor fell into the hands of the Inca nobles in Cuzco. The new ruler had only to be a direct descendant of the sun god Inti. Any of the Inca's many sons were eligible. The court nominated a man by the name of Gentle Hummingbird—Huascar.

There were those who disagreed. The army—headquartered in the north—much preferred the battle-hardened Atahualpa to the hummingbird raised in Cuzco's court. The empire split in two.

Huascar, with the backing of his nobles, demanded Atahualpa's presence. Atahualpa wisely demurred, sending instead a slew of sumptuous gifts. Back and forth along the Inca Road between Quito and Cuzco, the battle of wills raged for five long years. At last Huascar, in a fit of pique, had Atahualpa's messengers tortured and his gifts burned. The gauntlet was thrown down.

A nation barely recovering from a disastrous smallpox epidemic suddenly found itself engaged in a bloody civil war.

The Gentle Hummingbird had little chance against the ruthless Turkey. When Atahualpa won his first battle, he had the skull of the opposing general, another brother, lined with gold and turned into a drinking vessel; his skin was used to make a drum. The next engagement proved decisive, for Huascar himself was captured and his army routed. He was taken back to Cuzco and forced to watch as his family and advisors were slaughtered. Their bodies, including children and unborn fetuses, were tied to poles around the city as a bloody warning to all those inclined to challenge Atahualpa's rule.

Atahualpa retired to the hot baths of Cajamarca to enjoy his hard-won victory and the prospect of ruling one of the world's greatest empires. Just over the horizon, a ragtag band of 160 Spaniards was making its way from the coast to intercept him. Atahualpa knew all about the bearded white foreigners and had been keeping tabs on them since their arrival. He was unimpressed. How could such a tiny force possibly threaten a nation of ten million people?

He was dead wrong.

A small prop plane landed at the military airport and we clambered on board. I sat beside a bespectacled man with iron gray hair and the ramrod stance that belied his civilian clothes. He was a colonel, he told me, one of only two surgeons assigned to the Condor mountain region. His specialties were trauma, pediatrics, hernias, internal problems, parasites, and obstetrics, though of necessity he was unusually well-versed in amputations and other particulars of war. He treated at least three mine-related injuries each month. Most survived. The ones that didn't....He shrugged. If a call came in at dusk on a rainy night, there was little the rescue helicopters could do until morning. Every month he taught the new soldiers tourniquet techniques and how to handle severed extremities in the field.

"What would you do," I asked, "if there were no war?"

He smiled and his eyes turned sad. "Obstetrics," he said wistfully. His hands made an involuntary motion, as though cradling something very fragile. "To see a baby born—it's a miracle."

We landed on a remote runway carved out of a dense carpet of green, near a cluster of houses that I hadn't seen on any map— Patuka, a military base deep in the heart of the Ecuadorian jungle. The colonel dropped us off amid a row of identical cement bungalows and drove off to do battle with torn limbs and shattered bones and to dream of the sound of a baby's first cry.

We settled in to await the orders of the Ecuadorian military. It didn't occur to us for several hours that no one knew we had arrived. I was tempted to just shoulder my backpack and catch a ride into the jungle, but it seemed a poor way of repaying the colonel's generosity. In the end we agreed to wait. I watched a thick rope of army ants crawl through the bathroom window, stumble across a tortured landscape of peeling gray paint, and disappear into an unused drain. John fiddled with his camera and rechecked bulbs and batteries. As darkness fell, flying ants swarmed through every window, crack, and crevice. Soon we were sealed in tight, drenched with sweat and hunkered down in silence under a ceiling fan that barely stirred the torpid air. By 9 p.m. I was ready to brave the ants, the military, and even the possibility of getting lost forever among the identical houses of our military neighborhood for a single bite to eat.

Three sentries later we wandered into a musty dive with blaring music and boiled potatoes—and an unexpected sight. Braga. I was so stunned that it took me a moment to recognize him from the helicopter crash. That day up on the high and windy páramo felt like a lifetime ago.

We exchanged Brazilian bear hugs and then sat down to potatoes and a pint of beer.

"So what happened after we left?" I asked.

They'd spent five more nights at the site of the crash, sleeping under a tarp until a larger helicopter arrived to airlift the wreckage. Braga shivered with remembered cold. Apparently he had missed our tent more than he'd missed us. The downed aircraft was eventually shipped off to the States for repairs. An investigation concluded that the crash was due to "engine failure." After several beers, Braga suggested we try to catch a ride to the border with a MOMEP peacekeeping helicopter. We tipped a final toast to eternal friendship and took our leave.

The next morning we followed the *thwack-thwack* of descending rotor blades to a tidy set of prefabricated buildings tucked in among the MOMEP tents. Two men sat under an awning in the glutinous heat, drinking diet sodas. A third stuck his head out of a nearby kitchen when we introduced ourselves. "Y'all want a burger?" he asked as though we were old friends stopping in for a backyard barbecue.

They were American mechanics, hired on one-year contracts by an aircraft company to maintain and repair the MOMEP helicopters. All three wore wedding rings. I watched the sweat collect along their hairlines and bead the cans they cradled in their hands. "What makes someone take a job in a place like this?" I asked.

The two men at the table laughed. "The first year it's need. After that it's greed," one of them recited in a singsong voice. He had a small mustache and a large body that must have suffered in the heat. "My wife has MS," he added quietly, fingering his soda as though massaging unresponsive muscles. "This pays the bills."

The second fellow, Frank, was old and wiry with thinning gray hair wrapped tightly around his head. "I retired a few years back," he said, "and spent two years at home. My wife couldn't stand it anymore, so here I am."

A handsome young man emerged from the kitchen and put a hamburger down in front of me, fries for John. "I got a wife and kid at home. I came here because we really needed the money, and signed on for a second year so that we could buy a house."

They seemed eager to talk about home and family. "There's no such thing as a normal relationship down here," Frank said. "How can there be, when you're apart for months?"

I thought back to Achupallas—an entire village of women, their men all gone for 30 years to work the factories of Guayaquil.

Rob laughed suddenly. "I went home a few months back. My wife does it all—changes lightbulbs, pays the bills, has the car fixed. It's amazing how independent she's become." He shook his head.

"The most important thing," Frank said slowly, twirling his bottle by the neck, "is to have someone at home. It keeps you centered." Everyone nodded. I realized I was nodding too.

Frank offered us a tour of their quarters, but the topic stayed on house and home.

"Nobody brings women in here—it's a camp rule," he said, pushing open the door to a tiny room with a metal bed and footlocker. The humming air conditioner poured out miraculously cool air. "No one touches the women help. We even do our own laundry."

"What happens if someone ignores the rules?"

"One guy did. He was outta here in two weeks. It's better that way. Less stress."

I looked at the photos tacked to the walls. It struck me how much these lonely men had created a place like home.

Not everyone felt the way they did. "The Argentineans and the Brazilians hate each other," Frank said as we passed through the hangar to the helicopters. That wasn't surprising. Practically every South American country had been at war with at least one of its neighbors in the past 200 years. "They used to have fistfights on the base all the time. Then the commander forbade it, and now they fight off base. You can always tell if they've had women on R&R by how talkative they are on the way home. Sometimes they come in and they won't even say hello."

I made small talk, though it wasn't the air-conditioning or the ice-cold sodas that made me want to stay. These men weren't really here for career advancement, or for better pay. They were all working for someone they cared about back home. Their love showed itself in feeding strangers and the way they fiddled with their wedding rings. It attracted lonely souls like moths. It was hard to tear myself away.

The Ecuadorians eventually tracked us down, but were regretfully unable to translate their apologies into a working helicopter. All flights were grounded during the peace negotiations, they said. And besides, their only 'copter was temporarily out of commission due to a recent accident. They would, however, be happy to provide us with a military jeep and driver to take us to one of their point bases in the Condor mountains.

We were packed and under way in 20 minutes. The novelty of finally making progress toward our goal quickly wore away as we were scrubbed like dirty clothing along the washboard road. The incessant rain had gouged out craters deep enough to bathe in. Three, five, six hours passed. We left our eyeballs behind at every hairpin turn, searching for stomachs that were at least 200 yards back. Perhaps waiting for a helicopter wasn't such a bad idea after all.

We came to a sudden halt at the end of a long line of weather-beaten trucks. I hadn't expected a traffic jam in the middle of the jungle. We trudged past 15, 20 vehicles, their owners lying slack as fallen laundry in the grass. A mudslide had torn up the mountainside, leaving in its wake a litter of waist-high boulders and downed trees. A river now bubbled merrily where the road had been.

Traffic had been piling up since the wee hours of the morning. I asked around to see when it might be repaired. "Next week," a woman cutting grass said. "Later," a driver told us. "Who knows?" shrugged a man leading two horses piled high with sacks of rice. "Tomorrow," promised a truck driver with a leisurely wave of his hand.

"And that"—our driver pointed at a large settlement in the valley below us—"is Gualaquiza." After seven hours on the road, the avalanche had blocked us just six miles short of our destination. There was nothing to do but turn around and....

A ripple of gossip stirred the line of limp bodies. A bulldozer had arrived. With heavy metal on their side, the men rolled up their sleeves and took on the avalanche. In less than an hour we were passing through the shiny gates of Gualaquiza's military base, smartly saluted by starched uniforms and white hats, and deposited at yet another set of officer's quarters for the night. "Be ready," we were told. "Tomorrow morning, 5:30 a.m."

We were going up the mountain.

This time we were not forgotten. Before the sun touched the nearby peaks, we were under way in the company of a round-faced lieutenant with chipmunk cheeks and a jack-o'-lantern smile. His name was Duval. He outlined our itinerary with such casual confidence that for a moment I actually believed we could drive up the mountain, hike to the observatory, go on a de-mining patrol, and see an explosives demonstration in time to be back at the officer's quarters for dinner.

Everything went smoothly until we reached a wide and swiftly flowing river with a wooden ferry moored to the bank. The operator met us with that universal fluttering hand gesture that means something is not functioning. A wooden connector—about the size of a football, from the way his hands described it—had broken and couldn't be replaced until Monday. The ferry was out of commission. We turned around and drove back the way we'd come. We pulled up at a narrow footbridge and everyone climbed out.

"We're walking?" I asked, quailing a bit at the thought of hauling all our gear up the mountain. Duval and the driver cheerfully slung bags and packs over their shoulders and took off at a soldier's gait. At the far end of the bridge another truck was magically awaiting us.

"How'd you do that?" I asked Duval. He laughed and jiggled his walkie-talkie. We settled in among the cargo and rumbled off.

Twenty minutes later the truck pulled over. We got out and it drove off. I looked at Duval. He made that same wobbly hand gesture. "The shocks," he said, and crinkled his nose. "Not good enough for the mountain."

We waited. I read a book and eavesdropped on Duval's radio conversation, but could make no sense of it beyond that fact that we were Blue—or perhaps in sector Blue, and that everyone remained superhumanly polite despite the crackling static and repeated transmission failures.

A truck arrived. We got on board. We got off. A flat tire was removed. It rolled off down the road, guided by a jogging soldier with a stick. Duval was unperturbed. I hadn't seen a single house—let alone a vulcanizing shop—for at least five miles, but by now I had utter faith in the devastating combination of that two-way radio and his cheeky grin.

I wandered along the edge of the jungle, peering through the latticework of braided vines and knife-edged roots of banyan trees. It was filled with bird-of-paradise flowers and fluorescent frogs—as enticing as a children's picture book. The reality was far more lethal. The early explorers who tried to hack their way through disappeared without a trace, or lay down and died like flies. The few who survived described it as festering and malarial, and filled with stinging, biting, clawing things.

The stories hadn't changed much to the present day. In 1953 six Ecuadorian soldiers were captured by Peru while "inspecting" border markers. They escaped into the jungle and emerged nearly a month later in a state of semi-starvation. Peruvian soldiers suffered similar fates. New owners came and went. The jungle remained.

An open pickup arrived. We loaded up. I stood in back and drank in the dappled meadows wreathed in purple and white orchids. Butterflies danced among the dense green leaves and wispy clouds played tag among bromeliad-laden trees. It was a wild place, an untouched paradise. I felt joy bubble up inside of me.

A row of camouflaged trucks and gas tanks flashed by.

The border encampment crouched in a bald spot on the mountainside. It was filled with rough-hewn houses, a volleyball court, a flagpole, and a large cement sign that proclaimed their right to "Win, not die." The walls were painted with grinning skulls in rakish olive-green berets. Laundry hung over balconies and sweat-streaked bodies sent a dirty white volleyball back and forth like a bomb that refused to explode.

Duval rounded up a dozen soldiers. We marched behind them along a swampy footpath interspersed with rotting ladders that clung like vines to damp stone walls. An hour later we reached the summit to find yet another flag—an advertisement, it seemed to me, for a guided missile—and a tiny shack that boasted four sleeping bags and a row of nails to hang guns. The lookout soldiers alternated weeklong shifts, keeping watch on a similar Peruvian outpost less than ten miles away. It was a dreary existence, made more so by the clinging mist and airless hut. I was soon ready to head back down, but Duval wanted to show me something the Peruvians had done. It sounded like a propaganda stunt, but it was unlike him to insist, so I agreed to go and see. A hundred meters from the shack, a large yellow cross was planted squarely across the path.

"The Peruvians infiltrated two months ago," Duval said. I had heard him speak with cheery confidence, or with that careful lecturing tone he used to explain the construction of a mine, but this was something different. He was angry, raw and seething, and hurting too. "They planted mines—not just one, but 50, in a cluster—right on the path where we patrol every day. RIGHT ON THE PATH." He shook his head. "Two men were vaporized and six more became amputees. There were no bodies to bury." He paused. "Sometimes when we walk by here we find a piece of boot—and once a foot—but nothing else." He picked up a charred strip of cloth at the base of the cross, stretched it out, and laid it gently back in place. "Why on the path, where they knew we would walk? And why so many mines? Why?..."

The mood had turned as grim and forbidding as the rain clouds that were bearing down on us. We hurried down the mountain.

Back at Gualaquiza, I had seen a military video of a real-life de-mining patrol. The soldiers in the tape wore no protective clothing, nor did they use metal detectors. The Condor mountains, I was told, contained significant concentrations of natural metals that precluded the use of high-tech gadgetry. The terrain and heat made Kevlar clothing and heavy shoes unbearable. The soldiers simply wore their regular uniforms and used machetes, driving them into the earth at an angle and levering up the dirt, hoping to hit the mines from the side or below. They looked like farmers digging up their potato crop.

Duval showed me the two most common kinds of local mines. One was small and round, no larger than a hockey puck. It held 80 grams of TNT and was activated by screwing the two halves together until they were just barely snug. The other was a larger wooden box that contained 200 grams of TNT. Once again I sensed Duval's anger, this time directed at the larger mine.

"Eighty grams of CC," he said, "will sever a hand or foot. Two hundred grams blows off an entire leg—up to the femoral artery, so the soldier almost always dies." That must be it. Better a crippled comrade than none at all.

"And besides," he continued, "the smaller mines are far more damaging psychologically. Picture this—your best friend steps on a mine and blows off part of his leg. He is screaming and his blood is splattered on your face. You have to call in a helicopter to evacuate him. Your entire patrol is emotionally destroyed. It takes many resources to care for the injured soldier, and it is demoralizing for everyone to see him afterwards with a prosthesis." Duval hefted the larger mine. "If someone steps on this," he said, "he's just dead."

The demonstration was ready to begin. The man in front was already sweating heavily under a full suit of Kevlar clothing and two-inch soles. The land mines, we had been told, were all deactivated so John could walk among them freely while filming. I watched the point man carefully scraping away leaves, uncovering a mine, and digging it up with shaking hands. They were unexpectedly good actors. The mines were passed back along the line with exquisite care. I noticed a man crouched down near the front, his eyes fixed unblinkingly on John's feet. Something wasn't right. "Is this live?" I asked the soldier beside me as the next mine was handed back.

"Of course."

"John, they're live! Watch your step." I called forward. "Hey, Duval! You said they were deactivated!"

"I didn't want you to be scared!" he called back.

After three sets of takes, even Duval had begun to sweat. We gathered up the mines and turned for home. The soldiers found a bare spot and buried one of the smaller ones. Another man used a bit of knotted string to hang a heavy block, then both of them ran like hell. Even knowing that it was coming, the blast was deafening. The block looked like a shattered chunk of ice.

That night I dreamt of wandering through a field of exquisite purple flowers. I leaned down to pluck one and vaporized.

The next morning we piled aboard yet another military truck to visit a set of ruins 30 miles outside the base. I was secretly more interested in our guide than in the dubious possibility of finding Inca remains. A Shuar Indian, he had better reasons than anyone to hate the war.

The Shuar nation straddled the no-man's-land between Ecuador and Peru. Before the war, they lived as one extended family, traveling freely from village to village, trading salt and cigarettes, pigs, and chickens. Then the border came crashing down. Some families lost contact for the next 50 years. In other areas the effects were more insidious. Peruvian Shuar who grew bananas still crossed over to sell their products in the more lucrative markets of Ecuador. Saturday soccer games went on as before. Then, as the yearly anniversary of the war approached, tensions mounted. Trading was suspended, and bi-national spouses separated to go stay with their families for a month or two.

For those who joined the military, it was the most difficult of all. The Shuar played a crucial role as scouts and survivalists in the war. They were among the most devoted—and feared—fighters of all.

But what happened when a Shuar soldier looked down his gun sights and saw a brother in a different color uniform? Would his first allegiance be to his country or his people?

Maurice was short, dark, and handsome. His mahogany skin and uniform, mottled like a leopard's skin, blended with the jungle. He didn't walk—he padded, slithered, *flowed* along the narrow trails that wormed through the impenetrable undergrowth. His chest was twice as wide as mine.

His father had hacked his way 200 miles south from Cuenca to carve a future out of the same festering jungle that had sent the Spaniards home in body bags. He built a house, became a chief, took 2 wives, and fathered 17 children.

The ruins, when we finally found them, turned out to be an overgrown graveyard. We cleared the graves of tangled vines and wove wreaths of flowers. That earned me an invitation to Maurice's house for tea. He lived in a typical Shuar village consisting of twisted jungle wood, spidery children, and roly-poly guinea pigs. He had one wife and five kids. The boys were named Edison and Jefferson. His house had no doors.

Once we settled down, his daughters hauled out a vat of boiled cassava and proceeded to mash it into paste. The eldest scooped up a fingerful and popped it into her mouth. She rolled it back and forth between her cheeks, then spat. A stream of saliva-soaked paste landed back in the pot. Her younger sibling followed her example.

"The saliva," Maurice said, "is used to ferment the cassava." It was the women's job to sit and stir the mash, sucking in mouthfuls and spitting them back out. The pot was then covered and allowed to sit for a day or two, dosed with sugar, strained and shared with guests. It tasted like potatoes soaked in lemon and spiced with spit.

After two glasses I had swallowed enough saliva to digest my next three meals. We staggered out the door to take a walk. The houses were scattered through the valley, connected by a network of paths exactly one bare foot wide. Almost every balcony had a uniform or two hanging over the wooden rails.

"Maurice," I said. "You're in the jungle on patrol. You hear a noise. You raise your gun. You look down your sight. You see another Shuar. What do you do?"

"I shoot."

Shuar Indians were not recognized as citizens by either Ecuador or Peru until 40 years ago.

Duval was adamant. There was absolutely no way we could cross the Condor mountains into Peru. If we wanted to continue our journey south, we would have to take a bus ten hours back up the Pan American Highway to Cuenca, catch the overnight connection to Quito, take an international flight to Lima, catch another plane to Piura, then an overnight bus to Huancabamba, the northernmost Peruvian provincial capital along the Inca Road. All to reach a piece of land that I had actually been able to look at from the Condor observation post.

The next morning Duval took us to Gualaquiza's bus station. He got us the best seats, double-checked that our gear was safely stowed, and made me promise to call as soon as we reached Quito. Then he stood and waved until the bus pulled out. We passed three checkpoints during our ten-hour journey. At every stop a soldier came on board to look for us, make sure we were all right, and phone back to Gualaquiza with the news. It felt marvelous to be taken care of.

Peru and Ecuador signed a historic permanent peace accord. After 500 bloody years, a conflict begun in the time of the Inca might finally be laid to rest.

CHAPTER 9

A JOURNEY INTO
THE SPIRIT WORLD

FIELD NOTES: The result: a dozen guys leaping about like crickets, happily ridding themselves of evil spirits, and one sleepy woman looking like the embarrassed newcomer to an advanced aerobics class.

We flew south to Lima, then north to Piura, and finally boarded an all-night bus for Huancabamba, to sleep fitfully on badly rutted roads and stumble off at hourly intervals to present our passports to the checkpoint police.

We were heading for the Huaringas, a mountainous region of northern Peru dotted with sacred lakes and, we were told, more witches than sheep. Men and women came from all over the country to purify themselves in Huaringas's frigid waters and participate in all-night healing ceremonies. They brought a heavy burden of financial worries, damaged relationships, or sometimes just the need to look beyond the tangible world and see into the spiritual realm. As part of their cure they were given a dose of the hallucinogenic San Pedro cactus. It also kept them from dozing off throughout the long and grueling cleansing that could go on for an entire night and a day.

These healings were not just local oddities found in the "colorful characters and preposterous places" section of Lima's Sunday papers. The sorcerers had clientele from all walks of life—doctors and debutantes, lawyers and laborers. President Fujimori himself had paid a visit to the sacred lakes—doubling prices and tripling clientele for those lucky few who happened to be on hand when the helicopter set down.

Our bus pulled into Huancabamba's station at 3:30 a.m. No one made a move to disembark. The conductor didn't even try to open the baggage compartments. Not a single taxi or motor cart arrived to take advantage of 20 sleepy passengers with too much luggage and a long walk home. "Huancabamba," I read in huge letters on the bus station wall, "Mystery Capital of Peru." The place seemed completely bewitched, like Sleeping Beauty-land after she pricked her finger and sent everyone off to sleep.

Eventually we managed to scare up an ancient, wheezing station wagon and wrestle our gear past the drowsy bus driver. The passengers stayed rooted to their seats, waiting trancelike for a truck to arrive and take them up the mountain to the sacred lakes.

That afternoon we made our rounds of the local witches. I'd been briefed at great length on this subject by a fellow passenger on the bus. She was attending her third healing ceremony so that her son would do well in his coming school exams. "You must find someone that you trust to guide you on your journey through the spirit world," she told me firmly. "And make sure he hasn't just done a healing the night before." Apparently even witches had trouble focusing their energies when they were short on sleep.

We caught a ride into the mountains in a car called Crazy Love, driven by its owner, the Cat. The road was narrow and steep, and as muddy as a buffalo wallow. "This is nothing!" the Cat shouted, steering his rusty hulk through knee-deep pools. "Six months a year—during the rains—the people can't get into town at all!" It was, I pointed out, the middle of the rainy season. He laughed agreement. "If it rains tonight then you'll be walking back yourselves!"

He was taking us to Salala, a village that boasted the highest concentration of witches per square mile in the country. We were less than a third of the way there when the Cat pulled up at a ranch house with a sunny courtyard and several grazing sheep. He made us understand that the owner, a man by the name of Cipriano, was the *best* sorcerer around. He had, apparently, rethought his promise to take us all the way to Salala, since Crazy Love was not going to make it through the mud.

I was all for continuing, on horseback if necessary, to the village on the mountaintop. John wanted to stay. The Cat was suddenly sure that there were no healings to be had in Salala that night. We stayed.

The next morning, Cipriano emerged from his bedroom wearing a simple homespun poncho and rubber thongs. Aside from a glazed expression left over from last night's hallucinogenic cactus, he could have been a farmer on his way to harvest his fields.

We piled into an open-air truck with six other new arrivals—all men from a village in the Amazon Basin. I gathered from their discussions that they were in business together, but they refused to tell me why they had come to be healed, except to say that it was a matter of dire urgency. And that we would find out that night.

For the next three hours we bumped and ground along the rutted, mud-choked road. Late morning sunshine dappled the rolling hills around us. Yokes of oxen tossed their heads as they plodded back and forth across chocolate fields. Here and there a thatched adobe hut sent thin fingers of smoke drifting slowly through a cloudless blue sky. I could see farmers heading home on their horses, their ponchos spread out around them, thinking, no doubt, about the potato stew simmering on the cooking fire and the sheep to be gathered before noon. It was a utopian setting, exactly how the 16th-century Europeans had envisioned indigenous Andean life from the early Spanish reports.

At last we pulled up at a hitching post with a dozen horses. The six men jumped out, grabbed an animal apiece, and took off. We followed more slowly with Don Cipriano's apprentice and his bag of swords, seashells, and assorted sorcerer's tricks.

The ceremony we were about to participate in was far more than just an interesting cultural experience. It is impossible to make sense of Andean society without some understanding of its shamanistic underpinnings. Curanderos and their philosophy define the entire psychology of indigenous life.

Curanderismo was around long before the Inca or their Spanish conquerors. It never tried to compete with either Christianity or Western science, in fact most of its adherents are devout Catholics. It simply inhabits a parallel reality. Unlike the painstaking methods of modern science, curanderismo functions on a mythological plane, doing battle against spirits, magic, and enchantments. It reflects a society that is more inclined to placate and accommodate its environment than to conquer or control it.

Shamanism may be a religion, but a shaman is not a priest. A priest's authority is the result of diligent study of a strict set of religious doctrine. A shaman's power stems from a personal psychological experience. The priest chooses to become a clergyman. The shaman experiences a revelation that makes him aware of his gift. He is in many ways more of a poet than a priest. He uses hallucinogens to diagnose the sick, control events, and make contact with the parallel world of ancestral spirits. Those participating in a shamanistic experience make a ritual passage to the unseen spirit world.

Curanderismo is particularly powerful in the Huaringas in part because Catholicism never managed to claim this sacred landscape from its original inhabitants. Although Christian deities are often invoked in the ceremonies, the curanderos keep careful control over their patients' psychedelic wanderings.

I sidled up to Cipriano's apprentice. He had already been in training for four years and expected to spend fifteen more before graduating to full-blooded sorcerer. "Why a witch?" I asked. Had he had some sort of mystical experience that led him to his chosen path?

He shrugged and shook his head. Witchcraft, he said, was the best paying job around.

"Does it run in your family?" I persisted. The gift of second sight was hereditary, I'd been told. Either you had it or you didn't.

He thought about it for several minutes. "My neighbor is a sorcerer," he finally replied. "He got me the job with Don Cipriano."

We arrived at the lake and formed a circle around a blanket covered with swords and seashells, a wooden skeleton, several fetishes, a statue of the Virgin Mary, Christ nailed to the cross, and a round-bellied Buddha. The assistant sorcerer started chanting, calling down the sun, the moon, the stars, the nearby mountains, the wind, the cloud, the trees...and on down to the grains of sand on our beach. We were handed stained seashells full of liquid tobacco and told to inhale the juice through our noses. Cipriano vowed to protect us from black magic, evil spells, loose women, bad luck, ill winds, poor finances.... He took a long drag from a bottle of cologne and spat it over each of us in turn. For the next hour we danced and clapped and rubbed baby powder in our hair and were subjected to a variety of scented liquids, all of which he sprayed over us through the gap between his front teeth. I was becoming intimately acquainted with the inside of Cipriano's mouth. I did my best to get into the spirit of things, without much success. The trouble was my own upbringing; I had grown up with two doctors for parents. The only real religion in my family was science. The results were rather unfortunate: a dozen guys leaping about like crickets, happily ridding themselves of evil spirits and one skeptical woman looking like an embarrassed newcomer to an advanced aerobics class.

The dancing thankfully over, we were told to strip down to our underclothes and jump into the filthy waters of the lake. After our cleansing we were supposed to climb back into our outerwear and toss our undergarments into the water. I waded through layers of rotting bras and panties from past ceremonies and dunked myself.

I was last in line for a final spiritual cleansing. Twenty-one people stood in front of me, all soaking wet and shivering in the bitter mountain wind. By the time it came my turn to be armored against illnesses of the head, the hair, the eyes, ears, nose, tongue...the back, the liver, the spleen...the ankles, heels, and toes... I was so stiff with cold that I could barely haul myself back into the saddle.

Mt. Cotopaxi (ABOVE) appears peaceful for the moment in Ecuador's Avenue of Volcanoes. Six-foot-two-inch John Armstrong attempts to negotiate a three-foot outhouse (BELOW).

The Otavalo Indians (ABOVE, LEFT) maintain their traditional customs while learning to negotiate a modern world. Otavalo on market day offers a young girl a chance to rest among the wares (BELOW, LEFT). Participants in the Festival of Mama Negra in Latacunga, Ecuador (ABOVE) wear a coating of black face paint made of tar and animal fat.

Farmers (ABOVE) thresh wheat in the remote Ecuadorian village of Achupallas. The frontier gold-mining town of Nambija (ABOVE, RIGHT) seems perpetually on the verge of sliding off the mountainside. Ancient mausoleums cling to the cliffs of the Chachapoya (BELOW, RIGHT).

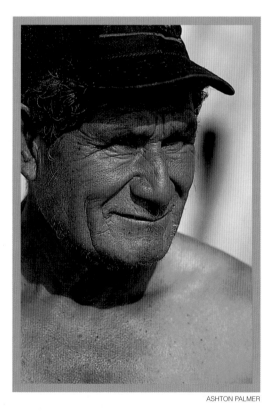

ASHTON PALMER

When built according to imperial standards, the Inca Road in Cochabamba, Peru (ABOVE, LEFT) was 27 feet wide and straight as an arrow. Buso, the father of Huanchaco beach (BELOW, LEFT), helped me to build a reed boat and, against custom, allowed me to accompany him fishing. My clumsy attempt (ABOVE) to paddle a "little horse" off the coast of northern Peru was a source of amusement for the local fishermen.

Carrying the sacred mural through the streets in the Lord of Miracles procession in Lima (RIGHT) is a great honor—and a heavy burden. In Lima's central plaza (BELOW), the colorful carpets are made of flower petals laid down by the faithful in the path of the mural. Crowds are so dense that it is impossible to move.

We arrived back at Cipriano's house exhausted from the grueling trek, the frigid swim, the early start—and braced ourselves for the coming all-night healing ceremony.

We were better off than Cipriano. This was to be his third healing in a row, and he was running on empty. His skin was sallow and guttered and his movements clumsy. He downed a shot of the hallucinogenic cactus and his eyes took on a glittery sheen. His garbled conversation gradually turned into a verbal stream that went on like a set of bagpipes. I never saw him stop to breathe.

He began with a long opening prayer to God and Jesus, beseeching them to give us a successful ceremony and promising to practice only white magic and to repudiate all practitioners of the black arts. The rapid-fire intonations gradually widened to include the sun god, the moon, thunder and lightning, local deities—everything and everyone short of the kitchen sink. We were once again given the dreaded tobacco-stained seashell filled with thick black tobacco juice. "All right," Cipriano said. "Shell in the left hand, snort it up the left nostril. Repeat after me between gulps. "Ashes to ashes. Dust to dust...." I silently begged forgiveness of Mother Earth and poured the contents of my shell onto the ground behind me, and tried not to listen to the retching and choking all around. More tobacco juice. Right hand, right nostril. I knew the tobacco, along with the mescaline-based cactus, was supposed to heighten our senses and help keep us awake, but I just couldn't bring myself to bathe my sinuses in that foul black liquid again. Mother Earth took another hit.

"Does anyone know a Carlos?" Cipriano said suddenly. There was an uncertain silence. He waited three beats. "How about an Olga?" Someone raised a hand. "Yes!" Cipriano shouted like a game-show host. "Tell me!"

Olga was a cousin, the man said, and had been causing a lot of problems in his business and marriage.

"I knew it! She's a bad woman. I can feel it. She's—" he stopped suddenly, as though having a conversation on the phone. "How about a Lucho?" Someone knew a Lucho, vaguely. Don Cipriano skillfully drew information out of his patients, skipping over his misses and parroting back his hits with such finesse that it seemed like he had come up with them himself. He made us stand for hours, chanting a strange mix of Christian prayers, invocations, and white witchcraft. We danced in circles, tossed off our sins, and raised our arms for luck, for life, for love.... I lost all sense of time as the waves of nonstop human voices washed over me, bells ringing, assistants walking up and down the line spitting fine sprays of cologne or herbal waters until we were wrapped in clouds of perfumed air. He was using all the elements of religious rit-ual—mesmerizing repetition, sensory overload, disorienting dark-ness—to create a kind of hypnosis, an abrupt shift in environment meant to catapult the mind into an entirely different plain.

At last Cipriano motioned us to sit on a row of grimy mattresses that lined one courtyard wall. I nudged a flea-bitten dog away and sank gratefully onto the lumpy pad. The San Pedro hallucinogen had done nothing more than turn my stomach into a seething ball of nausea. The man sat down next to me. He was jabbering unintelligibly and smelled like a cologne factory. I curled up with the dog.

Some time later one of the apprentices shook me awake and ushered me into Cipriano's room. He was about to start his private consultations, and I was invited to listen in. The six men from the Amazon did indeed own a business—trucks and buses—that had been making "millions." Suddenly bad things started to happen:

lost contracts, fights with their wives and in-laws, accidents, and debts. They were here to find out what had gone wrong.

"Bad luck is plaguing you," Cipriano was telling them as I tucked myself into a corner. "Your trucks don't have much work. Damn, don't tell me my friend. I see a woman."

The man looked up. "The wife of my brother."

Cipriano nodded triumphantly. "Don't tell me! I see her crying...." He hesitated for a beat. "I don't like the way this woman is acting. She does not want you all to work together." The man clearly agreed.

"Do you keep your heart clean? Are your trucks clean?"

The man nodded quickly. "We are always clean. We maintain ourselves. But"—he twisted a cap around in his hands and the words poured out of him—"I am on the point of losing my house. I have a debt. Everything is loaned. I go to visit friends and money disappears. My child needs an operation. Every time we try to start afresh it goes badly." He launched into a long story about a new car he had bought that broke down and couldn't be fixed.

Cipriano held up a hand to stop him, his eyes once again focused in the distance. "In your house I feel something," he said abruptly. "An animal." he paused for several seconds. "Next Saturday at 5:00 a.m. go to the door and give a benediction to your house in the name of God. Then sprinkle holy water around in every room. This will scare away the animal that is living under your floor. Then all will be well."

John was next.

"You are married, yes?" Cipriano said.

"Yes."

Cipriano looked pleased. I remembered his assistant asking me that question earlier in the afternoon.

"Why do you not have kids?"

"I got married late and we separated before we had children." John said, squirming uncomfortably at the line of questioning. "How will this trip go?"

"Fine," Cipriano said. "Always there will be bad things but you will surmount them. You must have faith. There is a woman in your future...." He glanced at me and before I could stop myself, I shook my head.

"Who is she?" John was asking.

"I have it in my mind," Cipriano said. "But it is fading. No, Damn! It's gone."

And then it was my turn.

"You have good objectives," he told me. "Both of your parents are living."

"Yes."

"One of them was an orphan."

"No."

"You have a brother."

"Yes."

"And a sister."

"No."

He was starting to flounder. "You are going to go forward because you have a strong character. You are going to have success and prosperity." He paused and gave me a sly look "You are also waiting for matrimony, later, but you have been in love before."

I nodded, not sure what I was agreeing to.

"But it has always gone badly. You have bad luck in love."

"Why?" I asked. He'd caught me despite myself.

"You should be more careful. Take more precautions. Don't think that this person is perfect and then he isn't. Wait longer before jumping in."

He'd obviously been talking to my mother.

"And," he added, "it is good to maintain a perfume."

"I beg your pardon?"

He thought a moment. *"Amor Salvaje"* he said. Savage Love. "You must buy this perfume and do a cure from Saturday to Saturday before the sun comes up. Raise your perfume. Take it in your mouth and spray it around the room where you sleep. Ask God for his favor and his intervention. This will fix your problems. It always does." Amor Salvaje, he added, was conveniently on sale after the ceremony.

"Do you know a John?" he asked suddenly.

I laughed. "Yes." Obviously his apprentice had forgotten to pass on our names along with our marital statuses.

"Who is he?"

I pointed at the camera. "Looking right at you."

This caught Cipriano completely off guard. He gave John a startled look. "He's John?"

"In the flesh."

He turned to John. "Your name is John?"

"Yes, it is."

"Ah, that's good." He looked over our heads for a moment, then stood abruptly. "The spirits are tired. It is time to close."

We returned to Huancabamba with the six Amazonian businessmen. They were pleased with the results of the healing ceremony and quite sure that their luck was about to change. Don Cipriano had given each of them minor chores or rituals to perform, and all had been told that they were good men and that they would prevail over their current difficulties. They were once again ready to succeed.

I spent the afternoon washing baby powder, cologne, and lemon seeds out of my clothes and hair. The provincial capital had running water twice a day, either cold or colder, depending on the temperature outside. What came out of the tap was the exact same shade of muddy brown as the river flowing past the marketplace. The city had once been a major hub in the Inca Empire, an administrative center and outpost against the oft-rebellious Cañari Indians. Not a single Inca stone remained, though rumor had it that the church was built on Inca foundations, and that heathen bones still lay beneath the earth where true believers now recited their rosaries. What I really hoped was to find some remnant of the Inca Road, for this was where the Spaniards first laid eyes on it in 1532. And what a sight it must have been. "I do not think anything so grandiose as to equal this road had been built in all human history," one chronicler wrote. "It crosses deep valleys and the highest mountains, passing snowy peaks and waterfalls, cutting through solid rock, and skirting tortuous mountain torrents. In all of these places the road is solidly built, held up by terracing along the slopes. It is cut into the rock along the banks of rivers and protected by supporting walls. At the snowy summits it is provided with steps and benches where travelers can catch their breath, and for the entire length it is kept open and clear of rubble at all times." This was in contrast to the roads of 16th-century Europe, where one needed to have "a falcon's eye, a dog's mouth, and a deer's foot" to arrive safely at one's destination.

Sadly, by the time I reached Huancabamba, the great highway had disappeared without a trace, not even the memory remained of where it once had run. I tracked down a local schoolteacher who told me that the closest Inca ruins were in Caxas, an ancient city some eight hours away. In short order, he had located a pickup and found another teacher who knew the way.

We began at the ungodly hour of 4:00 a.m. The pickup hammered the stony road into submission, carved trenches in the Earth's soft sides, left muddy tracks where once soft moss had grown. The mountain gods retaliated. The glittering Andean sky turned sickly, dark and gray. As we wound our way down the final pass into Caxas, we were waylaid by a thick bank of icy, clinging fog.

At first the "city" seemed like nothing more than rolling pastureland and freshly tilled fields. Only gradually did I see the long lines of bumps and ridges that lay just beneath the grass, like Masaii beauty scars. Caxas stretched out to the horizon, and for the first time I realized how grand this ruined city must have been. A wide band of deeper green ran arrow straight along one edge. The Inca Road. I scampered down. The fog thickened in the valley like well-simmered stew. I found the place and called to John.

"This is the road?" he said, staring at the grass between his feet. "How boring."

He had a point. But the ruins were something else. I wandered among the knee-high walls, imagining what Hernando de Soto must have seen when he first arrived—paved streets, squares, and fortresses, a temple large enough to house 500 virgins, block after block of houses....

Actually, that wasn't quite true. The first thing de Soto saw was three corpses hanging from a tree at the entrance to the city. They had been caught trying to enter the temple of the sacred sun virgins. Inca justice was swift and merciless.

In 1532 the inhabitants of Caxas had just been through a bloody civil war and were thoroughly sick of all things Inca. The newly arrived Spaniards were given gifts and made welcome. In return, de Soto, "a man full of good impulses, a gentleman and a soldier," ordered the city's 500 sun virgins brought outside. The sight "excited the soldiers like the fruits of paradise." He then gave each man the woman he liked best. Once everyone was satisfied, a city elder was invited—in chains—to guide the conquerors to Cajamarca and their historic rendezvous with Atahualpa and destiny.

For years I had dreamed about discovering an ancient city, of pulling back a thick mass of vines and uncovering a perfect wall of stone. No one knew exactly how deep the Caxas ruins lay beneath the earth or what might be waiting under five centuries of accumulated dirt. All I had was my belt knife, but I went at it with unbridled enthusiasm. I tugged away bits and pieces of moss and vegetation and scooped out handfuls of earth to reveal a second row of Inca stones underneath the first. John had long since wandered away and the schoolteacher came by to watch. When he was a child, he told me, the walls had been twice as high and the grounds littered with perfectly rectangular stones. "What happened?" I asked. He shrugged. People pilfered them for houses and stone fences—they made particularly good foundations— and some had even been used to build the local school.

I stared at my newly uncovered row of Inca stone. Perhaps some things were better left in peace. I slowly filled the earth back in.

The map made it look easy. From where I stood in Huancabamba, it was a straightforward journey overland to the provincial capital of Chachapoyas. The thin white road followed the Huancabamba River due south a distance shorter than the length of my thumb. It then turned into a thicker yellow line that almost proclaimed itself a two-lane highway. Along the way it only seemed to cross a single mountain.

But maps can be misleading. They flatten towering ranges, fill in canyons, and resurrect—with thick, unbroken strokes—roads that have long since washed away. I've often wondered why they can't make maps with a more useful scale than miles: like the distance a man can cover while chewing a wad of coca leaf. The Indians have been reckoning time that way for centuries.

On the scale of masticated coca wads, the mountains of central Peru would balloon out to the size of the Sahara and the coastline would choke up like a drawstring. And the Amazon—that would just be filled with broken squiggly lines indicating the unknown— or perhaps infinity.

I asked around. The road south from Huancabamba was indeed washed out. We were told to head back to the coast, take the Pan American Highway south, and then cut east into the mountains. The next morning we were rattling over grooved roads to Piura.

We knifed back and forth along the edge of the Andes, traveling for miles along mountain-hugging roads in order to descend a few hundred feet. The countryside shriveled up around us like a carcass in the desert sun. Fluffy sheep turned into rangy goats, damned to a lifetime of spiky grass and bitter leaves. Vultures hovered overhead. All around us jagged mountains gnashed the sky like dragon teeth. At last the bus's wheels discovered tarmac along that thin ribbon of desert that hugs the sea. I barely saw the sandy beaches as we raced by. My mind was already high up in the misty mountains of our destination. Among the People of the Clouds.

CHAPTER 10

THE PEOPLE OF THE CLOUDS

FIELD NOTES: The next morning our chariot arrived.... A 20-year-old Toyota with a steering wheel that wiggled like a loose tooth and the tiredest tires you've ever seen. A veritable deathmobile.

The Chachapoyas," I had read several months ago in a cubicle at the whisper-quiet Library of Congress, "has more undiscovered ruins per square kilometer than any place in Peru." The article was entitled, "South America's New Archeological Frontier." A giant yellow circle immediately appeared on my map marking the rugged northern mountains, two hundred miles from nowhere.

It was only later that I realized why the ruins had lain hidden for so long. "Chachapoya" comes from the Quechua words *sacha* and *puyu*, meaning trees and clouds. The entire region lies under a heavy layer of perpetual cloud cover and dense, impenetrable vines and trees. The area is so inaccessible that only two years ago an immense discovery had been made: more than 200 mummies, countless pieces of pottery, textiles, and other artifacts—all within a few miles of a major population center.

Relatively little is known about the Cloud People who dwelt in this forest long before the Spaniards—or even the Inca—arrived on the scene. This is in part due to the ceaseless activities of the *huaqueros*, the grave robbers that pilfer burial sites in search of salable ceramics and textiles. Their source of information is usually the local farmers who come upon a cave or burial mound while burning the forest for new fields. Grave robbing is against the Peruvian Preservation of National Antiquities Law, but the farmers are poor and the robbers rich, so few items make it into government hands. Most large discoveries—like the 200 mummies—only come to light when archaeologists notice a massive influx of ceramics on the black market several months after the looting has already begun.

The Chachapoya people were master stonemasons and extraordinary climbers, building elaborate mausoleums hundreds of feet off the ground in cliff-side caves. They left behind paintings of bloody decapitations and snarling jaguars, but wove textiles of the finest thread and almost inhumanly complicated patterns. They were conquered by the Inca but proved almost impossible to absorb into the empire. They rebelled relentlessly. The Inca retaliated with forced transmigration on a massive scale and, eventually, with genocide.

But where the mighty Inca failed, tiny microbes succeeded. During the first two centuries of Spanish rule, the Chachapoya population dropped from half a million to less than ten thousand—most felled by European diseases. Today there is almost nothing left of these mysterious people who venerated serpents and held both their enemy's heads and beautiful textiles in high esteem.

The bus station in Cajamarca was a dirt yard surrounded by tin shacks. "Buses to Chachapoyas city run on Wednesdays and Saturdays," the ticket lady said. We were in luck. It was Saturday. I bought tickets. "How long is the ride?" I asked. It couldn't possibly be the 16 hours posted on the schedule—Chachapoyas was only eighty miles away.

"Five hours," she said.

Hallelujah! I glanced down at my tickets. "But these only go to Celendín."

"You have to change buses there."

Damn. I knew it was too good to be true. "When does the Celendín bus leave?" I asked.

"Twelve-thirty."

I looked at my watch. "We won't get to Celendín by 12:30."

"You can take the next bus from Celendín."

"On Wednesday?"

She nodded and snapped her plastic window shut. I wandered back to John and explained the unexplainable. A taxi driver took this moment to amble over and offer us his services and station wagon to Chachapoyas for the bargain-basement price of $200.

I saw John perk up. He hated buses. A car to Chachapoyas would be a luxury indeed. We bargained, settled on $100 plus gas and went off to have breakfast together.

His name was José Luis. He had driven his white station wagon to every corner of Peru—"Sixty-two hours from Lima to Leymebamba," he told me proudly. "No sleeping." He had four children, all girls. He badly wanted a boy but was too afraid to try again. The armload of dolls at Christmastime alone was going to bankrupt him. He seemed intent on getting us to Chachapoyas in eight hours, no matter what the cost. His hands gripped the wheel, his burly forearms straining as he wrestled the car around hairpin turns on the steep mountain road. By the time we had reached Balsa, a dusty town four hours into the ride, I was draped over the backseat, trying unsuccessfully to keep my stomach in the car with me despite the slingshot curves.

The first time we bottomed out on the deteriorating road I felt relief, guessing correctly that it would put a damper on our one-man race. Soon I was wincing as fist-size stones began hammering the underbelly of the car like an impatient stranger at the door. José Luis began to sweat.

It was nearly midnight by the time we limped into Leymebamba. One particularly vengeful rock had done in the oil pan, and we were leaking too badly to risk the final four hours to Chachapoyas. I put José Luis up for the night, paid him for the car ride and his Christmas dolls, and wished him luck on his journey home. Then John and I set out to find a late night meal before catching the 3:00 a.m. bus that would take us to Chachapoyas city.

The main square was full of Saturday-night drunks all walking like wobbly bowling pins. They stared intently at the sudden appearance of foreigners, then looked back at their bottles for an explanation and recovered with another drink. I stopped at a corner grill roasting skewered meat and potatoes and bought us both a meal. The meat was made of unidentifiable internal organs. The potatoes were riddled with soft, slimy lumps.

"What is it?" I asked the grill tender.

She glanced at the potatoes. "Worms."

"Inside?"

"It's like that sometimes."

"Ah." I decided not to tell John.

The next morning we slept in, missed the bus, and eventually wandered into Leymebamba's museum. A young man wearing incongruously white gloves was explaining the difference between Chachapoya and Inca artifacts. He had a farmer's body—compact and curved—sculpted by years behind a plow. He pretended not to notice when I reached out to caress the hand-carved spindle worn smooth by working hands 500 years ago. When the tour was over Federico pulled off his spotless gloves and carefully placed them in a drawer, revealing thickly callused palms and the tattered nails of a potato farmer. I invited him to coffee. He sat with his hands between his knees and his shoulders slumped, and told us in post-doctoral detail about virtually every ruin within a 30-mile radius. He assumed we wanted to go to where the 200 mummies had recently been found, and offered to hire several mules and guide us there. I asked for something a little less discovered. He agreed, but suggested we see the famous mummies before we left town.

Two hundred desiccated corpses, most of them still wrapped in their original shrouds, looking like a bunch of potato sacks—how interesting could that be? I walked into the tiny, climate-controlled room and stopped dead in my tracks. A woman stared back at me, wispy hair lying across her forehead, hands shielding her face and lips drawn back in an eternal scream. The flesh had melted from her fingers, leaving behind enlarged joints and prominent fingernails. She was so altogether lifelike that I almost looked over my shoulder to see what she was screaming at. Beside her lay several infants, their papery skin hanging in folds like bodysuits a size too big. It was an extraordinary feat to preserve a corpse so well in a region famous for its endless rain and moisture-laden air. The local caretaker proudly described the process in graphic detail. The viscera were pulled out through the anus and the resulting cavity stuffed with a mixture of herbs and natural powders. The body was then wrapped in layer upon layer of cloth. It took modern archaeologists days to unwrap a single mummy, stopping every few minutes to photograph and sketch the textiles down to the last stitch.

Mummification was a common burial technique throughout the Andes, though the Inca developed it into a veritable cult of the dead. According to their religious beliefs, if the body remained intact, the soul would live on forever. They paraded the mummified remains of their departed rulers around on feast days, took them out to visit equally stiff and desiccated acquaintances, and assigned young maidens to attend their every need.

But eternal afterlife could be a heavy burden—to those who remained behind. Inca mummies expected all the same privileges they had enjoyed while alive. They continued to live in palaces staffed with servants and surrounded by their families. A system called *panaca* gradually evolved that allowed each dead Inca's royal retinue to use his conquered holdings to pay for his eternal upkeep. In time most of the best agricultural land was held by such legacies, and the families of departed rules acquired great political power. Each new Inca ascending the throne thus inherited a gift-wrapped kingdom with nothing inside. In order to support himself financially, he had no choice but to conquer new territory.

The result was one of the mightiest empires in all of South America. A fringe benefit of worshiping the dead.

Federico arrived at dawn with two horses and two mules in tow. Soon we were high above Leymebamba, hiking along an ancient Inca roadway still maintained by a yearly tithe of communal labor. Federico described with pride the foreign archaeologists and treasure seekers he had come into contact with over the past few years. I was more interested in our potato-farmer-turned-curator than I was in lists of bone-collecting countrymen. Federico stood about five feet four inches, with gold-rimmed teeth and stooped shoulders that belied a wiry build. At 34 he was still living with his parents. They were old, he explained, and needed care. He was unwilling to take a wife until they passed away because he didn't have the financial resources to support two households and didn't think a man's wife and mother belonged under the same roof. He was exceptionally good with the animals, calming them with a quiet confidence that spoke of a lifetime out in the fields.

Late that afternoon Federico led us to a small stone house surrounded by well-tended pastureland and fat, fluffy llamas. It had carefully cut foundation stones and Inca carvings at the base of each terrace post. The owner appeared and helped us unsaddle the horses, and for a moment I could almost believe that we were travelers along the old road and had stopped for the night in one of the empire's many way stations.

The owner's name was Willerman. He bade us sit by the fire while he boiled up some coffee and made potatoes for our evening meal. Willerman had spent 20 years as an administrator in distant Lima. Faced with the prospect of watching his two sons grow up in a landscape of cement and smog, he had "retired" to Leymebamba with his wife to take up the far more arduous farmer's life.

But what kind of children could one raise within old stone walls, with neither running water nor electricity? I soon found out. Juan Gabriel, Willerman's twelve-year-old son, paced back and forth across the packed-earth floor. He called down the heavens. He laughed. He cried. A mesmerizing hour passed while he recited Spanish poetry. He did it all from memory.

We rose with the sun, fueled our bodies with weak coffee and cold potatoes, and set off to pay a visit to a city of the dead. Diablowasi—the Devil's House—was a vast cliff face pocked with hundreds of burial chambers, each built to house a grinning, shrouded mummy for the rest of eternity.

From a distance the sheer wall seemed smooth and unblemished. As we drew nearer I saw a sprinkling of small discolorations. Gradually they sharpened into doors and windows, surrounded by exquisite masonry that blended like makeup with the fissured rock. Closer still I could see skulls with gaping smiles scattered across their thresholds and an occasional tattered rib cage propped up against an outer wall.

We slashed our way through the clinging undergrowth to the foot of the cliff. More skulls lay embedded in the ground around us, their eye sockets sprouting tentacles of braided vines. We picked our way around the shattered skeletons tossed down by grave robbers in their frantic quest for ceramics and other black-market products. Some of the headless torsos still had papery skin attached, and almost all were wrapped in priceless textiles. I fingered a thin strip of finely woven cloth. It was damp with rain and already beginning to rot along one side.

I edged along the cliff face to the first set of chambers, but they had all been ransacked. According to Federico, the Peruvian Institute of Culture didn't have the proper equipment to rappel down the cliff, so no one knew if the higher mausoleums were intact or not. Sadly, modern-day grave robbers had a reputation for being as ingenious as their Chachapoya forefathers. It was unlikely that the caves above us held anything of worth.

Before we left I asked Federico if we could gather the more beautiful textiles on the ground and bring them to the museum in Leymebamba. He shook his head.

"If we remove anything without special permission and proper verification from the government then we can be charged with all of the looting that has happened here."

"How long would it take to get permission?"

"To remove archaeological artifacts?" He shrugged. "A year, perhaps."

Six-hundred-year-old weaving required by law to rot away. I thought briefly of slipping a small piece into my backpack, to take home, frame, and hang on my living room wall—Why not? A few more months of rain and it would be gone forever. But the memory of the grave robbers and the damage that they had wrought would forever stain its beauty. I laid the cloth back on the ground and turned away.

We returned to Willerman's house to be greeted like long-lost kin. The place had become something of an icon to me—built of Inca stone and filled with warmth, laughter, and generosity. Sadly, Juan Gabriel was no longer there. He had left that morning for Leymebamba with nothing more than a knife and an overcoat.

His father wasn't the least bit concerned. His son, he told us with a twinkle in his eye, was almost certain to retrace our eight-hour trek in less than three.

He was, however, worried about our itinerary. It was nine hours—Andean pace—to our next stop in the village of Cochabamba. Even Federico, despite an almost superhuman patience with our endless filming and photographing escapades, was afraid we might not make it over the high pass with enough daylight left to get down the other side. We swore a solemn oath to keep up no matter what and slunk off to bed.

The true Andean walk isn't a walk at all, but rather a slow jog that carries on for miles despite a heavy load of kindling at 10,000 feet. The next morning we were forced to eat our words. Even the mules had to break into an occasional trot to stay ahead of Federico's compact, loping stride. Gradually we left the cloud forest behind us and climbed up and up and up along an ancient Inca road. The stairs were so steep that the horses nearly panicked on the slippery, rain-soaked steps. Our animals weren't the first to balk at Inca architecture. When the Spanish first arrived, their horses, carrying swarthy men in full battle gear, almost succumbed to the unexpected altitude and bitter cold. Inca roads were built for small men with cannonball calves, enlarged spleens, and expansive lungs, not heavy armor and spindly legged steeds.

Or gringos. We kept up a steady trot as the path narrowed to a llama trail. Trees shrank down to bushes, then twisted up in arthritic agony and disappeared. We were back in the páramo—the grass-covered highland plains that soaked up the six-month rainy season like a giant sponge and doled it out in dribs and drabs to the rivers flowing down to the Amazon and the Pacific Ocean. The mist rolled over us and the mercury plummeted. Now we had to keep running to stave off the bitter cold seeping through our layered clothes, making us feel as fleshless as the shattered mummies. When we at last caught up with Federico he was staring fixedly into the heavy fog that swirled around us.

"Are we lost?" I asked him after several minutes.

"No," he said. "It is just that there are obstacles." He indicated the mist.

I tried another tack. "Any idea where the path is?"

"Yes. When it clears." He handed me the reins and set off to find the missing trail. In seconds he had disappeared.

"We're lost," John said flatly as I snuggled up against one of the long-suffering horses for warmth. I wasn't particularly worried. Beneath those silly white museum gloves I had seen the hands of an Andean farmer. If the weather didn't clear, then we could always do the unthinkable and go back. To Willerman's house.

A ghost appeared and the fog reluctantly coughed up our guide. He had found the path.

The peak. A howling wind tore away the mist to reveal a splendid landscape of jagged peaks rising like crocodile teeth out of fleshy green valleys. We broke our promise and stopped to film. When we turned around, Federico and the animals had disappeared. We had nothing but the sweat-soaked clothes on our backs to ward off the freezing night. We held our breaths and plunged downward toward a gemlike lake that lay several thousand feet below, hoping desperately that darkness wouldn't catch us trying to retrace our steps.

We found the horses first, making their way home. Federico showed up next, proudly waving four fat trout that he had caught in the waters of the lake. Confronted with his broad smile and cheerful wave, our fears at the summit seemed ridiculous. We were, however, only halfway to Cochabamba and the sun was sinking below the mountaintops. It was time to hurry.

We dropped back down into a liquid, milky fog. The temperature skyrocketed and within an hour we had gone from teeth-chattering cold to T-shirt warm. We had crossed the Andes in three short days, from the dusty desert of its western slopes through cloud forest to its treeless peaks, and down again into the watery world of the Amazon.

Cochabamba. Grassy streets that had never seen a car and flocks of sheep that grazed the sidewalks into shape. Its main square was a real-life nativity scene: donkeys, horses, pigs, and sheep. The local schoolteacher offered us his room for the night and his mother generously cooked up Federico's fish.

Once a major Inca administrative center, all that remained of Cochabamba's heritage was a single massive doorway, two crumbling Inca baths, and a few stones so large that the farmers simply plowed around them in their fields. What had happened to the thousands of carved stones that once made up this ancient town? The answer was so obvious that I didn't see it for a while. Almost every stone fence had perfectly rectangular cornerstones. The first two rows of every house were as neat as cinder blocks. Even the ancient aqueduct was still in use, though overgrown and half-plugged with moss. The vast bulk of the conquered stones had been reincarnated as the village church. It seemed a sacrilege to subdue a people, convert them, ransack their greatest engineering achievements, and use their own stones to build the temples to the newcomer's God. And yet...the Inca had done the same to those who had come before. This village wasn't a museum, it was a living piece of history. Perhaps the ancient stonemasons would have wanted their hard-won labors to be used by living, callused hands.

Federico bustled around like a worried hen, making sure that we had animals to take us on our final leg to Pusak. He seemed completely unconcerned that he would have to retrace his steps over the high pass and all the way to Leymebamba in a single day. When he finally gathered up his meager belongings, I realized how much I'd miss his company. If only we could go back with him. But, no, his parents were expecting him, and he had crops to tend. I watched as he turned and waved one last time at the edge of town, then disappeared.

Pusak. Rattan baskets filled with week-old bread. Sandals made from butchered tires. Blue plastic awnings turned brittle by the sun and aged to the color of human skin. Six micro-stores selling carbon-copy odds and ends. A haze of dust hung over the central square where the village boys played pickup soccer. An old woman sat on the corner selling overripe bananas out of a condemned wheelbarrow. I downed a bottle of lukewarm soda, trying to remember the icy winds and frozen fingertips of less than a day ago.

The car I had hired to take us back to Leymebamba was nowhere to be found. The soccer game ended abruptly as both teams settled down to vivisect the foreign novelties. I ate a dozen black bananas. No car. I watched the limp skins visibly decomposing on the searing sidewalk. The soccer teams watched me. By eight o'clock the moon was up and the kids all left for home. We had the sidewalk to ourselves—and nowhere to go. The owner of the wheelbarrow sold us a final bunch of bananas and then unexpectedly invited us to spend the night on the floor of her tiny store, just off one corner of the square.

Her name was Mamita Teresa. She was friendly and talkative and had a white skunk-streak in the center of her coal black hair.

Two decades ago her husband had left her for another woman and she had yet to find a replacement man.

She lived alone in the tiny attic above the store, where the ceiling was so low that years of stooping under it had turned her spine into a question mark. She had four children, all of whom had fled Pusak to make their fortunes. They called from time to time, she told me proudly, on Pusak's only telephone. By the time the lady at the post office ran out to get her, the entire town was buzzing with the news.

Electricity would not find its way to Pusak for a few more years, but Mamita Teresa, like most villagers, had a tiny television set. It ran off a car battery which could be recharged across the street for the princely sum of 21 bananas. Why would anyone buy a television before they had a Coleman lantern, a proper toilet, or a refrigerator?—for the same reason, she told me, that she filled her wheelbarrow each morning and parked it at the village square, a mere 20 feet from her small store. It gave her a window on village life, something new to think and watch and talk about. Here television was the chance to see beyond the edge of town and into a mysterious land of fax machines and jet planes, pelicans and polar bears.

The shelves of her store were lined with a few old mangoes, dusty bottles of beer, and a grim assortment of wilted vegetables. Almost everything edible had been sampled by both rats and roaches, but the floor was spotless. Even more miraculous, a large cement sink crouched in one corner of the room. Without further ado I clambered into it and hunched under the faucet to wash off days of grime and sweat. Beer bottles bobbed around me and something squishy rolled under my knee. A rotting carrot. I blew out the candles, snagged a beer and more bananas, and went to bed.

Mamita Teresa tugged gently on my sleeping bag. It was 5:30. A 20-year-old car was parked outside our door. A grizzled old man lay curled up around the gearshift, snoring heavily.

His name was Santiago. I examined his car with some concern. The tires were smooth as a baby's bottom and the spares were even worse. It was a veritable deathmobile on these narrow, winding mountain roads. No problem, Santiago insisted. He patted the steering wheel and it jiggled like a loose tooth. "This car is solid as a rock," he said—better even than the one he had meant to bring, which had developed a cracked windshield in Leymebamba and was the reason for his overnight delay.

Before we left Mamita Teresa suggested we take some provisions with us—a few oranges, a bag of peanuts, or perhaps a carved stone figurine? Many foreigners, she told us with a conspiratorial smile, came to Pusak to buy antiquities. Of course if I wanted mummies or ceramics, she could place an order with the grave robbers and they would go out and gather what I needed. Tiny, good-natured Teresa—a broker for the local bone-collecting mafia? It was like discovering that the neighborhood granny who used to bake everyone cookies was running a bordello out of her basement.

I turned down the illegal artifacts but jotted down the phone number at the village post office. Teresa had been kind to us—I wanted to call from far away and make the postal woman run out to get her so that the whole town would know.

Santiago was more than just a taxi driver—he was a lifeline between outlying villages that had few phones and fewer roads. He was the general store and switchboard operator—wheeling and dealing with almost every driver we met along the way. He stopped frequently to make rapid-fire trades, offering several crates of mangoes for transport of two bales of hay to town, or pulling over to pick an armful of avocados in return for once hauling a man's wagon out of the mud. He seemed to remember every debt and bargain he had ever made, along with dozens of random bits of information about each farmer, his family and crops, attitude and politics and scandals. And he knew the road.

"Just last year," he said as we crept by a steep cliff face that pitched sharply into the valley below us, "a red Toyota with a driver and three passengers drove off right here in the middle of the night. The car went almost 80 meters into a ravine and—thanks be to God—no one was injured; a small cut to the driver's head was the only casualty. They say it was because it didn't roll but instead went headfirst and was slowed down by the vegetation." A good trick to remember if I was ever going off a cliff. "The car," he continued sadly, "was completely destroyed."

"And over there"—he pointed at a deceptively wide shoulder overlooking a river several hundred feet below—"a truck with many passengers disappeared and was not found for several days. I was there when they hauled it up. It seems the driver was an apprentice and that alcohol was involved. A terrible thing." He looked pointedly at his 17-year-old son beside me in the backseat.

The problem wasn't always alcohol, or inexperience. Sometimes the road itself was to blame. During the rainy season it was known to slide right off the mountain, like ice cream off a Popsicle stick. Or, conversely, death could fall out of the sky in the form of house-size boulders, crushing the cars like Ping-Pong balls. During the last rains, a single massive stone had sliced away 30 feet of road, cutting Leymebamba and its satellite villages off from any contact with civilization for several weeks.

We stopped for a lunch of warm potatoes in a dusty, no-name town. Santiago bantered with the owners and we watched their six-month-old play with a tiny kitten on the cement floor. When it came time to go, I noticed he was carrying a plastic bag that wriggled and squirmed as though it had a snake inside.

"What is it?" I asked.

"Hush. Don't say anything," he hissed, waving me off with one hand. It wasn't until we were well clear of the town that he fished around inside the bag and produced the bewildered kitten.

"You *stole* a cat?" I asked, scooping up the baseball-size ball of fur.

"It was just a joke!" Santiago quickly explained. "I didn't think he'd really give it to me. It belongs to the neighbor and is always coming around their restaurant. They wanted to get rid of it." He shrugged. "I'll give it to my daughter."

The half-pound bundle of curious claws spent the next six hours exploring every nook and cranny of the car, our gear and food and clothes. I held it, warm and purring, in the palm of my hand. I couldn't remember the last time I'd felt a soft caress against my skin. I fell asleep to the sound of Santiago singing forlorn love songs to keep himself awake and the gentle purr of trembling fur against my neck.

The early morning bus back to Cajamarca didn't arrive until half past noon. Yes, we could get on board, the conductor said. No, there were no seats. Gear and passengers were already stacked up in the aisles like cords of wood. An old woman sitting near the driver noticed my spindle sticking out of a corner of my backpack and room was quickly made for us up front. She examined my thread and passed it around to the other women, who clucked among themselves, agreeing that my fleece needed to be cleaned before another inch was spun. Every woman within arm's length grabbed a handful of the fleece and began picking through it, tugging at the burrs and bits of alpaca dung, teasing out the fibers. A cloudlike pile of woolly fluff rose in the center aisle. Then, one by one, they took their turns at the spindle.

Time was measured in the balls of alpaca yarn that found their way back into my lap. Four balls, four hours into the ride there was a sudden explosion and the bus coasted to a halt. Everyone piled out and squatted in straggly patches of shade. The driver and conductor rooted among bags and boxes to find the rattiest spare tire I had ever seen. Its patches had patches. The peeling rubber along its edge looked like the rings on a 500-year-old tree.

A giant socket wrench appeared, followed shortly by a hammer. By the time I saw them rummaging around in the toolbox for a chisel, I knew we were in trouble. One look at the tattered lug nut sent me searching for a mossy spot along the roadside to take a nap. It was going to be a long day.

The sun was sinking below the mountains when arthritic fingers plucked at my sleeve. We all clambered back on board, leaving behind a lonely black smudge and the stench of burning rubber.

Darkness caught us still high in the mountains. The conductor, a veteran of a thousand journeys along this road, wrestled the steering wheel around tight turns and sharp-edged cliffs. From time to time he directed his young assistant to fiddle with a tangled knot of wires that ran alongside his seat. An hour after dark he stopped long enough to send the boy outside to disconnect a driving light. Our imperturbable driver was starting to get perturbed. Twenty minutes later another light went out, then a third.

The alternator was shot, he told me quietly, and the batteries were running down. The flat tire had forced us unexpectedly to drive at night. By the looks of it, we'd be lighting the way by candlelight long before we reached the halfway point of Celendín.

But we had other problems. There were at least 80 people on board. Whenever the bus had to negotiate a tricky corner, the conductor was forced to stop and let off half his passengers so that the overloaded vehicle didn't collapse the soft shoulder and slide into the void below. The smart thing would have been to get out and walk the last 30 miles with my pack. Instead I took the coward's route. I went to sleep.

We arrived in Celendín well after midnight. Most of the passengers stayed on board to wait out the next five hours for the early morning connection to Cajamarca.

I said farewell to the women who had shared my spindle. They had given me something more than four balls of well-spun yarn. The sweater I planned to knit would forever remind me of their gentle faces and gnarled hands.

The angular bus seats had not been made to accommodate John's lanky frame. It seemed best to get him to a hostel immediately. The next morning I knew better than to even mention public transport. I set off early in search of yet another taxi that would take us the final 50 miles south, through a land of tall evergreens and rolling pastureland, of grazing sheep and well-tilled fields— to Cajamarca.

CHAPTER 11

TWILIGHT OF AN EMPIRE

FIELD NOTES: 160 vs. 10,000,000. You'll never guess who won.

Cajamarca was a pearl set in the cool green Andes, too often bypassed by tourists hurrying to see Cuzco and its more tangible treasures. What Cajamarca didn't have in well-cut stones it made up for with its central role in one of the most extraordinary battles of all time, between the last Inca ruler and a motley band of Spaniards.

It was November 15, 1532. A hundred and sixty of Francisco Pizarro's men crested the mountain ridge overlooking Cajamarca. Their intention was to intercept Atahualpa, the recent victor in a five-year civil war against his half brother Huascar. But what the Spaniards saw on that ridge made them forget their dreams of gold and glory. Enemy campfires blanketed the valley below "as thick as the stars of heaven." Although the would-be conquerors were quaking inside their heavy armor, they dared not show it or "the very Indians we brought with us would have killed us." And besides, they had nowhere to run. They were deep in the heart of a hostile empire. The world's second-highest mountain range lay between them and the safety of their ships.

They spent that night writing out their wills. A priest circulated to offer them last rites. "Many of the Spaniards made water without knowing it out of sheer terror," an eyewitness wrote. Only Pizarro was unperturbed. Indeed, he seemed to welcome the overwhelming odds, thinking that his men would fight more fiercely if there were no possibility of retreat. "Make fortresses of your hearts," he told them, "for you have no other."

Atahualpa, on the other hand, was taking his leisure at the royal Inca baths only a few kilometers outside the city, surrounded by his faithful entourage. He knew all about the Spaniards. He had, in fact, been keeping a close eye on the bearded, white-skinned strangers ever since their arrival several months earlier. But they were only a handful of men—what could they do in a land of ten million loyal citizens?

The next morning Pizarro sent an envoy to ask for a meeting with the Inca emperor. De Soto and his men rode out of camp through a gauntlet of 8,000 seasoned warriors. It was the ultimate war of nerves. Knowing the Inca fear of horses, de Soto suddenly charged forward and reigned in his mount within inches of Atahualpa's head. Frothy saliva sprayed over Atahualpa's tunic. He didn't flinch. Those among his men who did—on his behalf—he later executed.

Atahualpa agreed to meet the next day in Cajamarca's central square. Quietly, he ordered his men to wait until sunset, believing incorrectly that the Spaniards could not ride their horses after dark.

In the meantime de Soto returned to the Spanish camp. Pizarro immediately hid his men in the buildings surrounding the main square. They spent the day in tense anticipation. Atahualpa didn't arrive until late the next afternoon. So confident was he of his superiority that he chose ceremonial regalia rather than military array. He rode a litter lined with parrot feathers and gilded with silver and gold plates. His collar was made of emeralds and his robe interwoven with golden threads. He was preceded by an honor guard of Indians wearing livery and playing flutes, drums, and conch-shell trumpets. Dancers and choralists sang praises to their chief, and young boys swept the ground clean before their god-king passed over it.

The dancing ended and Atahualpa's litter came to a stop. The square was empty but for a robed Dominican friar bearing a cross in one hand and a Bible in the other. He strode forward and presented Atahualpa with the Holy Book. Atahualpa raised it to his ear, heard nothing, and threw it to the ground. This was all the excuse the Spaniards needed. "I absolve you in the name of St. James!" the priest cried aloud. "Throw yourselves upon them forthwith!" All hell broke loose. Cannons fired. Horses charged. A three-foot-thick wall crumbled under the force of Atahualpa's panicked warriors fleeing the terrifying scene. Pizarro made straight for Atahualpa. Although his royal pole bearers—all Inca nobles in their own right—were being hacked to pieces, others continually jumped in to take their place. Pizarro grabbed the emperor and threw him to the ground.

When the cannon smoke finally cleared, Atahualpa was in chains. Seven thousand of his warriors lay dead in the square and surrounding fields. Not a single Spaniard was injured with the exception of Pizarro, who had suffered a minor hand wound defending the royal Inca from a blow by one of Pizarro's men.

They say Rome fell in a day. The Inca Empire fell in less than an hour.

Atahualpa was more than just a ruler. He was a deity. With his capture the empire was effectively decapitated. No one, not even his most courageous generals, dared risk an attack on the Spaniards that might result in the murder of their captive god.

But Atahualpa quickly came up with his own plan. He had been watching these crafty strangers and knew their lust for gold. In a desperate bid to free himself, he offered to fill a room once with gold and twice with silver—a kingly ransom the likes of which the world had never seen.

For the next nine months the Royal Road became the golden road as treasures flowed into Cajamarca from the four corners of the empire. Priceless works of art, plates pried from the walls of the sun god's temples, and silver figurines all offered up in exchange for the life of their living god.

Atahualpa passed the time playing cards and practicing his Spanish. He even learned to read a bit, an accomplishment that made the "low-class pagan" more educated than his illiterate captor, Pizarro. He was allowed to keep many of the trappings of his status, including a bat-skin cape much admired by the Spaniards. A flock of women were in constant attendance. At mealtimes he had merely to point to what he wanted and it was fed to him. If a stray hair fell from his head, a royal handmaiden immediately picked it up and ate it, for Atahualpa was terrified of sorcery. His spit was similarly disposed of.

Things were starting to look up for Pizarro's men. Tons of precious metals were pouring in from the farthest reaches of the Inca Empire. The conquistadores, once the dregs of Spanish society, were suddenly decorating their horses with solid silver shoes and playing cards with bricks of gold.

At last, the ransom was complete. Unwilling to release their potentially lethal captive, the Spaniards trumped up fake charges against him and reneged on their agreement. Atahualpa was tried for treason in a kangaroo court and sentenced to be burned at the stake.

The Inca believed that in order to enter the next world, they must depart from this one with their bodies completely intact. For Atahualpa immolation was a fate far worse than death. At the eleventh hour he agreed to convert to Christianity if they would commute his sentence to death by strangulation.

Once he was safely dead, the Spaniards again reneged—this time by cutting his head off and displaying it on the city gate. Crowds gathered to worship the grisly relic, which reportedly grew more handsome with every passing day. At last the Spanish took it down one night and buried it. Too late. The legend of Inkarri had already taken shape, and persists to this day—that Atahualpa's head is hidden in a secret place and growing a new body. Once he is again made whole, he will rise from the ground and return his people to their former glory.

There were other Inca nobles, also direct descendants of the sun. Some were installed as puppet rulers by the Spaniards and offered themselves wholeheartedly to the Spanish cause. Others formed an insurgency and harassed the conquerors throughout Peru for the next 35 years. But all that was just an epilogue to the fateful day when 160 desperate Spaniards took on a mighty empire—and won.

CHAPTER 12

THE PATRIARCH OF HUANCHACO BEACH

FIELD NOTES: "Women are for cooking fish, not catching them," he said.

The trip was at a crossroads. The Capac Ngan—the Inca high road—ran due south from Cajamarca to Cuzco, down the spine of the Andes. A second road ran west, across the foothills of the Andes to connect with the coastal Inca road at Chan-Chan, once the capital of the ancient kingdom of Chimu.

The sunshine and sea breeze beckoned. So did the Chimu, a civilization that rivaled the Inca in their engineering and artistic achievements. But between Cajamarca and the sea lay a wide swath of unforgiving desert.

Most of Peru's coastline is one long ribbon of sand and rock. It is paralleled by the Humbolt Current, which carries cold water from the Antarctic almost as far north as the Equator. The coastal winds always blow onshore, cooling the air over the land. The results are mild temperatures and little moisture from the sea. The Andean mountains to the east act as a barrier against the rain. But the same current that takes away the rain also bestows upon the coastline its greatest blessing—the upwelling of cold water—creating one of the richest sources of marine life anywhere in the world.

Every once in a while a valley cuts across the endless sand, siphoning water from the spongy Andean highlands and returning it to the sea. These enclaves—fertile river valleys with ample food and freshwater—were quickly colonized, resulting in the development of some of South America's most advanced civilizations. One of these was the kingdom of Chimor.

Chimor had its roots in yet another ancient culture that reached its zenith around A.D. 600 on the banks of the Moche River near the modern city of Trujillo. The Moche were a sophisticated, warlike people who conquered several neighboring valleys and built irrigation canals capable of sustaining a population of 50,000 inhabitants. They hunted sea lions from their tortora reed boats and shot the deer that came down to graze along the riverbanks. They developed systems of field irrigation that spread for miles across the barren desert. They kept domesticated dogs and cultivated beans, squash, maize, peanuts, and peppers. They traded for lapis lazuli as far south as Chile and for the exotic spondylus seashells all the way north to the Gulf of Guayaquil in Ecuador. They even perfected an electroplating technique that allowed them to gild copper objects. Although they never developed a system of writing, they were seemingly possessed with the desire to preserve for posterity every detail of their civilization. They were master sculptures and artisans, and used their formidable skills to leave behind an almost photographic representation of their daily lives. Fine line-drawings of horrific bloodletting ceremonies. Armed warriors with conical, crested helmets and blazed tunics. Men and women engaged in every conceivable sexual act. Severed heads. Panpipes and flutes. Their ceramics were so detailed that we even know some of the diseases from which they suffered: veneral disease, blindness, and perhaps cancer.

Then, some time between A.D. 650 and 700, disaster struck. Torrential rains from El Niño wiped out their irrigation canals, causing widespread famine. The Moche sank into obscurity.

But not for long. Within two centuries they rose again, reincarnated as the kingdom of Chimor. Earliest construction of the Chimu capital at Chan-Chan dates back to A.D. 800. The Chimu would eventually become the largest kingdom to rule Peru before the rise of the Inca, conquering nearly 1,000 kilometers (620 miles) of coastal territory. They built Chan-Chan into a splendid city with walled temples, mausoleums, parks, and artificial lagoons. The surrounding population was composed almost entirely of weavers, metalsmiths, and potters.

Chimor was thriving just as the Inca began their great expansive drive. Conflict was inevitable. Slowly, inexorably, the Inca armies forded the trackless desert. But in the end, armed force wasn't necessary. The very river that gave the Chimu life in the desert led to their downfall. The Inca Emperor Topa Yupanqui simply cut the flow of water to their capital at Chan-Chan and the Chimu fell without a fight. Once the kingdom was digested, its technology was disseminated throughout the Inca Empire.

I was just five miles out of Chan-Chan, slogging through a blisteringly hot and bone-dry stretch of sand, when I stumbled upon the remains of the Inca Road. Although the once high walls were largely washed away, the road itself was clearly visible, 30 feet across and stretching like some prehistoric runway in a straight line to the horizon. Just beyond it lay the sea.

Huanchaco is a tiny dot on the coast of northern Peru. It is a pretty town, with white sandy beaches, foaming surf, sun-browned fishermen and...tortora reed boats. They were nearly exact replicas of the ancient vessels found on Moche pottery dating back to A.D. 600. They had graceful, tapering bows and truncated sterns. The fishermen called them *caballitos*—little horses—which is exactly what they looked like as they rode the incoming surf. As legend has it, caballitos were the offspring of the balsa boat that first brought the Chimu dynasty's founder, Tacaynamu, to Peruvian shores.

I had come to Huanchaco to find out more about the ancient boats from the fishermen who still used them. I also hoped— secretly—to build a little caballito of my own and to learn to guide it through the surf.

Elvira was the owner of a Huanchaco hostel called, appropriately, Caballitos de Tortora. She had all the joyful energy of a half-grown Labrador and a similarly endearing charm. When she heard about my quest, she immediately sent me to meet a man named Buso, the padre of Huanchaco beach. I found him mending nets, surrounded by four of his eight sons. Buso was barrel-chested and barnacled. He didn't have the sculpted curves and corrugations of chiseled bodybuilders, but Buso was enormously strong. He was the kind of man who could walk into your kitchen and pick up your refrigerator, then walk out with it, whistling.

Several other fishermen gathered around to listen respectfully to our negotiations. I knew that if Buso chose not to work with me then I might as well pack up and go home. I told him of my dream to build a boat, to ride it in the waves....He listened in silence while I made my pitch, then shook his head. "Women," he told me, "don't go out in boats." I tried to change his mind with massive doses of personal charm and charisma. When that failed utterly, I discreetly offered cash. He clucked a few times, staring out to sea. Exceptions could be made, he said at last. He walked off with a wad of bills in hand. There was obviously more to being the padre of the beach than just knowing the whims of the sea.

I had done some paddling in my life and even a bit of white-water kayaking, back in my college days. The boats looked unstable, but the principles were probably the same. I clambered into the depression in the stern and took up the paddle—a simple piece of split bamboo with the internal dividers knocked out. I drove straight out through the surf, reveling in the way the boat bobbed over the cresting swell. All went well until I turned around to ride my first wave back in toward the beach. The boat's long line made it almost impossible to surf straight down the front of the frothy crest. Given the slightest opportunity, my seahorse immediately made a 90-degree turn and started rolling like a log. The bamboo paddle did little more than slow down the inevitable while digging painfully into my uncallused palms. After several tries, Buso suddenly appeared, swimming slowly through the icy water. He hopped on board, repossessed the paddle, and pointed out that I was sitting in the hole that was normally used to store fish.

The boat cut through the ocean like a surgeon's scalpel in Buso's capable hands. He took us farther out into the larger surf, then slipped back overboard and directed me from the water, his face crinkling into a fatherly smile.

I caught a last wave into shore and Buso emerged, soaked and shivering. He picked up the 250-pound boat, settled it on his shoulder, and walked off. I grabbed the paddle and ran after him. "Tomorrow," he said, his voice muffled under the caballito's weight, "we build your boat."

The next morning we set off to hunt tortora reeds with Buso and his son Carlos. We walked just above the high-tide mark, where a ridge of sand fell off steeply into a series of deep, hand-dug troughs, each the size of a backyard swimming pool. They were filled with the fleshy green spikes of tortora reeds. Each trough, or *posa*, grew enough reeds to build five caballitos per year—a good thing, since the average boat only lasts a couple of months before succumbing in its daily battle with the sea.

Buso handed me a scythe and I stepped gingerly into the thick mud. The stalks had to be cut at an angle no more than two inches above the waterline, leaving behind vicious-looking spikes that felt exactly like a field of *punji* stakes. I worked my way through the knee-deep mud, cutting and piling reeds. Something slithered along my instep. "Anything live in here?" I asked Carlos with poorly feigned indifference.

"Crabs," he said. "And snakes, sometimes."

"What kind of snakes?"

He pointed his chin at the ocean without pausing in his work. "From the sea. They come in on the tide."

Sea snakes, the most venomous serpents in the world. I tucked in my toes and kept cutting.

Once we had three large piles, we hauled them out onto the sand and laid them in the sun. The drying process normally took two weeks, allowing the pulpy green reeds to harden and gradually turning them the color of ripening corn. Buso, who obviously didn't want us underfoot for that long, immediately took us to a batch of well-seasoned reeds just a little way down the road. We gathered and cleaned them, then carried them back to the narrow street in front of Buso's house.

His front entryway opened into a two-story warren of tiny rooms and a cavernous kitchen that could feed an army. And so it did—seven of Buso's ten children were still living under his roof. All but two of the boys had become fishermen, and his two girls had married into the trade. Several had already started families of their own, to which Buso added a few orphaned kids he had picked up like driftwood on the beach. He counted under his breath, "12, 14, 18, 23...." All in all there were 25 mouths to feed each day. To make ends meet, he maintained a small garden a little farther inland and kept a pig in a bricked enclosure just off the kitchen.

His wife appeared, warm and round and quietly capable. "The Queen of Huanchaco," he called her fondly, and her eyes disappeared into the folds of her smile. Carlos slipped two fingers into the eye sockets of a fish and dangled it over a four-month-old strapped into a baby carriage. "Teaching the next generation to fish?" I asked. "No, no," he said, quickly putting the fish back in the pile. "She's a girl."

There was one faded black-and-white photograph hanging in the living room—a small boy sitting on a miniature reed boat. "You started young," I said, recognizing Buso's wide cheekbones and smile in the four-year-old's face. He nodded. "I only studied to third grade before going out to sea."

"Why?" I asked, expecting to hear a story of financial hardship and family tragedy.

"I never wanted to be in school," he answered with a shrug. "I liked the water better. Paddling a boat. Reading the waves. In the ocean I know exactly what to do." His indifference to his school-work did not go unnoticed by his teachers, who regularly called him onto the carpet. "'Don't you want to be a doctor, a lawyer, a professional?" they asked. "I am a professional!" he told them proudly. "I am a fisherman."

Over the years, while others were memorizing Plato and learning how to do square roots, he studied the sea in all her fickle moods. He learned about the fish that swam just beyond the breakwater's edge, and the storms that sometimes came roaring over the horizon with all the fury of a wrathful god. And, gradually, he became respected for his knowledge and his understanding of the ocean's depths. Now, at 60, with thick fingers and eyes that were already starting to turn milky from the glittering waters, he was the undisputed master, the father of the sea.

We gathered three of his sons and went outside to begin construction on the boat. They moved with an almost military precision that could only have come from years of building and rebuilding these short-lived craft. One son sorted the reeds into longer and shorter piles while another sat off to one side and carved a bamboo paddle. Buso and his eldest, Carlos, began wrapping the reed bundles with frayed twine salvaged from an earlier boat. Around and around they went, pulling each wrap tight until their hands turned white and the twine wore ridges in their callused fingers. They swatted away my attempts to help. "Women don't build boats," Buso said.

Beneath their expert hands the graceful line of a caballito gradually took shape. The shorter bundles were laid inside the longer ones and the two halves married with twine. In little more than an hour the boat was done.

Buso had agreed to everything except my going fishing with the men. First, he said, he wanted to see me carry my own boat down to the waterline. Then I'd have to surf it successfully among the breaking waves.

The beach was three long blocks away. Newly built, my boat weighed a little over half that of the waterlogged caballitos fresh from the sea. Still, that was nearly 140 pounds in a package that was twice as tall as I was.

I felt Buso's hands mold my back into the proper shape and then help lift and settle the caballito onto my shoulder. It sat perfectly balanced front and back. I suddenly realized that, despite his stubborn stance against women and fishing, he really wanted me to succeed.

The rest was easy.

My maiden voyage. I paddled out and prepared to do battle with the surf. I waited for a moderate-size wave—large enough to make a good impression but not so large that it could put me in a body cast. I straddled the boat—there had to be a reason they call it a "horse"—and dug in hard. Nothing happened. The wave rolled by. The shore crowd clucked and shook their heads. I tried again—a larger wave this time. Nothing. I checked surreptitiously that someone hadn't thrown an anchor overboard. I had—my own legs. They were causing so much drag on the caballito that I might as well have been tied to a pole.

I pulled my feet up and stretched them out in front of me. This raised my center of gravity so high that the next wave inevitably— and immediately—set things right. I tried again. And again. When I finally managed to get the caballito moving in the proper direction while I was still on top, I received a crash course in how not to steer.

For two hours I struggled in the surf while Buso stood on shore with his feet spread wide and his hands behind his back, alternatively shaking his head or breaking out in a proud parental smile. It wasn't until I got back to shore and faced a line of clucking fishermen that I realized what a stir I had caused. "Never mind," Buso said. He clapped me on the back. "Tomorrow we're going fishing."

Four a.m. found me hunkered down in the back of a caballito, trying desperately not to upset the boats—or throw up—while Buso's son paddled me through the surf. I had decided after all not to take my caballito out with the fishermen. Who was I kidding, anyway? One look at their powerful biceps and rippling shoulders told me I'd be lucky if I reached the fishing grounds the day after they dropped their nets.

The sea was glassy smooth beyond the breaker line. Early morning fog lay plump and heavy on the water, turning sky and sea into a seamless gray bubble through which we seemed to paddle endlessly, going nowhere. I felt silly sitting in the depression where the fish were usually kept, like a useless piece of cargo. I watched Buso guide his boat easily through the water. He seemed to have no trouble keeping up with his sons. They must be proud of him.

His son Carlos smiled in agreement, but added, "last year he almost died. Now we don't let him go out alone anymore." Buso had taken his boat out fishing by himself early one morning, despite not feeling well the night before. He got a sudden attack of nausea and diarrhea, and shook so badly that he fainted and fell into the sea. He climbed back into his boat with difficulty and clung there, shivering, until the sun rose. "He lost all the strength in his body; he could barely lift his paddle. He collapsed as soon as he reached shore. We found him on the beach. He had cholera. It took him a month to get well again."

"Does he know you keep an eye on him?"

Carlos gave me a quick glance over his shoulder, grinned, and shook his head.

"We take turns. There are seven of us."

The shadowy forms of the other fishermen began to appear out of the swirling mist. They were all anchored, stern to the swells, their tapered prows rising and falling in the oily-smooth water. Buso and Carlos unfolded a long net and dropped it between their boats. We drifted slowly downwind, dragging the net behind us while Buso called out to the fishermen, joking with them about their catch, their families, and their boats. I tugged at a line, more to tease Buso into automatically slapping my hand away than to do anything useful.

"Women," he said loud enough for the other fishermen to hear, "are for cooking fish, not catching them."

"Papa, I think I've caught a siren," Carlos called back, and won my heart forever. Perhaps there was hope for the next generation of Huanchaco beach.

On the other hand, my backside was freezing from sitting in the icy water and my hands were blue with cold. Hanging around a warm fire roasting fish might not be such a bad deal after all.

Buso's boat was called *The Maestro*, The Teacher, and Carlos was the "disciple." He and Buso worked together in almost telepathic silence. When Buso did give orders, they were gentle, and Carlos obeyed without the slightest hesitation. Buso was transparently proud of his sons and the way they handled themselves and their boats. He experienced a joy in life that I seldom see in those who work desk jobs, or in families with latchkey kids. I wondered if, despite the cholera and the admonishments of his teachers, Buso hadn't chosen the right path after all. He had found a place where many of us, to some degree, yearn to be.

CHAPTER 13

THE WALKER

FIELD NOTES: I felt like toothpaste being squeezed out of the tube.

The ancient road south out of Huanchaco had largely disappeared beneath the sands of time and the asphalt ribbon of the Pan American Highway. I wasn't surprised. Even at the height of its glory, the coastal Inca Road was often marked with little more than stone cairns and wooden signs. In some places it was just a trail of footprints. In the 1540s the famous chronicler Cieza de León called it the "pole road" for the rows of wooden posts that marked its passage. Those that followed in his footsteps less than a generation later noted that most of the poles had disappeared and that a guide was needed to cross the desert sands. The wood had all been used by travelers to make fires.

The ancient road hugged the coast wherever possible, cutting inland to skirt deserts where there was no water source for more than 62 miles. Vestiges of broad thoroughfares with adobe sidewalls could still be seen in some of the more fertile valleys. Three hundred miles south of Huanchaco, the Inca Road ran smack into the outskirts of Peru's sprawling capital city and disappeared.

Lima was one vast cloud of six-million-person-created smog and traffic. It looked like an unrepentant smoker—clogged arteries, wheezing heavily, yet still sucking down more noxious fumes.

The city center is gradually decaying as its wealthier inhabitants escape to the suburbs in search of room to breathe. Along Lima's outer margins, the shantytowns fester with drugs and violence. These "young towns" absorbed the bulk of the 12-fold increase in the city's population in less than 50 years. Lima is like a tropical ulcer, growing from the inside out.

Its wealthier pockets have all the earmarks of a modern industrial society—more cars than taxis, more taxis than bicycles. BMW dealerships and fast-food restaurants. Dogs that are leashed and have a discernible parentage. In Lima the word Inca has become more closely linked to "Kola"—the national soft drink—than to its own history.

I found a tiny room outside of downtown Lima. It was just large enough to hold a single bed and was lit by a hanging, 20-watt bulb. It was huddled in a corner of a cement roof like a pile of accumulated debris, ready to catch the next tornado back to Kansas. Every morning rows of starchy blue jeans and crisp white sheets appeared on the clotheslines that crisscrossed the roof. They rustled with the scent of lemons and formed a protective barrier against the smog that swirled up from the streets below.

Showering was an elaborate ritual of opening valves under the laundry sink and beside the water heater. The faucet below the showerhead tingled with electricity. Only once did I turn it off before I dried my hands.

At 5:00 a.m. every morning I'd wake to a thunderbolt of bodies against the corrugated roof and the sound of desperate, metallic scrambling. I thought they were rats—until they settled into a rusty gutter, and began to coo.

My plan was to spend two weeks learning the Andean pan-pipes, poring over maps, and researching the next leg of my journey down the Inca Road. I also hoped to track down a Peruvian I'd been hearing about since I first arrived in Ecuador. A young man with the unusual nickname of "El Caminante"— The Walker.

He had made his fame—and gotten his name—by a single, audacious act. In 1995 he put on a tattered backpack, slipped his feet into a pair of leather sandals, and caught a bus to the northernmost tip of Peru. His goal was to walk the entire desert coastline of his country, alone.

And that is exactly what he did.

What had started as a simple, solitary act, a moving meditation, quickly caught the imagination of a nation in search of heroes, and in search of itself. Reporters scoured Peru's desolate coastal landscape, impatiently awaiting the seemingly unstoppable Walker. Lima's largest newspaper ran a series of excerpts from his diary, snatched up and read by millions of smog-and-traffic city dwellers. Somewhere along the way, El Caminante realized that he was inadvertently following what once had been the Inca Empire's mighty coastal road.

His interest piqued, he researched the network of Inca highways and discovered the seven principal connecting roads between the coastal route and the legendary high road through the mountains. Without further ado, he put on his backpack and added another 1,700 miles to his well-worn shoes and a priceless amount of field data to the little-known geography of the disintegrating system of royal Inca Roads.

I had come to Lima to meet El Caminante—Ricardo Espinosa in real life—to compare notes and archaeological data on the road ahead. More than that, I wanted to get to know this man, this carefree wanderer who would undertake a hero's journey in the same way that most of us would go out for a cup of coffee. I needed to know what made him tick.

I was sitting at our prearranged meeting point on the steps of McDonald's when it suddenly occurred to me that I had no idea what Ricardo looked like. The book he had written—filled with lovely images of sea lions and crescent beaches—didn't show a single photo of his face. Then, through the crowds, I saw a lanky man float up the stairs with what seemed like an absolute absence of effort. That's him, I thought, and then was greeted with an utterly welcoming hug.

"I don't eat meat," he murmured, and whisked me off to a vegetarian restaurant. "The food's not all that good," he apologized, "but I like the people." They were Hare Krishnas, and they greeted him like a long lost brother—which is exactly what he was. He had joined their sect as a 20-something in search of wisdom and stayed just long enough to help them launch a successful vegetarian restaurant in Cuzco. I felt awkward poking into the private life of a man I had met barely an hour earlier, and immensely curious. Curiosity won.

"I grew up in a perfectly normal, middle-class Lima family," he told me with a shrug. As a child he wanted for nothing, was well-educated, and carefully programmed to become a useful cog in the machinery of modern society.

But early on there was already something unusual about him—something more than the kinky brown hair he now wore in a ponytail or his exceptionally light skin. "When I was 14," he said, "I had a...breakdown, more or less. I suddenly realized that the adults I looked up to didn't have all the answers to life." The resulting crisis of confidence in the world around him sent him into a downward spiral of isolation and despair.

Eventually he made up his mind to finish high school and then head out to seek his own truth in the far corners of the world. Despite acne and the anxieties of the teen years, the beginnings of an iron will were already starting to take shape.

He celebrated his 19th birthday. School was done. He packed his bags and left. He spent nearly a year working as a farm laborer in rural Peru, and finally ended up living with a former Trappist monk in a remote mountain village in Argentina. It wasn't an easy life. "We worked eight hours, meditated eight hours, and slept from 10:00 p.m. to 2:00 a.m. each night." He took vows in everything from poverty to chastity. "Once you were there for nine years, you were granted the right to never leave the place until you died, and to be buried there." It didn't sound like such a great deal to me.

Ricardo obviously agreed. Within a year he had met an Iranian woman who ran an ashram in India. "You could feel her power," he said, his eyes lighting up, his hands fluttering along the edges of an imaginary aura. "She knew many things about me that she could not have known." He accepted her invitation to study at the ashram, repacked his bags and left.

"Then, while I was on my way through Lima en route to India, I got married."

I stopped in mid-bite. "Just like that? You make it sound like falling off a ladder."

He laughed. "It was. You must understand—I had hardly any experience in such things. A friend invited me to a party. Halfway through the evening, his girlfriend got angry and stormed out, and he ran after her. They never came back. The hostess dropped everything to take care of me. We spent the next 30 hours together. It was," he said thoughtfully, "like falling off a ladder."

A whirlwind romance with a Trappist monk. Could it work?

He shook his head. He stumbled through several explanations, his voice and hands faltering for the first time. She had come from a well-to-do family and was used to money, yet was desperately searching for a way out of a life that had become devoid of meaning. He had spent years traveling the path to enlightenment, and was convinced he could show her how to find happiness.

"You rescued her," I said.

He nodded. "Here is an image...." He tried steepling his hands as I had seen the Hare Krishnas do. "Imagine an endless line of people walking through the desert. They are wearing suits and jackets and carrying an enormous amount of luggage, some so burdened that they're sinking into the sand with every step. Out of this line comes one man, naked, walking a foot above the ground. He is dancing with joy. You say to yourself, "How wonderful it must be to live like that man." You tell him, "Teach me how to be like you." You climb onto his back. You bring all your luggage with you. Then one day you look down and see that he is slogging knee-deep through the sand. "You tricked me," you say. "You aren't what I thought you were."

The divorce took seven years. By then there were two boys, three and five years old. The whole ordeal had left quite an impression on him.

"I am completely happy being alone," he said with conviction. "I don't need people. When I am out walking in the desert, I never crave the companionship of others. I don't think to myself, "I wish so-and-so were here." I prefer the tranquillity and solitude of my own company."

And yet he was so obviously at ease with others—witty and fun and friendly, sociable and, I had to admit, downright charming.

"Don't you think that one day when you're 65 you'll look back and wish you'd found a partner to share the rest of your life?"

"Whenever I think of myself in the future, I see an old man sitting in a cave, throwing rocks at anyone who comes too close." His eyes were twinkling, but he was serious.

"And after you finish walking the Inca Road?"

"Someday, perhaps I'll sculpt a mountain."

"What would you sculpt?"

"A bird"—he thought for a moment—"an eagle, perhaps."

And somehow I knew that he would do that too.

Lima is blessed with lovely beaches and a turquoise ocean. It is cursed with a thick blanket of smog that curled itself around the city like a cat for eight months out of every year. The heavy haze keeps sunlight from seeping in and pollution from leaking out. It leaves a thick brown varnish on buildings, cars, and old people in the park. It creeps through broken windows and inseminates

unused basements with a furry coat of mold. It even has a name—
garúa.

For the few months of summer, the smog retreats and the sun
breaks through. Despite the daily health warnings published in the
local papers, I started hauling myself out of bed at dawn, donning
running shoes, and jogging down to the beach.

One morning I plodded past a tiny cardboard shack huddled in
the shadow of Lima's most expensive seaside restaurant. Its owner
was manhandling a pair of oars.

"Heading out?" I called.

He stuck a hand through several holes in his net. "As soon as
these are fixed."

"Can I come along?"

He looked me up and down through eyes spider-webbed with
thin red veins.

"Sure."

Forty minutes later we clambered on board his heavy wooden
boat and put out to sea.

He and his helper pulled hard through the surf and rowed along
the shore to the edge of a stone jetty. They positioned the boat
between the waves and the leading edge of rock, and held it there
in a magnificent ballet of oars and spume and waves and granite.
His name, he told me, was Willy. He lived in the closetlike shack
on the beach with three other men and rowed out each morning
to work the waters off some of Lima's filthiest beaches.

He threw his net again and again into the trash-strewn water,
shouting at his helper to reposition the boat, tugging gently at
the line and hauling it up empty. He shook his head. "El Niño," he
said bitterly. A year ago it had swept the coast, raising the
temperature of the water by several degrees. The fish all fled.

"Nothing left but stones and seaweed." Soon the fishermen were forced to leave as well. He himself had traveled inland to Huaraz and worked as a painter for nearly nine months. He threw the net again in a perfect circular arc that covered an area of water the size of a beach umbrella. It sank out of sight. He waited a moment, tested the line, and pulled it in. Empty.

He had three children—two boys who lived with his wife in a nearby town and a daughter by his mistress. The boys were still studying, and the girl.... He looked over my shoulder. "Son of a *bitch*."

I whirled around. Dolphins! Four of them, rising through the foot-thick layer of gray spume, cutting back and forth along the surf line in search of fish. I sat, entranced by their shiny skin and supple movements while Willy raised his fist in futile anger at the graceful beasts.

"Dolphins! Ha! Pigs of the sea! They're protected now, dammit. Can't eat 'em. They'll scare the fish away. Damn!" He turned back to me. "Very tasty. Better than turtles."

After three hours in the roiling surf even the shiny-backed dolphins had lost some of their fascination. I had long since given up on the perpetually empty net and was waging an inner battle against my stomach's queasy rumblings. The sun had finally burned through Lima's smog and my unprotected nose was bubbling like an old paint job. Willy had promised a two-hour trip, but the frustratingly empty net only added to his determination to stay. Our haul to date—a three-inch crayfish—flopped around in the bilge, narrowly missing freedom every time we bailed the boat.

Another hour passed. And another. It was far too dangerous for me to disembark on the rock jetty, an enticing 15 feet away. My stomach was in full mutiny against the rolling swell. I let go my pride and began to bargain.

"Okay, how about three more tosses and if you don't catch anything, then we go home?"

He agreed to head back if the net stayed empty for the next hour. Ninety minutes later there were two rocks rolling around in the bottom of the boat. We renegotiated. An hour after that a sea urchin came on board.

"They're inedible, Willy," I pointed out.

"I caught 'em," he countered. We had an identical conversation over several clumps of seaweed and an empty soda can. I considered throwing up but was afraid it might attract the few guppies still hanging out in the tidal zone, and we'd be stuck there forever.

At last Willy grimaced, dug around inside his mouth, and pulled out a bloody molar. We rowed for home.

It was late afternoon. I was wobbly with sun and crossing my legs after eight hours without a toilet in an open boat. I leaped ashore as soon as the boat touched gravel and sprinted for a taxi. Willy called me back. He whispered to his helper, then invited me into his shack. We sat, making small talk for half an hour. At last the man returned, flourishing a plate of ceviche—raw fish soaked in lemon and onions. Willie presented it to me with a broad smile—there really was a bloody hole back there where his tooth had been. I looked out over the filthy water, knowing exactly where the fish came from. Then back at Willy, offering me his entire day's catch.

I ate the fish.

By sheer luck my days in Lima coincided with the Señor de los Milagros procession—the largest religious gathering in all of Peru.

More than one million faithful thronged the streets for ten days while a copy of the mural of the Lord of Miracles made its stately way through the city's narrow, crowded alleyways.

The image had an unusual pedigree. It was painted in 1651 by an "ignorant but inspired" Angolan slave on the wall of his room. Four years later an earthquake decimated Lima, destroying everything in its path—except the mural, which was left miraculously intact. A popular cult rose spontaneously around the invincible "black Christ." The local priest, annoyed at the sudden competition, sought authorization from his superiors to tear down the wall. They obligingly sent an Indian with a fat brush and instructions to paint over the image. He approached the mural, suffered violent convulsions, and fled. A second man was hired with the promise of better pay. He took one look at the sacred image, was struck dumb, and retired in confusion. The church was losing patience with such insolent behavior on the part of an adobe wall. This time they sent a soldier, a less likely candidate for spontaneous conversion. He cried out at the beauty of the image and refused to do it harm. Immediately thereafter the sky was obscured by heavy clouds and a torrential rain began. The people somewhat belatedly took up the cause and forced the ecclesiastic authorities to retire.

Thirty-two years later another earthquake sent a copy of the mural cruising through the streets on what was to become a yearly procession that continues to this day.

I wanted to feel what it was like to be part of a million-person procession. I also wanted to film it, but I was short a cameraman. Perhaps the Miraculous Lord would provide.

He did. Welby Leaman was a young Yale Law School graduate working for Peru's tourism promotion board. No, it wasn't really a part of his job description, he said with a laugh. Yes, he'd be happy to do it.

I liked Welby immensely. He had long-fingered piano-player hands and a Mennonite upbringing that manifested itself in his tiny one-room studio and a habit of walking virtually everywhere. He was humble and hardworking, and could usually be found propped over his computer, alternately dozing and plugging away at his reports until well into the wee hours of the morning. And he was smart. I wondered if he knew what he was getting into.

We arrived downtown to find the entire city center decked out in the Señor's color. Purple balloons, purple beverages made from purple corn. Purple pudding, banners, flags, and floats. Whatever wasn't purple was plastered with the Lord's image, from umbrella handles to clocks, bathroom scales, and crucifixes.

We headed for the headquarters of the "Brothers"—the men in charge of organizing the procession and carrying the heavy mural through the streets. The building looked more like a corporate headquarters than a religious retreat. Efficient-looking men wearing ties and good shoes slipped silently in and out. Somewhere in the background I thought I heard the quiet buzz of a thousand cell phones charging.

With press passes in hand, we dashed off to a nearby shop selling purple dresses. An old woman slipped the procession costume over my head, wrapped a white penitent's rope firmly around my waist, took one look at my filthy sneakers and told me to go barefoot.

Lima's main plaza was draped in the almost tangible odor of carnations. Piles of flowers freckled the entire square. Determined knots of women tore flowers limb from limb and gathered the petals into growing mounds of confetti color. On the rectangular street that ringed the plaza men sketched out religious scenes in chalk and filled them in with moistened sawdust. I soon found myself butchering flowers beside weathered women stained yellow with scented pollen. This group lived in the town of Barranca, they told me. They volunteered weekly at a soup kitchen and came every year to offer a flower carpet to the Lord of Miracles. They were from the countryside, they said, and understood how hard life was.

The flower paintings began to take on shape and color as an endless rain of petals accumulated on the street. I wandered from drawing to drawing, marveling at the quiet faith that could lead so many people to sculpt offerings that would last a scant few hours before being trampled by the coming crowds. What a waste, I thought, wanting to take pictures, film the paintings, and create some testament that would make all this work worthwhile. The women laughed at my frustration. "This is faith," one of them said, sweeping her arm to encompass the work of thousands. She was right. It wasn't about the final product. It was the process, the act of worship, that mattered. The fleeting nature of the offering made the gesture that much more meaningful.

Still, I wanted something more than a fading memory of the mingled smell of sawdust and flower petals. Welby and I set off to case the buildings around the square. We soon found ourselves on the sixth floor of a building, overlooking the plaza. It was an unearthly scene—pools of light in the midnight darkness illuminating a vast carpet of doves and olive branches, chalices, and bleeding hearts. Suddenly I realized the depth of the women's faith. Like the legendary Nazca lines, these works of art could only be fully appreciated from above. The artists themselves would never see the results of their own labors. It was an offering in the truest sense of the word.

We returned to the church at 5:00 a.m. sharp and waited bleary-eyed for the Lord of Miracles to begin his lengthy trek through Lima's streets. Five thousand faithful sat in the cold stone courtyard, their unwavering gaze on the huge church door. I looked around at the stoic older faces, wrapped in shawls and fingering candles and beads with gnarled hands.

At last the enormously heavy copy emerged from the church on the shoulders of 16 purple-robed brothers. We slipped under the ropes that separated the inner core from the teary-eyed spectators and entered another world. The palanquin swayed back and forth in a slow, mesmerizing rhythm. All around it, white-veiled women carried charcoal burners that they fed with tiny silver spoons. Sweetly scented wisps of incense caressed my cheeks and tickled my nose. The women sang as they walked barefoot in the path of their Lord. The crowds had burgeoned and the streets were packed. A river of people surged around us like the tide.

The sun crept across the sky faster than the mural shuffled through the streets. Soon the day turned suffocatingly hot. The palanquin was made of solid oak and decorated with a thousand pounds of silver. The 16 gray-haired bearers were having a hard time of it. Sweat poured from their faces and soaked their robes. One man staggered repeatedly, clearly on the verge of collapse, but refused to give up his place of honor. The other brothers propped him up and mopped his brow.

The central plaza was a wall-to-wall press of people, all standing on tiptoe to get a better view. They were a tangible presence, as solid as a stone embankment along which a river flowed. We walked directly on the flower paintings that carpeted the road between the crowds. Despite the seething mass of humanity that stood waiting for the mural, the paintings were completely undisturbed. And in the wake of the procession not a single flower was left to commemorate a long night's labor.

The crush of people increased steadily until even the brothers were having trouble squeezing through the crowd. Welby and I decided to make a break for the building we had been in the night before.

It was only 50 feet away, but it could just as well have been 5 miles. At first I held my camera bag in front of me like a cowcatcher and, murmuring a nonstop monologue of apologies, tried to forge a path through. I felt like toothpaste being squeezed out of a tube. Twenty feet later I was solidly stuck. In a last, desperate bid for freedom I ducked down and crawled through a scaffolding of legs, still shouting my apologies and periodically popping up like a prairie dog to figure out where I was. Even that soon became impossible. I stood in toe-to-shoulder gridlock, locked in place by knees and thighs and breasts and elbows. A woman fainted. She didn't fall. Gradually we melted into a single, living mass—our breathing synchronized so that when one exhaled the other had room to breathe in. We were united not as much by shared devotion as shared location.

The mural, indifferent to our suffering, shuffled down the street.

The fifth-floor balcony was crowded with Europeans and wealthy Limeños, watching the spectacle from their ringside seats. From this high up, the entire plaza was a mottled mass of pinheaded people. A small island of purple and white churned through the flower paintings. Music floated up, and the air carried just a touch of incense.

"You should go see it from below," I told an English couple standing next to me. I offered them my press pass to allow them entry to the inner circle.

The woman reacted like I had tried to sell her a pox-infected blanket. "Why on earth would we want to do that?" she asked, peering over the edge of the balcony at the crowds. "It looks beastly down there."

I remembered the feel of moistened sawdust beneath my bare feet and the clouds of incense wrapped around me like a silken veil. That mingled odor would forever transport me back to this place.

I offered the pass to several other people on the balcony, but no one was interested. If only I could find one of those wizened women who sat with me in the chilly predawn darkness and burst into tears when the mural first appeared.

The Lord of Miracles slowly wound around the square and disappeared.

A young girl pauses with her llama in the shadow of Cuzco's ancient Inca walls (LEFT). The twelve-sided stone in Cuzco (BELOW) stands as a symbol of the Inca's superb engineering skills.

Machu Picchu (ABOVE, LEFT) is the most visited of the Inca ruins in South
America. The Inca built entire cities of stone without knowledge of either the arch
or the wheel (BELOW, LEFT). Manco Capac, the very first Inca on the shores of
Lake Titicaca, arrives during the yearly reenactment (ABOVE).

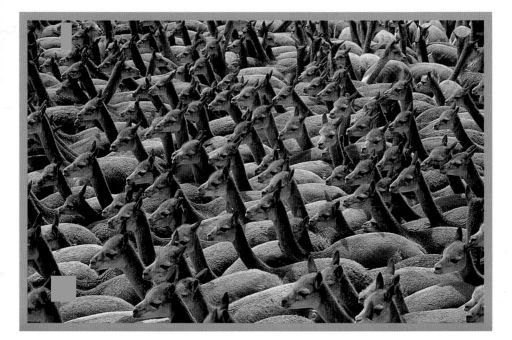

Sixteen hundred corralled vicuñas, the Golden Fleece of the Andes (ABOVE), will soon be tagged and sheared following a roundup. I enjoy a quiet moment in a sacred place—the Island of the Sun on Lake Titicaca (ABOVE, RIGHT). Being dressed to dance with my troupe, the Devils, during the festival of Oruro (BELOW, RIGHT) involved spike heels that were two sizes too small, panty hose, false eyelashes, a flowing wig, and a mask that cut off most of the air intake through my nose. All performed in penance to the Virgin.

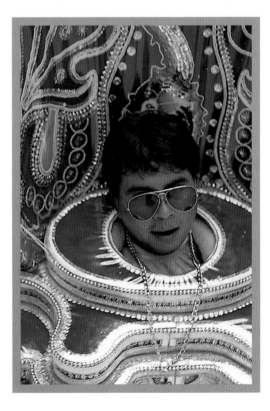

Other Oruro dancers chose even more exotic garb. Some wore eight-foot rhea-feather hats (ABOVE, LEFT). This man (BELOW, LEFT) was so restricted by his own costume that he couldn't reach up to wipe the perspiration from his face. A moment of supreme emotional catharsis takes place in the Catholic church at the end of the procession (ABOVE).

Twenty-five thousand dancers participate yearly in Oruro's grand festival (ABOVE).
I ride into the sunset across Bolivia's salt flats (BELOW).

CHAPTER 14

A MANGO IN THE SURF

FIELD NOTES: Never walk alone at night through the Bolivian hinterlands, particulary if you are carrying nothing but a bell.

I slogged through ankle-deep sand and watched the horizon flicker and dance. Ricardo—The Walker—had been on this road for nearly five months. How had he found food and water in the desert? What I had taken to be merely a triumph of discipline and tenacity—like hiking the Appalachian Trail—must have been in reality a far more dangerous exercise in survival.

"It was," he told me when I got back in the car. We were heading down the coast south of Lima, visiting some of his old stomping grounds. The expensive four-wheel-drive I had rented for the trip was leaking gasoline like a sieve. Our 5:00 a.m. start had left me bleary-eyed and foggy brained, but his tales from the road were an instant pick-me-up. He was a mesmerizing storyteller.

"There was one time," he said, "when I very nearly died. I knew I was approaching a long stretch of desert, so I asked the local fishermen how far it was to the next water source. They told me 75 kilometers (46.5 miles). I assumed that I could cross it in less than three days. When I finally pulled out a map and saw that it was nearly twice that far, it was already too late to turn back. I just put my head down and walked." He smiled unexpectedly. "At one point I looked up and saw a perfect mango rolling around in the surf right at my feet. And a little after that, a carrot—without a blemish. It was extraordinary."

We arrived in Nazca just before noon and pulled up at a dusty hostel far outside of town. Ricardo had warned me of the dangers of driving a single vehicle through the unforgiving desert, so we had arranged to meet Lucho, the owner of the jeep, and continue down the coast in tandem. Lucho ran an adventure trekking company and hoped to open this particular route to his four-wheel-drive clients. Ricardo needed to revisit some areas that he had walked and substantiate certain facts for the second edition of his book. I wanted to see some of the wildlife in several of the remote coastal zones and visit Puerto Inca, the only significant set of Inca ruins still extant along the coast.

But first our jeep had to be repaired. What had begun as a slow drip was now a steady stream of leaking fuel. Lucho slid under the wheel, pulled off the oil pan, and applied a wad of what looked exactly like chewing gum. As we were loading up to leave, Ricardo noticed a second puddle under the engine itself. Oil? We pulled out the filter. It was shiny-wet and apparently intact. I put a finger in the puddle. Power-steering fluid. The motor had burned out. Lucho headed into the nearby city in search of replacement parts and we settled down to wait.

The heat made the mosquitoes slow and drowsy, though we were too lethargic to take advantage of their plight. My sodden laundry, spread out on nearby bushes, dried before my eyes. We melted like chocolate into our cloth lawn chairs. I poked at Ricardo until he gave in to my pleading and told me about his year with the Trappist monk in Bolivia.

"Good Friday has taken on a strange meaning in the Bolivian Andes," he began. "They believe that since Christ is temporarily dead, people can do as they wish and they will not be held accountable. Once I saw a village catch a man stealing sheep on Good Friday and cut him into 150 pieces." He hesitated for a moment. "Harsh justice in a harsh land."

"When I was at the monastery I was in the habit of walking alone at night—sometimes until dawn. One evening I decided to investigate some distant ruins. I carried nothing but my shovel and an antique bell I used as a talisman. I was dressed, according to my vows, in simple white and"—he paused, rubbing his chin— "I had a beard.

"Halfway there I stopped for the night at the house of an old nun who ran an orphanage. Almost immediately after I left, she started having stomach pains and nausea. Two days later she died...."

He paused, then suddenly asked, "Do you know what a K'arasiri is?" I did not.

"An evil spirit. Known for putting spells on people and then stealing the fat from their stomachs to sell to people who make candles for mass, or as a lubricant for sewing machines. A K'arasiri can be recognized in several ways. He is a religious, light-skinned man. He dresses all in one color—for example, white. And he carries a cane and a small bell that he uses to put his victims to sleep."

Shortly after the old nun's death, rumors began to circulate. Two girls insisted that they had seen Ricardo walking in the night and had immediately felt a paralysis in their legs. They were later found, insensible and frothing at the mouth. A woman claimed that he had caused her mentally handicapped daughter to become pregnant.

Good Friday was just around the corner.

"I knew I was going to die and decided not to run from the inevitable," Ricardo said. "I simply went about my business, walking in the streets and greeting everyone I passed. I think it was my confidence that kept them from coming after me. They expected me to be afraid."

Despite his narrow escape, he was still not welcome around town. He was single and did no manual labor—both hallmarks of a sorcerer.

But everything was about to change.

"We got a message that the bishop was arriving in 25 days to inaugurate our new medical center—a building that was at least four months from completion. I threw myself into the project, working day and night. I drove the laborers without mercy, but for every two adobe bricks they put on their backs, I myself carried four. During our last week I hardly slept, painting and finishing the last minute details." He took a breath. "We made it. The bishop came for two hours and left."

"After that," he smiled, "Everyone treated me with respect. One woman even brought out her two children to greet me in the street."

Lucho arrived in a cloud of dust. Replacement power-steering motors were not to be had outside of Lima. He unhooked the power steering, pronounced it "fixed," and off we went.

We reached the rocky headland of San Fernando less than an hour before dark. We raked the skies with binoculars in search of condors. The largest birds in the world, their wings span 9 feet and they weigh more than 20 pounds. They were known to frequent this part of the coast where they feasted on the pups, placentas, and carrion of the ubiquitous sea lions. Ricardo had seen 24 condors when he passed through 3 years ago. But that had been before El Niño, and now the beaches were littered not with basking bodies, but with bleached-out skulls and broken teeth. The local fishermen told us that 95 percent of the sea mammals were dead or gone and the condors had all fled. We scanned the skies in vain.

Our jeep, still hurting from its Band-Aid fix, deteriorated steadily under the onslaught of trackless sand and slippery slopes. The frequent repair stops gave me the opportunity to pick the prickly pear cactus fruit that grew like red-and-yellow golf balls against a gray landscape. Occasionally I slipped over the next hill and watched the wind snatch streams of sand off of the sharp-edged aklé dunes. I envied Ricardo his solitary weeks of walking this magnificent terrain and his nights spent under the stars. What happens after 19 weeks with no company but your own thoughts? Do the voices in your head begin to fade away? Do you forget about taxes and the things you wish you'd said—or not— and whether you left the light on in a room downstairs? Surely life would be purer once all the clutter cleared itself away. Your only goal to set one foot in front of the other, to round that point and then the next and the one beyond. Ideas must buzz around like insects in a Coleman's light, grow bright, and burn away. At the same time there would be more room for grand imaginings, for hopes and dreams tucked away since childhood, for visions of the future in its infinite possibilities.

And yet the more I learned about Ricardo, the less I understood him. A highly intelligent entrepreneur who excelled at business ventures—and an acetic monk, a mountaintop meditator, who turned his back on the world to find the Truth deep inside himself.

He led a simple life, he told me, and had no interest in personal possessions. He could at any moment walk away from the trappings of modern society without regret and return to life in the desert—and yet his office was filled with the latest computers, a fax machine, and a full-time secretary, and he went nowhere without a cell phone attached to his belt.

He had an almost extrasensory understanding of human psychology and an abiding interest in people, yet he insisted that he had no real need to be in the company of others. Although he had met—and remembered—ten thousand people in his coastal trek of Peru, there wasn't a single photo of another human being in his book.

An enigma.

It was 4:30 in the morning and we were sitting in a blind at the edge of a deserted cliff. I sidled up to Ricardo. "Penguins?" I asked quietly, not wanting to appear too much a fool. "In the desert?" He nodded solemnly. And there they were, standing stiffly upright in a tight and unhappy bunch atop the cliff. A slow-motion drama enfolded as they clambered laboriously down the rocks. They used their flippers like ski poles to keep from tripping over their own webbed feet. A sea lion appeared. The penguins huddled in tense consultation. The sea lion grew bored and slumped away. The penguins gathered their courage and leaped into the surf, where they were magically transformed into sleek ballerinas, swooping and diving among the waves like seagulls playing in the wind.

A day later we reached Puerto Inca, the Holy Grail of the coastal Inca Road. The once-thriving fishing port was built around a crescent sandy beach with deep blue water. Ruins terraced the hillsides all around. As we clambered up to see them, Ricardo emerged from the almost trancelike state he had fallen into during our grueling days in the jeep. Puerto Inca, he told me, was connected to Cuzco by a major Inca Road. Royal runners could relay fresh seafood all the way to the emperor's table—280 miles—in just 36 hours. More importantly, vast quantities of seaweed traveled this route up into the Andes, providing both vitamins and iodine—the cure for goiter—to the ill-nourished mountain folk.

No one knew why the inhabitants of Puerto Inca had abandoned their gemlike cove. Pottery shards lay everywhere among the ruins. Perhaps the smallpox epidemic had devastated this close-knit population and the few survivors fled. Maybe the fall of the empire had left the fishermen with no outlet for their goods. Or perhaps their water source had dried up—like the Chimu farther north—forcing them to forsake the abundant sea. What they left behind was impressive: interlocking houses that fit together like the pieces of a jigsaw puzzle. A huge temple complex lined with rectangular rooms still roofed with stone. Dozens of beehive storage chambers that had once been filled to bursting with fish and octopus, mollusks, crabs, and seaweed. The stone walls of these chambers were cemented with a mixture of ash, burnt seashell, and rice husks—a potent natural insecticide that allowed them to store their dried seafood for months at a time.

We spent the day climbing the surrounding hills, then followed the Inca Road back into the desert by the light of a full moon. Ricardo had agreed to accompany me for the first few miles of the trek back to Cuzco.

His gentle presence had made the time pass like a children's game. He exuded a tranquility that was impervious to physical exertion or emotional fatigue. Had he earned it in a monastery after months quiet meditation, or did he just pick it up like a mango in the surf one day along his trek?

On the way up the mountain, he slipped my heavy pack off my back and settled it onto his own shoulders. It was a simple gesture, but it suddenly made me realize how much I yearned to travel with someone who could share those moments of triumph and tired camaraderie. I fell back a step or two and walked behind him in the darkness so that he wouldn't see my tears.

CHAPTER 15

THE HOLY HUB

FIELD NOTES: They came THIS close to wiping out the Spaniards....

Cuzco lies in the hollow of a valley, 11,000 feet above the sea. It is the navel of the Andes, the center of the Inca Empire. The city could well have been the source of the El Dorado myths that lured explorers to pillage the length and breadth of South America. At the height of its glory, many of Cuzco's buildings were fronted with sheets of gold. The main temple, Coricancha, sported an immense golden sun that apparently caught the early morning rays and blazed with the power of the sun god himself. Coricancha, the "golden enclosure," contained a garden with life-size replicas of llamas, ears of growing corn, bees and flowers, butterflies and lumps of earth—all made of solid gold. Its exquisite masonry was hidden behind 700 gold plates, each weighing about four and a half pounds. Small wonder the Spanish made straight for this legendary city as soon as Atahualpa was safely dead.

Despite their fear of the Inca ruler's power, the conquistadores understood the value of having a royal figurehead under their control to ensure the obedience of the indigenous population. Pizarro craftily chose Manco Inca, a son of Huyna Capac, Atahualpa's father. Manco had supported Huascar in the bloody civil war and was therefore popular in the south. When Pizarro and his men arrived in Cuzco, many of its citizens hailed the Spaniards as restorers of the legitimate Inca line.

The hapless population was soon to see the error of its ways. Unlike the Inca, who allowed conquered chieftains to retain many of their privileges and much of their power, the Spanish abused Manco mercilessly from the very first day. When Pizarro left for the coast to found the city of Lima, his younger brother raped Manco's favorite wife. Finally realizing the position he was in, Manco attempted to escape. He was captured, dragged home in chains, and thrown into prison. His jailers urinated on him and burned his eyelashes with candles. All possibility of cooperation between the Inca ruler and his captives ended.

This time Manco tried a different tack. He told Hernando, another of Francisco Pizarro's brothers, about a secret shrine that contained an effigy made of solid gold. If Hernando would just release him to go and pray at it, he said, he would bring back the priceless statue as a gift. The Spaniard foolishly agreed.

Once out of Cuzco, Manco immediately called a revolt. With a legitimate god-king once again at their head, the people flocked by the thousands to join him. In an extraordinary example of Inca organizational skill, warriors were recruited, armed, clothed, fed, and transported to the outskirts of Cuzco without the Spanish having the slightest clue. The first Francisco Pizarro heard of it, in distant Lima, Cuzco was already under siege.

Manco had captured the lightly guarded Sacsayhuaman, an enormous saw-toothed fortress that towered over Cuzco. From there his warriors showered red-hot stones onto the city, setting its thatched roofs on fire. The battle lasted for most of a year. Cuzco was effectively cut off from the rest of the country. The besieged Spanish survived only through the efforts of a few Indians who smuggled them food. Some of these were traitors who hoped to ingratiate themselves with the new rulers. Others feared Inca retaliation for their prior collaboration with the conquistadores.

In utter desperation, the Spaniards mounted an attack of 50 cavalry on the fortress of Sacsayhuaman. The tactic was successful but Juan Pizarro, Francisco's younger brother, paid for it with his life. Manco and his men were forced to retreat to the distant Inca fortress of Ollantaytambo. Huge flocks of carrion-eating condors descended to gorge upon the thousands of dead Inca warriors that littered the battlefield. To this day that sight has been memorialized by the inclusion of eight condors in Cuzco's coat of arms.

I closed my eyes and ran my fingertips along the length of Coricancha's outer wall. I couldn't feel a single joint in the perfectly curved stone. The Inca were right. They set their highest value on good workmanship, whether textiles, ceramics, or masonry. To their final day they never really understand the Spanish lust for shapeless blocks of metal.

But currency soon became a fact of colonial life and with it, capitalism. What the church and the conquerors failed to destroy has slowly been engulfed by creeping commercialism. Inca stonework is so common in central Cuzco that it has become one with the modern cityscape. Banks and hotels, jewelers, and travel agencies are all built in and around old Inca walls. It is impossible to tell where history ends and modern times begin.

It isn't just shop owners who know how to take advantage of a pretty wall. Dozens of young girls dressed in their native finery and clutching the halters of doe-eyed llamas stake out strategic spots against old stone backdrops. They charge tourists the equivalent of a day's farming wages for the right to take their photo. Though Cuzco long ago lost its place as the political center of Peru, it is still a supremely sacred place, a mecca for mystics and adventurers, artisans and archaeologists. Tour agencies line the central square, their placards offering everything from hiking treks to horseback riding. Old women flourish handmade alpaca sweaters like matadors. Antique weavings, hammered silverware, and dragon masks. Cuzco had something for everyone. For me, as I sat in the central square and watched the street lamps blink on like a year-round Christmas tree, it was, quite simply, the most beautiful place I'd ever seen.

CHAPTER 16

TAKING THE BULL BY THE HORNS

FIELD NOTES: Important lesson—when you are faced with 300 pounds of angry bull, do not stand directly behind your cape.

The year was 1536. Manco's rebellion was in bad shape. The Inca defeat at Cuzco had dealt them a crushing psychological blow. Many of his followers, seeing little hope for the Inca cause, drifted away.

Those that remained retreated northwest along the Sacred Valley to the massive Inca fortress of Ollantaytambo. There they dug in and awaited the inevitable. It didn't take long. That same year Hernando Pizarro arrived with a force of 70 cavalry supported by a large number of native and Spanish foot soldiers. Manco's men showered the attackers with boulders and arrows, spears and stones. In a brilliant move, Manco opened water sluices and flooded the plain below the fortress, hampering the Spanish horses and heavily armored men. Hernando beat a hasty retreat, which quickly turned into a rout as the victorious Inca warriors chased them down into the valley.

Their victory was short-lived. Soon after, a large Spanish expedition returned from Chile and threw themselves into the fray. This time they attacked with a cavalry that was four times the size of Hernando's fighting force. Manco had no choice but to abandon Ollantaytambo and retreat into the impenetrable jungle with what was left of his followers. There they built Vilcabamba—the last stronghold of the Inca—a city of 60 immense stone buildings and some 300 smaller ones. Using it as a base, they ventured forth to wage guerrilla war against the remoter Spanish outposts. When Manco eventually died, several of his sons took up the struggle in his name.

In 1572 the Spaniards finally wearied of the Inca thorn in their side and launched an expedition to eliminate the last vestiges of native rebellion. When they reached Vilcabamba, they found it deserted and burned to the ground. Undaunted, they continued their pursuit and eventually captured Inca Amaru—the last of Manco's sons—hiding along the banks of a river with his pregnant wife. He was taken back to Cuzco, put on trial, and beheaded in the town square.

We reached Ollantaytambo just in time for the festival of the three Christ Children. The celebration was off to an inauspicious start. All three villages had arrived at the main square with their sacred statues at the same time, and a fight had broken out over which of the palanquins had the right to lead the way into the church. Several worshipers, their faces covered with crocheted masks, began to wield their symbolic whips in earnest. There was much blowing of ill-tuned conchs, great puffy clouds of incense, and a certain amount of ungentlemanly shoving among the elder men. Eventually those with the loudest conchs and sharpest ceremonial staffs simply forged their way through the crowd. In Ollantaytambo, it seems, the meek do not inherit the church.

Right around the corner, we ran into a much more tangible test of strength and courage. Six thousand locals were gathered on the hillside surrounding a high-walled patch of dirt the size of a hockey rink. A herd of 20 bulls with wicked horns bellowed and pawed in an enclosure to one side. Several local men in spangled red costumes and thick shoulder pads strutted up and down while waiting for the release of the first animal. It didn't take long. Coal black and madder than a nest of hornets, the bull charged through the gate and came to a stiff-legged stop in the middle of the ring, clearly trying to decide which of the matadors to gore first. They all dashed for the protective wooden barriers set up at intervals along the wall. The bull pawed the ground. One of the men edged forward and jiggled his pink cape. The bull charged, the cape swirled, and the crowd cheered. Not to be outdone, the other matadors emerged and soon the bull was racing around the ring, flailing at one waving cape after another. It took him about three minutes to realize the futility of his efforts, after which he simply stood in the center of the arena until a rope was tossed around his horns and he was hauled, willingly, back out the gate.

There wasn't a sword or spear in sight. These were working animals—no one was going to damage a perfectly good bull on some flashy stunt. If anything, it was the matadors who were at risk.

The only thing that stood between them and 500 pounds of horn-tipped muscle was a cape no thicker than a shower curtain.

"What do you think?" John asked.

"I think I'm going to give it a shot," I said. I could already feel the incipient rumblings of terror-based diarrhea.

"Yeah, sure," John said, and turned back to the fight.

The organizers were equally skeptical. "Later," they said, meaning when the fight was over and everyone, including the bulls, had gone home. I checked out the animals. One was a half-grown calf with three-inch, horny nubs and a friendly face. "When is he coming out?" I pointed at the calf. "Three bulls," the man said, and held up an equivalent number of fingers. Excellent. I climbed back up on the wall just in time to see one of the matadors get slammed in the stomach by several hundred pounds of angry beef.

There was a huge difference, I discovered, between envisioning an act and stepping up to bat. At least I wouldn't have the chance to change my mind. The whitewashed walls were far too high to climb back out.

Two down, one to go. The chief matador kneeled directly in front of the entrance gate. When the next bull shot out, he swung his cape off to one side. The bull's horn swept by less than an inch from his ear. John was asking me about the spectacle, though his voice made no more impression than a mosquito's whine. What if I didn't do it? I'd spend the rest of my life wondering if I could have handled myself in the ring. I'd play the scene back and forth in my mind, picking it apart, combing through it for the key to my own cowardice.

I jumped.

I made straight for the protective barrier. "Teach me!" I shouted to the nearest matador. He handed me a cape and showed me how to swing it off to one side. *Body to the left, cape to the right*. Now all I had to do was wait for the little calf with the training horns....

The next bull exploded into the ring. He was huge, evil-eyed, heavy-horned, broad-beamed, and still wearing the rope that the handlers had been too afraid to pull off. To my horror he made straight for the only man in the ring without a costume—a drunken, potbellied fellow wielding nothing more than a six-foot wooden board. The bull pushed the drunk against the wall and tried to hook the plank aside with one horn. The crowd went wild. Several matadors rushed forward to distract the animal. I held my breath. The only one who didn't seem worried was the drunken guy, who held one hand over his head in a victory salute throughout the entire confrontation. Okay, I thought, a drunk can do it. How hard can it be?

It was hard. I had been secretly hoping that ten years of judo training would hold me in good stead. But every time those rage-tipped horns came barreling my way it was all I could do to keep from standing rooted to the spot, arms held rigidly in front of me, praying that my pink superman cape would miraculously hold back half a ton of moving flesh. *Body to the left, cape to the right*, I recited like a mantra. The bull obliged by following the cape no matter what else I did wrong. Gradually the world around me came back into focus. I tasted the swirling dust that turned my teeth a dirty brown and felt the tattered cape between my fingers. A single voice began to register above the roar of the crowd.

"You are an idiot!"

I turned to see an Australian standing on the wall, a sloppy beer in his hand. "I beg your pardon?" I said.

"YOU ARE A F&%$%G IDIOT!"

"Would you care to come down here and say that?" I asked. The crowd cheered and practically threw him into the ring. At that moment I realized why I was there. I was the clown. From then on the matadors strutted their courage and their fancy clothes while the drunken guy and I teased the bulls—whenever their backs were turned. We hugged and high-fived when things went well, and he rescued me when I did wrong. The bulls became almost secondary to the cheering crowd. Anyway, it was easy. *Body to the left, cape to the right.*

A bull swept by, turned his head at the last second, and caught me solidly in the ribs. He lifted me off the ground with the curved end of his horn and threw me over his shoulder.

The world went thick and viscous. Sound slowed down like a record playing at the wrong speed. I felt a trickle of blood run down my ribs, and a feeling of relief that my red vest would hide it from the crowd. I struggled, quietly and with utter concentration, to breathe. I didn't want the bullfight organizers to realize what had happened and regret allowing me into the ring.

Breathe. I retreated behind a wooden barricade. Gradually the noise and cheering crowd swam back into view and I discovered that there was a smile fixed to my face. Breathe. It was getting easier, except for the two ribs under my breast that felt as though someone were trying to pry them apart with a crowbar.

At that moment the drunk discarded his trusty board and ran after the bull bare-handed. Just as the animal whipped around he grabbed its horns, pushed his substantial belly against the animal's head, and held on. The bull stopped dead. A half dozen handlers rushed forward to rope the bull and shove the drunkard roughly away. I was amazed. For all his clowning, he was the bravest man in the ring. I remembered watching him from the wall and thinking that if he could do it, so could I. I was dead wrong, but the thought had given me the courage to face my fear. He had shown me how.

That night the throbbing pain began, tossing me about in my narrow bunk like a ship at sea. It was nothing compared to the ice-pick agony when I shouldered a full backpack the next morning and set off to hike the Inca trail to Machu Picchu. The lovely stone steps, so perfect—and perfectly steep—were suddenly unending, sharp-edged and slug-trail slippery. It began to rain. I knew there were extravagant orchids drooping languidly on either side, streams tumbling over furry, moss-lined stones, and perhaps even a snake or two coiled high among the trees. I saw none of it. My eyes were focused like rifle sights on the trail ahead.

Hours passed in the incessant dripping of intermittent rain. At noon we crested the mountain pass and began our long descent into a valley on the other side. No matter how carefully I set my feet, the weight of my backpack compressed my battered ribcage like an accordion. What I had thought was pain on the way up, I redis-covered as a pleasant memory on the way down.

At last, we staggered into the shelter where we planned to spend the night. It was a pimple on the mountainside—already over-flowing with hordes of disgruntled hikers, each staked out in a six-by-six-foot area of packed mud, their sweat-stale laundry hanging from sodden packs. The thought of a sleepless night on the unfor-giving ground amidst the refuse of 50 other campers made me want to weep. I found our porters, who had put down John's backpack and were trying to brew tea.

"How far to Machu Picchu?" I asked.

They thought about it, then shook their heads. It was already two o'clock. We'd have to cover the same distance we'd already come in less than half the time.

It wasn't ego that was driving me, or even misery. It was the vision of bliss and luxury. While researching Machu Picchu, I had met the owner of a five-star hotel just below the ruins, and he had invited us to stay there as his guests. After four months of bug-infested cots and icy baths, the Pueblo Hotel would be nothing short of paradise.

"Lead the way," I told the porters. "Whatever it takes. We'll make it."

They set off at a trot, balancing their loads with both hands tucked behind their backs. My world once again shrank to a pinpoint—this time centered on the sinewy calves of the man directly in front of me. He wore cheap sandals and moved with the airy grace of a racehorse despite his heavy load. I lost myself in the delicate machinery of his pulsating tendons and ligaments.

We struggled up one last flight of steps and passed through an ancient stone gate. Machu Picchu lay below us. The sight took what little breath I had away. Even the porters stopped to stare.

Then a bus pulled out of the parking lot below the ruins and drove off down the mountain. Only one remained. If we missed it, we'd be walking three more hours into town.

We scrambled wildly down the switchback trail. Those mesermizing calves quickly disappeared around the bend as the porters went into overdrive. I panted into the parking lot, scrambled aboard, and watched the doors slide shut with a sound just like a body hitting the ground.

A part of me has always secretly held fancy hotels in mild disdain. Real travel, I thought, had somehow to involve discomfort, long delays, open sores, and lots of biting bugs. I became a convert to luxury the moment I set foot inside the Pueblo Hotel. The receptionist seemed genuinely happy to see us despite the growing puddle of muddy water that was leaking in equal measure out of our clothing and our filthy gear. Our rooms had fireplaces, endless scalding water, and fleecy, forgiving beds custom-made to heal a broken body. It was worth every excruciating step.

I had just decided never to leave my room again when a call came through from the National Institute of Culture. "Your request for permission to camp at Machu Picchu," a heavy voice said, "has been granted. For one night."

An entire night at Machu Picchu! If there was one place that could make the Inca Empire come alive, Machu Picchu was it. I could walk the stairs as they did in olden times. I could dance along the ancient walls under the light of the moon. No tourists, no tour guides; just me and the mountain gods.

"Tonight," the voice on the phone said.

Ouch. My bed suddenly got softer, the fire warmer. My body felt like I'd been run over by an angry bull.

"You must pick up your permission papers at the entrance by five o'clock."

I tried to sound perky and grateful. "I'll be there."

We arrived in the early afternoon, just as the first horde of Machu Picchu's 20,000 monthly visitors were starting back down the mountain. I climbed to the highest point and watched smugly as the tour guides herded their flocks out to the parking lot. In a few hours I would have the place to myself. As if on cue, there was a break in the clouds and an enormous rainbow arced across the sky. The mountain gods were on my side.

Almost as compelling as the ruins themselves is the story of their discovery. Or, more accurately, their rediscovery. Hiram Bingham was a 35-year-old professor of Latin American history at Yale University. He was a passionate student of Inca history and lore, and an authority on the revolutionary leader Simon Bolívar. During an expedition by mule from Lima to Buenos Aires, Hiram heard rumors of some ruins called Choqquequirau, the "cradle of gold." They were, he was told, lost in the mountains on the far side of the mighty Apurímac River, in an area covered by impenetrable forest. Bingham became convinced that this was the legendary Vilcabamba, the last stronghold of the Inca. But where to begin looking? Three hundred years of oral tradition had distorted the truth so badly that it bordered on legend. The dusty scribblings of the 16th-century chroniclers had precious little to add. It was somewhere in the Amazonian piedmont, he read. Nearby stood a white rock overhanging a spring with black waters, and an ancient temple. Armed with this meager information, Hiram set off to find it.

In the ancient Inca village of Ollantaytambo, in the shadow of the ruined fortress, his perseverance paid off. Some sugarcane workers described a spot called Rosaspata—a white rock overhanging a spring near a ruined temple. It exactly matched the description from the ancient texts. Hiram knew he was close. Further questioning led him to the ruins of Choqquequirau, an impressive fortress built with perfectly interlocking stones and terraces. It was a monumental discovery and yet, when Hiram returned and admitted that there was no gold to be found amid the seamless walls, he was met with disappointment.

Undaunted, Bingham prepared another expedition into the jungle. To fund it he pulled out his Rolodex of wealthy former classmates and wrangled money out of Yale University. Bingham was still after Vilcabamba—the legendary lost city of the Inca. He knew it was hidden somewhere on the other side of the Apurímac River, in a dark and brooding rain forest "designed by nature as a sanctuary for the oppressed."

The expedition set out from Cuzco and eventually reached the banks of the Urubamba river. By sheer luck a new route had been blasted into the jungle two years previously. The landscape was daunting—sheer cliffs, steeply angled slopes and dense vegetation. It was enough to discourage all but the most intrepid travelers from wandering off the established trails. The team settled in. Bingham was out having dinner one night when a local tavern keeper told him of some well-kept ruins on the shoulder of a nearby mountain. Bingham was skeptical. He had already followed several similar leads and discovered nothing but the rubble of a farmer's shack. Nevertheless, he offered the man a silver dollar to lead him there the next morning.

July 24, 1911, dawned cold and rainy. None of his colleagues were inclined to accompany Hiram up the mountain—they had their hearts set on doing laundry and campsite chores. Bingham set out with his tavernkeeper guide and a government-appointed watchdog. He crawled across the Urubamba on an improvised bridge composed of long, thin tree trunks lashed together.

Two thousand feet up the mountain, the group stumbled across a smoky farmer's hut. The tavernkeeper, seduced by the warm fire and pleasant conversation, ordered his son to guide Bingham the rest of the way. The boy was not yet ten years old.

Bingham persevered. And then it happened. "Suddenly I found myself confronted with the walls of ruined houses built of the finest quality of Inca stonework." He later wrote in his diary.

Therein lay the difference between Bingham and me. I would have said, "*Whoa*," followed closely by "*Yippee!*"

Bingham wandered through a broad plaza, past fountains, a temple of the sun, a royal mausoleum, and dozens of houses. "Surprise followed surprise in bewildering succession," he wrote. Two enormous foundation blocks with 32 corners in three dimensions. A polygonal stone at the summit where Inca priests symbolically tethered the sun to keep it from straying away during the winter solstice. "It seemed like an unbelievable dream."

To his dying day Bingham was convinced he had discovered the legendary Vilcabamba. He was wrong. But if Machu Picchu wasn't the last stronghold of the Inca, then what was it? The site wasn't mentioned anywhere in the Spanish chronicles, for it had already been abandoned by the time of the conquest. Judging by the amount of food that could be produced from the agricultural terraces, Machu Picchu supported no more than a thousand inhabitants. Lack of water was a constant threat, for if the city's aqueduct dried up then water had to be hauled up from the river 2,500 feet below. For a while archaeologists thought it might be a sacred city to the sun virgins, since 80 percent of the skeletons found were female. Although it was set high on the spine of a mountain and surrounded on three sides by the Urubamba River, Machu Picchu was not a fortress, for it lacked any serious man-made defenses. Besides, it made no sense to construct such an elaborate city in an area that had little strategic importance and brought only a trifling amount of acreage into agricultural production.

When archaeologists dated the stonework they realized that Machu Picchu had been built a hundred years before the Spanish conquerors, in the time of Pachakuti. It was, they decided, Pachakuti's country estate.

I was hauling our equipment out of Machu Picchu's guardhouse when I felt the first symptoms of a bladder infection. I dug out a dose of antibiotics and went back to work.

An hour later, the last of the tourists had filtered out and my internal irritation had become a sharp-edged pain. The antibiotics weren't having the expected effect. I dug around and found a second, more potent medication, then watched the last tour bus begin its long descent down the mountain. We were alone.

Yet another hour ticked slowly by. It started to rain. John sat at the bar, tapping his fingernails on the countertop while I monopolized the bathroom, waiting for the antibiotics to take hold. My bladder was ulcerated and bleeding and my temperature was rising steadily. It had taken six weeks to get permission and it was only for tonight. I couldn't give up. I sent John ahead with a helper to set up the tent.

The rain and fog continued unabated. We were in for a dark and stormy night. So much for my mystical retreat among the mountain gods. If only there were people still living here among these old stone walls. Then we would be eating steamy, soft potatoes, drinking home-brewed beer, and making friendly conversation around a warm fire.

So that was it. My great Inca experience was missing a crucial ingredient. The Inca. The inhabitants of Machu Picchu were long since gone, but I had seen another place where people still lived the ancient ways—Ollantaytambo.

The next two days were the sheerest agony, alleviated by the Pueblo Hotel's sumptuous opulence. At last I felt well enough to head back to Ollantaytambo—to the forgotten streets of its old town, where dirt-encrusted villagers led llamas laden with their daily ration of kindling. To docile bulls that looked nothing like the corrugated, salivating, rapier-horned animals that I remembered from the last time I was there. Ollantaytambo had no need for sidewalks—the widest vehicle these streets were built for was a pregnant llama. Its stone aqueducts were open 24 hours a day for rinsing laundry, scrubbing children, and peeling potatoes. At almost every corner a pint of homemade beer could be had for less than 30 cents, and the laughter and camaraderie were free.

I sat beside an aqueduct and watched the animals plodding by on paving stones laid down many centuries ago by hand. Gradually the sights and sounds swam into focus—the clip-clop of cloven hooves and the gentle thud of softer pads. The gravel-throated roosters warning off potential adversaries, and the friendly one-word calls of lifelong neighbors coming home from the fields. What struck me even more was the absence of certain sounds. No sirens—police or fire. No ringing telephones, no fax machines or microwaves. No flushing toilets. Inside these simple houses there would be no droning background television, just the quiet pop and crackle of an open cooking fire. Perhaps the rumble of a grinding stone or the birdlike squeaks of guinea pigs. In this world people went to see each other if they had something to say. They cooked and ate around a fire, sat together in the evenings to spin or weave or to simply chat and chew some coca leaves. It made me wonder if all of our comfort devices—air conditioners, e-mail, television, and even telephones—had slipped into our lives like thieves, robbing us of some of our humanity.

I ran my hand along a craggy house façade, wishing that I were on the other side. In the distance I heard the sound of wounded plastic records playing on an overworked machine. Maybe it was a *chicha* bar and I could stop in for some companionship. I followed the noise through the darkening streets until I came upon a narrow alleyway. Men in bright red homespun ponchos staggered through a three-foot door to urinate against a wall and wobble back inside. They were Quechua Indians, all dressed in their Sunday best—and drinking hard enough to raise the dead.

I almost turned and walked the other way. Indians have a wolf-like wariness of both foreigners and their city-bred brethren, a habit deeply rooted in the memory of their mistreatment at the hands of the Spanish and virtually every governing body since. The vast majority had been slaughtered by European diseases, war and civil strife, conquest and enforced labor. Small wonder they cling stubbornly to their own language and resist any intrusion into their lives.

At that moment one of them motioned me over and waved a hand at the tiny door. Still I hesitated. A voice behind me said, *"Ole!"* An old man clapped me on the back and smiled toothlessly. Maybe the bullfight hadn't been such a bad idea after all. I followed them inside.

It was a wedding. Bride and groom stood stiffly behind a broad table, greeting new arrivals with severe expressions suited to such a solemn event. They were stalwart islands in a flowing river of home-brewed beer, cascading music, swirling dancers, and children darting out of eddies in search of bottle tops. The bride and groom were a luminously handsome couple, dressed in layer upon layer of intricate embroidery. When I greeted her with a few words of Quechua, her smile shimmered like the moon. "You're a lucky man," I told her husband. He smiled, too, with such transparent pride that I knew this marriage was made from love, not economy.

We danced and toasted the happy couple. I was surprised when they quietly slipped on wedding rings—the only Christian act I'd seen so far—but it was accompanied by neither speech nor ceremony and seemed little more than a reason to down another glass of beer. The single women sat straight as kindling along one wall. When they talked about the men, they hid their words behind their hands. I thought back to my night at Machu Picchu and was perversely thankful for the rain and illness that had brought me here. No amount of time amid empty stone walls could compare with this.

At last I took my leave and wandered back to my hostel. The streets of Ollantaytambo were empty and silent, but I knew now what has happening behind those walls. I ran my hand along the uneven stones. They felt friendlier somehow—alive, as though they carried an impression not only of their maker's hands but of the people still living on the other side.

CHAPTER 17

ANCIENT LIVES IN
MODERN TIMES

FIELD NOTES: Blood and raw alpaca heart for breakfast. Not my cup of tea.

The Inca called their empire Tahantinsuyu—"the Land of Four Quarters." The largest of these, Collasuyu, lay due south of Cuzco. It included southern Peru, all of Bolivia, the Andean section of Argentina, and the whole of Chile down to modern-day Santiago. For centuries its inhabitants resisted Inca domination—the Colla, after whom the area is named, and the Aymara, whose language is still spoken throughout the region. In 1420 Pachakuti began a campaign to subdue the tribes around Lake Titicaca. Shortly thereafter Inca Emperor Topa built the famous southern road that was eventually to extend 2,100 miles south into Chile.

Shortly after it leaves Cuzco, the Inca Road climbs up into the desolate Peruvian altiplano and eventually winds down through a marshy plain to what the Spanish called the "greatest lake in the Indies." Situated between two massive Andean ranges, Lake Titicaca is 80 miles long and 40 miles wide. At 12,500 feet it is the highest large navigable lake in the world.

I stumbled into Puno just as the sun began to roast the nightly frost off a bumper crop of bone-white stones. Puno was bleak. Perhaps it was the lack of oxygen, but the city's buildings were as gray as week-old corpses. Or maybe Puno's architects built their homes to reflect the landscape of barren rock, spiky grass, and wind-swept hills.

And then I saw the lake. It was a glittering sapphire set in lead. So blue it hurt to look at it, and hurt even more to turn away. It was a place where myths are born.

Legend has it that the very first Inca, Manco Capac, arrived on the shore of Lake Titicaca with his sister-wife, Mama Ocla, and a golden staff. He had instructions from his father, the sun god Inti, to wander the world until he came to a place where his staff would disappear completely when thrust into the ground. After many days he entered a valley where the soft and fertile earth swallowed up his golden staff. Upon that spot, a sacred city was founded: Cuzco—meaning "navel" in Quechua—became the center of the Inca Empire.

There is still some argument over where, precisely, Manco Capac first appeared. Some say he emerged from a cave on the Island of the Sun. Others argue that he arose from the waters of the lake itself. Still others insist that eight Inca—four brothers and four sisters—were sent underground by Inti and emerged from caves near Paccaritambo, 18 miles southwest of Cuzco.

Puno authorities choose, not surprisingly, to believe that Manco was born of the lake and that he first stepped ashore where the city now has its harbor. Each year they give substance to their claim by reenacting Manco's weeklong journey across the lake in a specially built reed boat. This was what I had come to see.

A modern, motorized yacht appeared on the horizon. I could just make out two stately Inca warriors standing at its bow, jostling for position with a dozen cameramen who kept their lenses trained on a wobbly reed boat that waterskied precariously in its wake.

The yacht pulled up at a random island and a 20th-century Manco and his sister-wife stepped ashore. The battle of the cameramen began. They elbowed past the native women laying down handwoven rugs for the royal entourage. They pushed to the front of the crowd, shooing children out of the way and squeezing past Indian women with faces as weathered as thousand-year-old trees.

I drifted away from the depressing scene. The ground beneath my feet felt springy and alive, like walking on a trampoline. This was a floating island—a mass of tortora reeds that slowly rotted underneath while being continually replenished from above.

I watched an old matron tie off her tiny dinghy and step ashore. What must her life be like? To be born, grow up, raise a family, and eventually die in a space no larger than a parking lot. To spend each day cutting reeds, catching fish, and tending a cooking fire. To live without electricity, telephones, television, or any other window on the outside world. And then, once a year, to be suddenly invaded by both the past and the future in equal parts—ancient Inca warriors and high-tech camera crews.

The woman glanced over at the square, dismissed them all, and disappeared into her hut.

The next morning Manco arrived in Puno to more speeches and a parade of brightly twirling dancers that escorted him to the city's stadium. A nervous alpaca was brought out and paraded around for all to see. It was forced to kneel. Its throat was slit, then its heart torn out and raised, two-handed, to the sky. Everyone took a bite and threw the remains onto a ceremonial fire.

That evening we headed up to the giant white statue of Manco Capac which overlooked the city, hoping to film an introduction to the day's events. John grumbled about the graffiti that splattered the base of the statue while I clambered laboriously up the back side and edged my way to the front, to sit at Manco's bare white feet.

"This is Manco Capac, the very first Inca, sent by his father the sun god to rule the world," I chirped. "And tomorrow we're going to meet him in person!"

"Okay?" I asked hopelessly.

"Awful," John said with painful candor. "Do it again."

I did, feeling as stiff and ridiculous as the statue above me. Take two. Three. Four. Five. "You sound like a car commercial," John said. He was right.

Take six. "Hello. We're here with Manco Capac. Tomorrow we're going to meet Santa Claus. My name is Mary Poppins. I've forgotten my umbrella. How on Earth am I going to get down from here?"

"I'm *rolling*," John said.

"I mean it." I looked between my feet at the distant ground. "How am I going to get down?"

"Forget it," John said, and folded up his tripod.

I scampered down the mountain to make the final arrangements for an event I'd been dreaming about ever since I'd caught my first glimpse of a mysterious herd of animals that flowed like liquid gold across the bleak and barren altiplano. We had been invited to a forgotten village called Picotani—to participate in an event that dated back to Inca times. We were going to a vicuña roundup.

CHAPTER 18

THE GOLDEN FLEECE
OF THE ANDES

FIELD NOTES: Thank goodness vicuñas don't bite. They do, however, kick like mules and jump like deer.

Four a.m. I had just enough enthusiasm left to drag myself out of my warm bed and into the back of an icy-cold truck. I didn't come back to life until nearly eight, when the sun was already searing my cheeks with its prickly, high-altitude glare. I clambered into the forward cabin with Marco, the government agent who was in charge of the region's vicuñas and their biannual roundup.

At 26, Marco seemed too young to be a full-fledged veterinarian and too old for the childlike enthusiasm that bubbled over every time he spoke about his beloved beasts. The vicuña, he told me proudly, has the finest fleece in the world, better even than alpaca or mohair. Its gossamer wool has been treasured since ancient times—only the Inca and his nobles were allowed to wear garments made of vicuña fleece. Modern roundups have changed little in the intervening years. Hundreds of villagers still gather to form human chains that stretch to the horizon. The frightened animals are gradually funneled into a stone corral. They are then tagged, relieved of their warm coats, and set free.

Vicuña fleece is more than just an expensive curiosity. It is a living remnant of the Inca Empire's legacy. At 2,500 hairs per inch, it is airy as a spider's web. The Inca prized textiles over almost any other commodity. It was one of the principal tasks of the sun virgins to sit and spin the vicuña fleece into flawless garments that the Supreme Inca would wear for a single day and then ritually burn. An act of sacrilege almost as painful as the Spaniards melting down the Inca statues into ordinary lumps of gold.

Once the conquistadores finished looting the empire's gold and silver, they turned their insatiable greed on the hapless vicuña. Their fleece was dubbed "the Silk of the New World," and they were hunted to the edge of extinction. By 1966 the vicuña—once a million strong—numbered fewer than 5,000. In a last-ditch effort to save these fleet-footed animals, the Peruvian government began organizing villagers, renewing roundups, and gathering the fleece to be auctioned off on the international market. Profits were returned to the village cooperatives. Overnight the vicuña became a rabidly protected resource, and poachers were suddenly as endangered as the vicuñas had once been.

We pulled up at a tiny store that squatted in a corner of a no-name town on the endless plains. Inside a shriveled woman crouched like a spider amid bags of candy and parrot feathers, amulets and sugar cubes. A dried snake with empty eye sockets glared at us from the shelf beside her ear and a tattered fox skin dangled from the wall. She and

Marco exchanged whispered words. "A *pago*," he told me quietly. An offering to the Earth goddess to ensure a successful roundup. I watched the old woman ladle handfuls of Mother Earth's favorite candies from a plastic jar. She seemed partial to sweets, and crackers too. Hopefully she wouldn't notice that the gold and silver figurines were really painted tin. The tiny lead llama made sense, but the large plastic chicken seemed a bit out of place. A toy truck, a handful of uncooked macaroni, a bag of colorful confetti. The old woman turned and rummaged about in a drawer, then triumphantly flourished what looked like a dried-up seahorse. "Llama fetus," she said. She wrapped it with exquisite care and placed it atop the pile.

Mother Earth was apparently no powder puff. She enjoyed a bottle of beer—or two, or three—a snort of tobacco, and a couple jugs of wine. Like all good Andean folk, she was mighty picky about her coca leaves. Only the best would do—fresh and unblemished, kept in a woven pouch together with a hunk of lime.

At last we were back in the truck and lurching our way up to the tiny village of Picotani. The engine coughed and spat to clear the line of the dirty gasoline we'd purchased along with the spit-and-polish coca leaves. Flamingos dotted shallow lakes and herds of fluffy llamas stood out among the rolling, treeless landscape. Few animals could survive in the thin air and harsh climate at 14,000 feet. The hardy villagers lived off their herds and supplemented their meager diet with *chuño*—the freeze-dried potato—and *charqui*. Made by cutting meat into thin strips and laying them out to dry in the sun, this Andean food was quickly adopted by the Spanish and eventually made its way into the modern lexicon—and Western convenience stores—as jerky.

We were given the nurse's room in the community center. Stitches, a sign said, were 30 cents apiece and injections cost a quarter. "Watch out for Yellow Fever!" A poster warned anyone who knew how to read. "INNOCULATE YOUR CHILD!"—at an altitude where mosquitoes were rarer than tourists and even less likely to survive the night.

We just had time to drop off our things before we were whisked off by a squat Quechua woman with trademark long black braids and voluminous skirts. Her name was Victoria. Her short legs propelled her along the rocky road at a pace that left me gasping in her wake. Apparently that shapeless poncho hid an industrial set of lungs.

Yes, she said, she had a small house in Picotani but spent most of her time in the countryside. I looked back on the half dozen stone buildings and wondered how, exactly, she defined "countryside." She raised alpaca and llama for a living, as did almost everyone. Once a week a truck arrived at 2:30 in the morning to ferry passengers to the nearest town, to do their shopping and return the same night. She had never been beyond that town, never watched a movie nor seen a tree. Her 12-year-old son wanted to be an English teacher, though we were the first English speakers he had ever laid eyes on. Despite—or perhaps because of—the isolation of her life, she was insatiably curious about the outside world. What was it like in the United States, she asked. I didn't know where to begin. Humpback whales? Television? Traffic lights? In the end it made no difference. We started talking about spinning wheels and soon were using ponchos to make Muslim veils and waddling around like penguins. I don't think she believed a word I said, but her son's eyes grew large and round, and I knew that one day he would be boarding that weekly truck, never to return.

The ceremony honoring Mother Earth was held in a bare room beside the empty corral. Everyone stood around with their hands in their pockets, stamping their feet and trying to pretend that the cement shed wasn't colder than an icebox. The head shaman unwrapped our purchases, carefully smoothing out each torn piece of newspaper—it was going to be a long night—and then meticulously building his offering. Crackers first, salt side up, then candy, chocolate, sugar cubes, confetti, more candy.... I was mesmerized by those bite-size bits of chocolate. I wasn't the only one who coveted Mother Earth's property. A small riot broke out beside me as the two-pound bag of coca leaves was dumped out on the table. People began grabbing leaves and arranging them—pointy end first, greener side up. I heard the occasional muttered, "Mama wouldn't want this one," as they surreptitiously stuffed their cheeks with the torn or broken bits. I tried a bite myself. The leaves were dry and bitter, sucking the moisture out of my mouth and shedding small pieces that got stuck between my teeth. "Don't chew it," Marco whispered. "Just tuck it between your teeth and gum."

Victoria quickly took me in hand. "It takes 30 minutes to build a wad," she said, supervising me until I had a walnut ball inside my cheek. I was to chew it for 45 minutes—no more, no less. Afterward I should remove it with my fingers and gently throw it away. One never swallows coca leaves, she told me firmly. One never spits them out. Coca leaves were chewed five times a day, and provided an orderly framework in a society that was essentially clock-free. Even the length of a chew was considered a unit of time, as in "it's two chews along that trail to uncle's house."

Coca chewing was invented, Victoria told me, when Santisima Maria lost her child. Griefstricken, she wandered into the forest and absentmindedly picked a few coca leaves. She put them in her mouth and discovered that they eased her suffering. When chewed according to the proper rituals, the leaves were supposed to be as comforting as a mother's arms.

Coca leaves have been used for centuries among the Andean people as a mild stimulant—similar to coffee—that dulls hunger, dispels fatigue, and enhances concentration. Chewing coca slightly elevates the heart rate and produces a mild vasoconstriction in the extremities, which helps maintain the body's core temperature. It is both an anesthetic and a medicine. It provides much needed minerals to high-altitude communities that rarely have access to leafy greens.

Socially it plays an even more important role. The closest Western equivalent to chewing coca is sharing a cup of coffee, but chewing coca leaves has far more significance than a shot of caffeine. Chewing coca together is like pouring coffee, saying grace over the cups, and then exchanging them. It is a way of indicating a serious problem and getting the other person to sit down and give it their full attention. Or, for those who don't wish to admit their difficulties, chewing coca and petitioning the mountain gods out loud in the presence of friends and family is an indirect method of asking for support. To refuse the leaf is an act of hostility, like refusing to shake hands. Sharing coca is an accepted means of sealing a contract, and has all the moral obligation of a sanctified union.

But most important of all, to chew coca is to be a *runa*—one of the people of the Andes. Several times a day, a chewer redefines himself or herself as a member of his community. Over the years coca has become the ultimate marker of indigenous identity. Once a man moves to the city, he immediately gives up coca chewing and with it, his ancestry.

The shaman was still hard at work. His candy house completed, he picked up a group of coca leaves, layered in a pinch of llama fat, and topped it off with a sprinkle of powdered incense. He raised the offering above his head and called it to the attention of the proper mountain gods, then placed it carefully along the edge of the candy pile. Another bunch of leaves. And another. He was directing the *sami* of the coca leaves—their vital essence—to the place that controlled the village's health, luck, and vitality. Coca was the quintessential Andean sacrament—it was even called the "host." It defined the relationship between the Earth, the people, and the ancestors. Using coca to maintain the proper channels of communication with the powers that be, the shaman allowed the successful transfer of the ancestor's procreative energy to the next generation. Coca was the key to life itself.

More sounds of celebration as a bottle of clear liquid appeared. It made its rounds of the circle until it came to me. I naively tossed it down. It instantly laid waste to the back of my throat, incinerated my tonsils, and landed like a Molotov cocktail in my stomach. I didn't realize until I had handed off the glass that I had also inadvertently swallowed my pigeon egg-size plug of coca leaves.

The shaman gathered up a handful of leaves and everyone surged forward. It was time, Marco told me, to see if Mother Earth was in favor of tomorrow's roundup.

The first casting of the leaves landed mostly gray-side up. That was bad. The shaman considered the potential implications of this disaster, then noticed that one of the leaves had fallen half off the divination cloth. No good. He gathered them up for a second try.

The leaves landed stubbornly facedown. He looked to the heavens, closed his eyes, and had a silent conversation with Mother Earth and the mountain gods.

At last the leaves fell fifty-fifty. Good enough, he said. Mother Earth was pleased. He whipped out a bit of string, bundled up the offering, and bolted out of the room. Everyone gave chase.

"What's the hurry?" I panted.

"We burn the offering at midnight," Marco said, "up there." He pointed at what had been a sizable mountain before the sun went down.

"You're kidding," I said. It was twenty to twelve. Did Mother Earth wear a watch? In a culture where time was measured by the growth of an alpaca's fleece, why were we racing hell-bent up a mountain in the pitch-black to talk to Her on the stroke of midnight?

They emptied a sack of marble-like llama droppings on the ground and poured half a bottle of moonshine over it. The pile lit explosively and burned with a blue-white flame. I sent a silent apology down my esophagus for having drunk the stuff. The offering was laid on top, where the candy burned merrily amid the llama fat. Several beer bottles were shaken up and sprayed indiscriminately over everyone. Then we stood around stomping our feet and stuffing ourselves with leftover moonshine and coca leaves while the fire slowly burned itself out.

The roundup was scheduled for the crack of dawn—only a few hours away. I wanted nothing more than to crawl inside my warm and fluffy sleeping bag. Not a chance. Our labors completed, we headed back down to the icebox room, broke out several Andean flutes and panpipes, and began to dance.

It was four in the morning before I crawled into bed. Three hours later the roundup began.

The corral was abuzz with activity. Hundreds of villagers were pouring in on trucks, motorbikes, horseback, and sturdy legs. A few of the more enterprising women had put up tents and were selling sickly sweet soft drinks and week-old bread. A soccer game began in a nearby field. Men and women immediately segregated themselves—the one group accessorized with beer and the other with children.

At noon the president of CONACS arrived. Dr. Martinez wore jeans and a baseball cap, and would have looked at home coaching Little League. He quickly ran us through the necessary pre-roundup speeches and in record time sent us scrambling up the mountain.

Vicuñas, Dr. Martinez told me, are among the few animals that have oval red corpuscles. The genetic adaptation gives them a higher density of hemoglobin and allows more oxygen to circulate through their bodies.

Oval blood cells, I thought. *That's the way to go.* The thin mountain air made me feel like I was breathing through a straw. Those vicuñas, I thought, definitely had a hand up on the evolutionary ladder....

"Chickens," Dr. Martinez continued, "share the same trait."

Victoria was far ahead, her legs churning like pistons. I bet she had oval hemoglobin too.

We reached the top of a ridge and untangled several long ropes with ribbonlike trailers used to scare the vicuñas into the corral. Victoria rushed around trying to organize everyone. "Make the rope taut! Hide behind those rocks! Faster, Faster!" Dr. Martinez was unfazed. The men had gone out an hour earlier in trucks to start moving the animals out of their remote mountain hideaways. It would be a while before the first vicuña topped the hill.

"There's a legend," Dr. Martinez said, "about the origin of the vicuñas." He had the soothing voice and rhythm of a natural storyteller. "When the Spaniards first came to South America they brought Catholicism with them. The apus—mountain gods—were afraid they would be displaced by this strange new faith. They called a meeting and discussed the situation among themselves.

The conquistadores, they decided, were only interested in gold. If they didn't find any, they would return to the lands from whence they came. The apus agreed that whenever they saw the Spaniards approach a source of gold, they would transform it into golden-fleeced vicuñas that would then gallop away across the plains.

The first vicuña appeared high above us, silhouetted against an ominously darkened sky. Two more followed, and soon they were flowing down the steep mountainsides in small bands of 10 and 20, more graceful than gazelles. They were the color of sunlit honey. Victoria leaped up and urged everyone forward. Dr. Martinez waved me back into the grass. It would be at least another hour before the men caught up with us. There was time for another story.

"There was once a village chief, 50 years old, who fell in love with a beautiful young girl of 16. She wouldn't have him, no matter how hard he tried to win her favor. After many months she grew tired of his persistent courtship and told him she would give in to his demands if he gave her a dress made entirely of gold. The chief immediately assembled the best artisans of his kingdom but they were all utterly incapable of spinning gold. In desperation he proclaimed a great reward for anyone who succeeded in creating light and airy cloth from the unyielding metal. Death would be the punishment for those who failed.

Then one day he and the young girl were returning from another fruitless visit to the kingdom's weavers when they stopped to spend the night beside a lake. The girl excused herself to bathe. The old chief decided that if he couldn't have her then he should at least see her naked, so he hid himself beside the lake shore to spy on her. While waiting he fell asleep and was visited in his dreams by a mountain god. "You have brought disgrace upon your people," the apu said. "Your punishment shall fit your crime: from this day forth you will be able to clothe yourself in the woman that you yearn for but never truly make her yours."

The chief awoke just in time to see the girl emerging from the lake. As she stepped out of the water, she was transformed into a vicuña and galloped away. The mountain gods decreed her sacred, so that only chiefs and royalty were allowed to wear her golden fleece. But, they said, the vicuña would remain forever wild.

And wild they still were. They thundered across the valley below us, gathering into a great tide, a river of flowing gold. Tiny dots of people were draped across the mountain ridge above us like a human garland, closing ranks behind the animals. Higher still the sky turned from gray to black, as though the mountain gods were angry at our imposition upon their sacred beasts. We gathered our rope with its colored strips of plastic and ran forward. The valley below us rippled with a seething mass of animals so dense that the vicuñas no longer had room to run. The human chain tightened behind them and forced them forward. At last they stood in tightly packed clusters just outside the corral, jostling and snorting, unwilling to take the final plunge into captivity.

A small white ball hit the ground near my feet, then another. It was round and hard as buckshot. Hail. The weather had changed from short-sleeve sunscreen to triple-layer underwear in less time than it takes to eat a meal. A great peal of thunder rolled across the plain. There were urgent cries to hurry. The hail grew to the size of peas, then marbles. A sudden surge of the crowd sent the vicuñas winging into the corral, and then we were running too, covering our heads and dashing pell-mell for shelter. I couldn't believe how much the hail hurt. We hid beneath the eaves of the shearing shed, watching the huge black sky bear down on us. Icy frosting covered the backs of the vicuñas. They tacked their ears back in misery and huddled together for shelter against the howling wind.

The unexpected storm put an end to our day's labor. There was nothing to do but drink and dance until the sun dried out their fleece. No matter—the roundup had been a spectacular success. More than 1,600 animals, the largest catch that Picotani had ever seen.

We were out early the next morning: I didn't want to miss the cutting of a single hair off the backs of our 1,626 vicuñas. The corral filled up with taciturn villagers returning from their all-night revels. Men and women remained firmly segregated while organizers passed out handfuls of coca leaves and roll was called. Each village was required to provide a certain number of volunteers. This system of *mit'a*, or work-share, was another vestige of Inca times. Once a tribal group was officially incorporated into the empire, it owed both the Inca and the sun god a yearly tribute of labor— repairing roads, serving in the army, or working the royal fields. To this day the villages use labor as a form of currency in a complicated system of give-and-take with in-laws, elders, neighbors, and friends. Fields are almost always tilled communally and serious consideration given to the potential payoff in future labor rights when it comes time to choose a godparent or arrange a marriage. Communal reciprocity—whether coca leaves or labor—is still the protective barrier against the outside world.

I listened to the litany of names, trying to wrap my tongue around the complicated words with the vowels pressed out of them, interspersed by machine-gun-like glottal stops.

I'd been practicing my glottal stops for months. I'd first come across them in written Quechua as these odd apostrophes that suddenly appeared in an otherwise ordinary word. They were supposed to sound like the speaker had managed to silence, but not quite suppress, a belch. The only reliable way that I could reproduce this sound—and the even more dreaded double-apostrophe- stop-stop—was to tap myself firmly on the sternum every time I hit a *p*, *k*, or *q*.

But the old Inca tongue had more mind-bending idiosyncrasies in store. Quechua speakers had a tendency to suffix everything. Their sentences are often one world long. LONG, as in *Much'ananyakapushasquakupuninyataqsumamarki.* In essence they take a simple word—"grass," for example—and start sticking syllables on the back end like wagons on a train. A pluralizer gets hooked up, followed by the suffix "without." Then, in rapid succession, "bull," "hunger," and "suffer" hop on board. Finally, they add one last pluralizer so that the verb doesn't feel left out. *Quihuacunaillaihuanhuagracacunacayarcanchu.* "Bulls get hungry without grass." Piece of cake.

All of this seemed tedious but not insurmountable as long as I was studying the language out of books. Then I met my first old man in an Andean village, bid him good day, and listened to his reply. It had something to do with the market and he'd driven over at least three glottal stops to get there.

Roll call ended and the vicuñas were officially dry. After another hour of democratic, coca-chewing Andean debate, five men grabbed a long piece of burlap cloth and waded in among the tightly packed animals, weaving back and forth to separate a dozen vicuñas from the main herd. I took off my jacket and jumped into the corral.

A vicuña flashed by. I grabbed two handfuls of fleece halfway down his back and off we went. He bounded along on powerful deerlike legs; I stumbled after him. My fingers were tangled in his wool, and as he turned his first corner, I sailed around behind him like an airborne water-skier. It wasn't at all clear who had caught whom. "I could use a hand here," I said in Spanish as we winged past the men holding up the burlap fence. It was possible that they didn't speak Spanish. They were, at any rate, too busy doubled over with laughter to say much of anything at all. Eventually, after a couple more loops in our tiny arena, the vicuña and I mutually agreed to part company. I ended up in a heap on the ground while he, rid of the 125-pound parasite clinging to his hindquarters, sailed over the burlap cloth and rejoined the herd.

That must be the problem. I had inadvertently picked the Hercules of the vicuña world. I decided to watch for a moment and choose an animal that was a bit more to scale.

It quickly became clear that vicuña-catching is a two-man sport. One fellow hooks the animal's long neck and the other sneaks up from behind to grab its convenient handle of a tail. At this point the vicuña can do little more than leap up and down in place while the men hang on to both ends as though they are shaking out a bedsheet.

I got off the fence in search of a partner. Not a chance. Apparently my value as a Good-Story-for-Months-to-Come far exceeded any useful contribution I might make to the roundup itself. I'd have to go it on my own.

This time I chose a tiny fellow, roughly half the size of Hercules. I grabbed his neck easily enough as he raced by, but he immediately tried to back away, putting his tail completely out of reach. We circled around a few times, eyeball to eyeball, while the burlap crowd doubled over again. Eventually I managed to hook an arm under his belly and pick him up. "Where to?" I asked the men. One of them glanced at my catch and pointed to a dozen babies waiting to be tagged. We got into line.

My vicuña was about the size of a Doberman pinscher. At first it seemed easier just to hold him in my arms where he couldn't use his feet. Unfortunately my arms started sagging faster than the line was moving, so I put him down and tried my hand at vicuña obedience training. "Sit," I said. He squirmed a bit but I had a firm hold on his upper body. He eventually sank onto his hindquarters while I rubbed his forehead and said silly things like, "good boy." I stole a glance at the burlap men to see if they were watching. They were. The vicuña chose this moment to shoot straight up in the air, using every ounce of energy he had stored in his springy legs. Vicuñas may share blood with chickens, but they have legs like grasshoppers. I was catapulted skyward and landed on my back with my arms and legs still wrapped around the vicuña. It seemed like the most stable position we'd been in so far, so there we stayed.

I was amazed at how fluid and graceful these animals were. They could change directions like a hummingbird, jump higher than a man, and weave their way through outstretched arms with the precision of an Olympic slalom skier. They never bit, rarely spat and, unlike mules, only kicked in self-defense. With their lovely long lashes and soft fleece, they looked as cuddly as teddy bears and as playful as dolphins.

We reached the front of the line and my little fellow acquired an ear tag, had his teeth checked, and was released into an outer paddock. My next catch was significantly larger and I was directed to a different line. After a 20-minute wrestling match I found myself facing an ancient man with a ratty school notebook. "Male or female?" he asked slowly. I had one arm around my vicuña's neck and my other hand clenched in a death grip on his tail. I could barely see over his back, and every time he jumped he snapped my jaw shut against my upper teeth. "I dunno. See fer yerself," I said, trying to keep my tongue out of the way. He leaned over, infinitely slowly. "Male," he said, and scribbled in his tattered book.

Eventually I caught a vicuña with fleece long enough to be sheared and was directed to the shearing shed. The place was a beehive of dark and dusty activity. A gas-powered engine ran four shearing stations and men were busy separating the stretched-out animals from their lovely fleece. The wool was then carried to a back room where the women sat around a table, trimming off the unwanted hairs and rolling the rest into little puffy balls. I fingered the soft fleece. I had secretly been planning to buy two pounds—nearly 300 dollars' worth—to make my mother a one-of-a-kind handspun vicuña sweater. I hadn't until this moment realized that the fibers were less than two inches long. They needed to be spun to almost machinelike perfection or the resulting yarn would fall apart.

By late afternoon most of the vicuñas were either shorn or tagged. I went out to join the line of women whose job it was to keep the animals in one corner of the outer paddock until it was time to release them back into the wild.

Andean mountain folk do not take kindly to strangers—an understandable consequence of 500 years of conflict with power-hungry administrators and cross-wielding missionaries. These women were no exception. They studiously ignored my greetings in both Spanish and Quechua and made no move to include me in their group. Feeling lonely and unwanted, I moved a few steps beyond the line, took out my spindle, and settled down to spin. They sent surreptitious glances in my direction. I pretended not to notice. They talked among themselves. Soon I was completely caught up in wresting my wooly fleece into something that resembled yarn.

"*Caramba!*" The voice rolled over me like thunder. I nearly jumped out of my skin. A stout woman with a body like a giant potato loomed over me, glaring at my spindle. She reached down and snatched it out of my hand, rapidly plucking the fleece clean with gnarled fingers. "You can't spin like that!" she said in a mixture of Spanish and Quechua. "Faster!" She snapped the spindle and it started whirring like a top, so fast I heard it hum. "Longer!" The silk-fine thread expanded between her hands, then rapidly twirled onto the spindle. "Hold it like this!" she demanded, her comments punctuated with bilingual obscenities. I watched her work for several minutes, then gestured cautiously that I was ready to try my humble best.

Nothing doing. She kept a firm grip on my fleece and didn't let go until the signal came to release the vicuñas and we were forced to move aside. Even then she handed it off to another villager—anything but the bumbling foreigner performing sacrilege on the sacred Andean arts.

The vicuñas made a dash for freedom as soon as the gap opened in the line. I watched them running—streaming, really—and heard the rolling thunder of their hooves. They moved like quicksilver over the treeless plains, and didn't stop until they were high up on the mountain ridge, silhouetted against the fading sun. Back where they belonged.

Our plans to drive back to Puno immediately after the roundup were interrupted by the truck, which had spent the day in pieces beside the corral. A wheel bearing was crushed beyond repair. Marco, with his usual quiet competence, had organized a ride as far as the sorcerer's store. With luck we'd catch the last bus back to Puno in time to drop John at a hotel near the airport.

John had the next day off and was making straight for Lima. Despite his stateside enthusiasm for a wild trek across the Andes, he clearly preferred surfing the city's beaches and sampling her haute cuisine to the remote and rugged hinterlands. Two of his surfboards had a permanent home at a friend's house in Lima's suburbs, and he spent every spare moment fighting other neoprene-sheathed enthusiasts for prime position on The Wave.

I chose to stay behind in Puno. Marco had made me an offer I couldn't refuse—proof that Manco Capac had passed this way while searching for a place to found his empire.

Marco showed up at my hostel the next morning at 7:00 a.m. sharp. Despite two grueling days in the field, he'd gotten up at dawn to find a new bearing for the broken truck and handed it off to one of his employees, who had volunteered to take it back *by bicycle* to Picotani village. A 12-hour ride, almost entirely uphill.

It wasn't the first time I had seen people respond to Marco's quiet command. Despite his city upbringing, the Andean villagers considered Marco one of their own. Even the vicuñas seemed to settle down under his gentle hands. Although he had spent his entire life in Puno, he dreamed of going overseas to study. For the moment he had to stay home to care for his father, who was old and ill. "Perhaps one day...," he said wistfully.

But in the meantime there was a place he wanted me to see. We hiked through a landscape that looked like giant sand castles half-melted by the sea. A two-story stone tower appeared unexpectedly among the worn stone outcroppings. Marco pointed out a small snake carved into one of the perfectly square blocks. "That," he said, "is the royal insignia of the first Inca. Manco Capac left a trail of those carvings on his journey to Cuzco."

The tower itself had an even more interesting lineage. "*Chullpas* are ancient burial chambers built by the *Machakuna*, the Old Ones," Marco said. They were a race of giants that lived by moonlight, before the sun existed. Then it came time for people to inhabit the land. The sun rose and daylight fell upon the Earth; the Old Ones immediately dried up and their flesh melted away. This understandably embittered them against humans, and they still occasionally seek revenge by seducing pregnant women in erotic dreams, causing miscarriages and birth defects. An evil wind blows from the places where their bones lie, making humans ill with chills and coughing fits.

The Machakuna are not gone; their world parallels our own. Bright moonlight reanimates their bones and they emerge. They eat and drink, visit one another and work their fields. In the syncretic world that the Andean people inhabit, even the Machakuna have a positive side. The Indians like to plant their potato fields near Machakuna graves, for they believe that the same ill wind that makes humans sick fertilizes the potatoes and makes them grow.

We climbed back up into the sand-castle playground and explored the burial caves that pitted the limestone walls. Marco told me about a camping trip he had taken with friends, how the music echoed off the rocks and the shadows danced along the walls like ghosts. Five years ago he'd found a cave that held the skeleton of a child, still intact. He'd filled the entrance with sand to protect it against grave robbers, but in the process fooled himself as well. He never found the spot again. He was glad.

Somehow, in my search for Inca roads and relics, I had forgotten what it was like to spend an unplanned afternoon with a newfound friend. We hadn't gotten any award-winning footage nor found a mummy that would grace the cover of *Time* magazine, but I would take away something much more meaningful to me—a day of personal, peaceful memories.

CHAPTER 19

A SACRED PLACE

FIELD NOTES: Imagine being able to live in Eden....

I knew where Manco Capac had sunk his golden staff into the ground to found the Inca Empire. I even had some idea of the route he might have taken to get there. It was time to retrace his footsteps to where it all began—the place the Inca called their Eden: the Island of the Sun.

Some say it was the birthplace of the sun itself. The Spaniards believed it held the legendary Fountain of Youth. Today the Island of the Sun has some 5,000 inhabitants who live and work the land much as their ancestors did. They speak Aymara, a dialect that existed long before the Inca first arrived. It sits smack in the center of Lake Titicaca, and beside it lies the Island of the Moon, where the Inca's sun virgins once dwelled. Modern politics have split the "greatest lake in the Indies" in half.

The sacred cave where Manco Capac once emerged now lies on Bolivian soil.

We caught a boat to the village of Cha'llapampa near the island's northern end and found the cave after two hours of hard hiking. It was a couple of stories high and not quite deep enough to keep out the rain. Our guide pointed out two jaguars that proved the presence of a supreme deity.

"Where?" I asked.

"There," he said, "an eye, the mouth, an ear."

I stood right next to the cave. I backed up 10 feet. I tried from 50 feet away. I couldn't see it. The place looked like an ordinary hole in an unimpressive stone wall.

We decided to try our luck at the Palace of the Inca on the other side of island. It wasn't really a palace at all, but rather an administrative center built in an elaborate maze of walls and doorways. The masonic masterpieces of Machu Picchu and Cuzco had spoiled me. I was disappointed. I headed out to sit near the entrance and watch the young boys scamper by, urging their sheep homeward with homemade wooden staffs. They looked like extras on a Hollywood movie lot.

The Temple of the Sun God stood on a lonely hillside facing the shores of Lake Titicaca. I stifled another pang of disappointment. Somehow I had expected something more spectacular from such a sacred place. We wandered slowly back, past women driving flocks of sheep along the narrow footpaths and carrying newborn lambs in their knotted shawls. Thatched houses perched among the grassy hillsides like scattered grains of rice. Footpaths meandered through the rolling landscape. There were no cars; the island had no roads. The birthplace of the Inca. I tried to imagine what it would be like to know exactly where your Eden lies.

I watched the distant farmers inch across their fields, sowing corn as they had a thousand years ago. The island exuded serenity. At last, I began to understand. A truly sacred place didn't need elaborate stone monuments. Whether it was the birthplace of a mighty nation or just a quiet corner of the world—it was a sanctuary.

We spent that night with a local couple. He was 74 and she was 69. They spoke nothing but Aymara, the language of their pre-Inca ancestors. His face was a spiderweb of wrinkles, creasing skin as dark and shiny as mahogany. She had twisted, driftwood hands and fingers that held a lifetime of handmade memories. Their home looked like the inside of a baker's oven—blackened walls and windowless, and no larger than a horse's stall. The door was narrower than my shoulders, and I had to get down on my knees to crawl inside.

Stalactites of tarry cobwebs collected smoky residue from the cooking fire. The few battered pots were still seasoned with the crust of last week's meals. The old woman and I found a common language in my spinning and her stew, taking turns at the spindle and with the stirring spoon. Her face took on the warm glow of the fire whenever she looked at the two-year-old clinging tightly to her husband's thigh. No, it wasn't their granddaughter, she told me. They had not been blessed with children. She was his nephew's daughter, sent to take care of them as they grew old. At first it seemed like a callous act, but as I watched the old man carefully ladle out the little girl's meal, adjust her hat, and rest a wrinkled hand upon her head, I changed my mind. There was a school just down the road, they told me in gestures and drawings in the dirt. She would go there once she was old enough. In the meantime there were chickens to be chased and sheep to herd and two pigs in the pen, and an entire island to explore without the slightest fear of strangers, cars, or trucks or drugs or even dirty magazines.

I slept in one of the storage huts, under sheaves of hanging corn and piles of alpaca blankets still burred with seeds and hay. The old man came over with his lantern to make sure that all was well. The little girl wrapped herself around his leg and peered at me with huge brown eyes. Once more his leathery hand dropped gently on her head in a feather touch as old as time itself.

A sacred place.

CHAPTER 20

LOST IN THE JUNGLE

FIELD NOTES: Four hours later they were still missing somewhere in the Bolivian jungle. I organized a village of nearly 300 people and we searched until 2:00 a.m. The next morning at 6:00 a.m. everyone went out again....

La Paz, just around the corner from Lake Titicaca, was Lima's country cousin—narrow, cobblestone streets to Lima's four-lane highways. In Lima it seemed like every motorist had a cell phone Velcroed to his ear. In La Paz the taxi drivers pulled over to use the antique phones-for-rent squatting on knickknack stalls. Lima overflowed with designer boutiques. La Paz sold its suits from streetside stands. It sold hair—too long black braids with snowy dandruff—purchased by Indian women to augment their trademark locks. Here "fast-food" meant wheelbarrows heaped high with grapes, or steaming potatoes wrapped in banana leaves. There wasn't a pair of panty hose or a purebred dog in sight. Only mutts.

La Paz had its share of glassy, high-rise office buildings and BMWs, but beneath the thin skin of market capitalism beat an ancient heart. The people of La Paz had managed to marry old and new in a seamless, scarless blend—and nowhere more clearly than at the Alasitas fair.

Once a year La Paz converted several city blocks into a monument to minimalism. The Alasitas festival was a shameless celebration of material desire. Fair goers went from stall to stall, buying up miniatures of all the things they wanted in the coming year—cars and trucks, hairdryers, homesteads, and sewing machines. But just buying dollhouse replicas wasn't enough to make their dreams come true. They then had to take their purchases to the nearest witch—perched conveniently between the stalls—and have everything blessed with incense, ringing bells, and a squirt of alcohol.

I sidled up to a man with a towering armload of trucks and buses. Did he really expect vehicles to rain down from the sky, with working carburetors and registrations already made out in his name?

"No no, you have to work for it," he said. "I am hoping to expand my business in the coming year. I want to buy three more trucks." There were four miniatures in his hands. Room for a little hope.

"But," he added as his turn came to hold his precious cargo over the dream-granting incense, "you must have faith as well. Hard work alone is not enough."

Although the festival offered everything from rubber sandals to apartment complexes, several items were obviously in high demand. Every third stall hawked solid bricks of fake money. U.S. dollars were far more popular than local currency—not surprisingly, since a thousand real-life bolivianos were worth about 80 cents. Foreign passports sold like hotcakes, as did university degrees. And for those who could afford to buy their blessing with a special guarantee, there was always the big stone statue of the Egeko himself standing in the center of the fair.

Egeko is the god of abundance and fertility—a dwarflike figure that stood ten feet tall. That day his head was one great mass of ribbons and confetti, and beer dripped like a chronic sniffle from the end of his nose. To get a blessing in his immediate vicinity was inordinately good luck. To time it for the stroke of noon on the first Saturday of the festival was the equivalent of a spirit-world guarantee.

I wandered among the endless rows of stalls, looking for something I truly coveted for the coming year. I travel too much to own a house. A truck seemed more a burden than a joy. Like everyone I could always use a bit more money, but I didn't really feel its lack. I had a passport and a university degree. No, what I was looking for couldn't be found among the cheerful little miniatures at the Alasitas fair.

I had been on the road for five long months. I was tired of watching people blink in and out of my life like fireflies—of struggling to make a meaningful connection across confusing cultural static, only to wave good-bye and wonder if the newfound friendship would survive e-mails and an occasional phone call until I might be by this way again. I missed the friends and family who were as comfortable—and as comforting—as a second skin.

And it seemed, if the god Egeko was in a benevolent mood, that my wish was about to come true.

Chuck is a computer engineer. I had met him ten years ago when I still had training wheels on my first hang glider. He'd been there to clean up my face when I broke my nose in a catastrophic launch. We'd tossed pebbles off the ramp when the winds went bad for six weeks straight. Somewhere between the blood and boredom, we'd become friends.

Chuck was a corporate-career rebel. For two decades he'd risen through the ranks of an engineering company. He wore a chest-length, bushy beard rather than a tie. It was years before he told me that he had a Ph.D.

He was a true technophile—not the kind who'd buy a wrap-around-the-room stereo and then bask in its reflected decibels, but someone who would wire up his darkroom to his home computer, which also ran the toaster and the coffee machine.

His house was filled with 30 years of carefully collected debris. Pebbles. Well-thumbed novels, rusty saws, old magazines. It was a personal museum with labels that could only be read with ESP. Occasionally he added to a jar of feathers that perched on his mantel. He called them his winged memories.

He always wore a seat belt, but on long trips he often read a book behind the wheel.

A part of him was mountain man. He biked. He hiked. He was an E.M.T. And sometimes—when he contra danced—he wore a skirt.

He had once taught me how to waltz in two twirly-whirly, soaring songs. With others I was still a bumbling bottle fly, but in his arms I flowed like water over tumbled stones. He led as confidently as a general on a battlefield. In his skirt.

Despite a certain wistful yearning for foreign adventure, in 46 years he had yet to wire together all his feathered memories and take wing across the world.

I had invited Chuck and his girlfriend to visit me in Bolivia. He called me in La Paz, telling me that she couldn't make it but that he had 12 days free. My exhaustion drained away. Chuck would offer me a new pair of eyes to rediscover the land around me. I could provide him with a relatively safe way to experience a completely unfamiliar world.

He arrived at 6:00 a.m. I sailed into his arms like a ship into a harbor in the middle of a storm. My bones dissolved with relief and gratitude. When I finally pulled away, I noticed he was 15 pounds heavier than his usual fighting trim. A cold, he said. The holidays. Too much winter snow. For the first time I wondered if this man—who carried survival gear in his car and always came prepared—had any idea what lay ahead.

Within an hour we were barreling down the eastern slope of the Cordillera Real, heading for the Yungas—the misty, jungle-filled valleys and gorges that lay between the barren altiplano and the impenetrable Amazon. In the days of the Inca Empire, gold was discovered along the Mapiri and Tipuani Rivers. Once the Spanish got wind of it, they flooded the Yungas valleys with so many conscripted laborers that the region became one of the continent's most prolific sources of the precious yellow metal.

But the Yungas held the key to another Inca legacy. It was a major source of legal coca production in Bolivia. Both the principal ingredient of cocaine and the cornerstone of Andean culture, coca leaves had come to symbolize the clash between ancient and modern, indigenous and Western life.

Halfway down the mountain we pulled up at a police checkpoint. Drug dogs sniffed up and down the line of trucks in front of us. While waiting our turn, I fell into conversation with the lieutenant in charge. The road we were on, he told me, was the only direct route from La Paz to the border of Brazil. That made it the number one drug artery in Bolivia. A package of raw cocaine increased eightfold in value along its length.

The lieutenant let me climb into one of the ten-wheelers that was undergoing inspection. Soldiers swarmed over the cargo like rats, slitting open cardboard boxes and probing their innards for evil intent. They tore the labels off cans and examined soldered seals. They carefully drilled through sticks of butter and rubbed the oily residue between their fingers, and sampled every single flour sack that lined one wall. I was surprised at both their attention to detail and their apparent dedication. Bolivia was second only to Colombia and Peru in the production of cocaine, and had a less-than-stellar record for drug enforcement. And yet these men were sitting in an open-topped truck in the persistent drizzle, systematically working their way through several hundred boxes without a single complaint. When they were done, they just as carefully taped over holes and resealed whatever they had undone.

The lieutenant was as patient with my questions as his men were with the cargo. Yes, they were searching for cocaine, but they also kept a lookout for ingredients used in processing the coca leaves—everything from cement to detergents. Even a five-gallon container of gasoline required official documentation to travel down this road. Earlier in the day they had confiscated 75 liters of turpentine from a passenger on a bus. Ten days ago they had found 22 kilos of cocaine hidden in a shipment of ironing boards.

How thoroughly they searched a truck depended on its origin, its cargo, and its destination. The one we were in was going all the way to the border of Brazil and, therefore, subject to careful scrutiny. And although the dogs were useful, they tired easily and could only work for 15 minutes at a time. Mostly the men relied on a pocketful of simple tools—small awls for drilling through containers, pliers, can openers—and instinct. The lieutenant reached up and, almost without thinking, checked a spare tire by letting out a tiny bit of air.

"What happens if you catch someone with cocaine?"

"It depends," he said. "Often they're just poor farmers paid to carry a crate of peaches in their car. We ask them to cooperate with us to catch the ones who are really to blame."

He clearly believed in what he was doing and was proud of his men's work. He had just recently been transferred from the jungles of Chaparé, where he'd led patrols to destroy the cocaine-making labs that flourished among the illegal coca fields of Bolivia's eastern rain forest.

...Cocaine-making labs...."Could we," I asked, "accompany one of those patrols on a raid?"

"You would have to speak with the head of the FELCN and get permission," he told me. "General Perez. In La Paz." I wrote it down.

Chuck looked dubious when I told him of this unexpected possibility. John was even less enthused. I tucked the piece of paper carefully into my passport before we climbed back into our jeep.

By now the sky had turned a brilliant blue, the sun was warm, and the mountainside sparkled with needle-sharp waterfalls that stitched intermittent holes in the dark green canopy. I remembered our lovely rooftop ride on the train in Ecuador and tried in vain to clean the dirty window of our rented jeep. When that failed I asked our driver to pull into the next turnout and stuck out my thumb. The very first truck stopped and cheerfully offered us a ride on top. The jeep followed some distance behind.

The road fit the truck like a surgeon's glove. There was no shoulder, just several hundred feet of abruptly empty space. In places I could drop a pebble and count to five before it hit the ground.

Our driver backed up to allow a fully laden fruit truck to pass. In misdirected gratitude they tossed us a three-pound papaya, which instantly became lunch. We drove under cascading waterfalls that poured off overhanging cliffs and past brilliant red bromeliads clinging to mossy mountainsides.

We spiraled slowly into the Yungas, the eyebrow of the Amazon— green and lush and intermittently cultivated with a patchwork quilt of coca fields. As we neared the bottom, the road turned middle age— wider, softer, and more sedate. We clambered down from our rooftop aerie and reluctantly returned to the company of our driver and his dirty jeep.

Don Rene, he called himself. He was 70 years old. He had a horseshoe of iron gray hair clamped tight to his balding head and an abrupt manner that implied he either could not—or did not— want to hear any point of view other than his own. Over dinner he regaled us with stories of his prior clients—of the two Swedish women who had insisted on getting out against his advice to take a stroll and had to hike five hard miles before reaching the turnout where he was waiting for them. Or the photographers who had arrived late at a rendezvous and had to find their own way home. He laughed heartily at his own jokes, but the relentless gringo-gets-it punch lines left me cold.

The next morning we rose early to help harvest coca leaves with a nearby farming family. They were one of the rare owners of legal coca bushes, all properly documented and registered with the authorities. The paperwork, the father told me, was expensive and limited their total acreage to two tiny fields. He had planted orange trees and coffee but nothing was as hardy, light, and disease-resistant as his coca crop. His standard of living had dropped considerably since the foreign eradication programs were put in place. "Why are you doing this to us?" he asked conversationally as we hunched over, side by side, plucking the tealike leaves. His hands moved in a blur of ridged and callused fingers, leaving behind naked stems and a bulging apron sack. My bushes looked tattered and torn, as though they had just been through a small but insistent hurricane.

"We were fine before foreigners started making cocaine. And now they hold us responsible and try to take away the coca leaves that have been a part of our culture since…" he paused, then shrugged— "time began."

He had a point. Coca pouches have been found in coastal grave sites as far back as A.D. 500. When the Spanish missionaries first arrived in South America, they recognized the importance of coca to indigenous religion and did their level best to wipe it out. The conquistadores, more inclined to gather gold than souls, saw coca as an opportunity. Coca chewing made it possible to drive their miners at a killing pace. Production of the tealike crop increased 50-fold. Once the Spanish government saw the light and started taxing the yearly harvest, coca became a major source of New World cash.

Then came cocaine. First derived from coca leaves in 1860, it quickly turned into the wonder drug of the Western world. It was touted as a cure for opium addiction, an anesthetic, and a general health tonic. Cigarettes were soaked in it and coca wine appeared. Coca-Cola—laced with cocaine—was marketed as a tonic for headaches and fatigue. It was finally banned in the early 1900s, but by then the drug had already taken hold. Unable to control the continuing demand for it at home, the U.S. government decided to eradicate cocaine at its source. F.D.A. planes started spraying pesticides over coca fields and local soldiers pulled out plants and burned down cocaine-making labs. Despite their efforts, Bolivia was still the world's third largest producer of cocaine.

None of which meant anything to the farmer next to me. He only knew that a hardy and profitable crop was now illegal. Still, when the field was harvested, he shook my hand and thanked us for our help and walked off down the path to his tiny shack without, it seemed, holding any grudge.

Afternoon found us back on the winding mountain road. Hoping to repeat a pleasant memory, we got out to hitchhike—against Don Rene's advice. "No one will pick you up," he warned, wagging an angry finger at me.

We asked him to wait at the next turnout—just in case he was right—and give chase if any truck drove by with us perched on top. "Idiots," he said as he shuffled off.

Within minutes the heavens opened up. Chuck snapped open an umbrella to shield John's camera while I stood in the rain and tried with increasing desperation to get the loaded trucks to stop. Don Rene was right. Five, ten, fifteen vehicles barreled by without the slightest inclination to hit the brakes. I had just decided to lie down across the middle of the road when I saw John whip around to track yet another passing truck. Chuck, intent on keeping the camera dry while staying clear of the wildly swinging lens, stepped backward off the road and silently disappeared. By the time I reached him, he was clambering back over the edge of a drop-off. I could see a slither trail of boot marks ending in a gully a dozen feet below. He smiled, wiped his muddy hands on a nearby leaf, and returned to the task at hand.

The rain kept falling, bloating our hands and wrinkling our feet. We finally admitted defeat and slunk up the road in search of Don Rene. The first turnout was disturbingly empty. I remembered his sullen face and had an ominous premonition that the gringo was about to get it again. Another truck hurtled by and I reflexively stuck out my thumb. To my surprise it shuddered to a halt 50 feet up the road. We swarmed up the ladder, shouting our thanks. We were too busy trying to jigsaw our equipment, elbows, and knees into the narrow rack above the driver's cabin to notice we had come to a stop. A second truck stood squarely across the road ahead of us. The driver was already wrestling with a rusty jack. Not one flat tire, but two—on a narrow section with no possibility of squeezing by. Traffic quickly piled up behind us. By the time the tires were off, nearly a hundred vehicles snaked around the mountainside, their anxious owners keeping a close eye on the rolling rain clouds and the gathering dusk.

And well they should. We were about to enter Bolivia's most famous stretch of road—the Death Highway. A hundred people die each year along this one-lane mountain track. It is also the site of South America's worst traffic accident. Eight years ago 110 passengers crowded aboard a new truck with its proud—and somewhat inebriated—owner at the wheel. It hurtled off a hairpin turn and plunged 200 feet straight into an abyss.

Crosses sprout at intervals along its length—the Bolivians call them "caution signs"—to mark the sites of prior fatalities. Apparently vehicles rain from the sky with such regularity that a small industry had sprung up at the foot of the ravine to strip cars and bodies of valuables before the police and rescue vehicles arrived.

I chatted with the worried drivers. I discussed, with apparent calm, the dangerous situation we were in. Unlike the others, I knew we could walk to the next turnout, climb into Don Rene's jeep, and be on our way.

The unexpected delay had forced John to dig into his reserve of batteries, so Chuck volunteered to find Don Rene and replenish his supplies. He returned an hour later, empty-handed. He'd walked the entire line of waiting trucks, and beyond. Don Rene had disappeared.

The spare tires—the same vintage as the flats—were finally in place. We climbed back into our narrow metal basket just as the last stain of daylight faded from the sky. As darkness fell, our rooftop aerie became a prime target for overhanging branches, trailing vines, and protruding rocks. Our truck driver hugged the mountainside and we ducked and dodged the dangling trees.

I had no idea what we were going to do once we reached the top of the pass. If we had to catch another ride back to La Paz, then we were in for a very long night. We had already passed a dozen empty turnouts and were facing the depressing prospect that Don Rene really had gone home. We tried excuses on each other—that he had driven to the police checkpoint to get a cup of coffee and a bite to eat. But wouldn't he have noticed the utter lack of uphill traffic, and come back to investigate? Perhaps all of the turnouts had been filled up by the traffic jam. No, he would have pulled over long before the pileup began.

Our explanations were getting hopelessly implausible when we suddenly turned the corner and lumbered past his mustard yellow jeep. We waved wildly and saw him pull out into the traffic several trucks behind us. What a relief. He passed one vehicle after another on the narrow turns until he was directly behind our truck. I signaled him to stop at the next turnout and asked our driver to pull over and let us off. Suddenly Don Rene gunned his engine, overtook us, and raced off.

"What's he doing?" I asked dumbly, staring at his receding lights. If our truck—or any truck ahead of us—got another flat tire, then we would once again be stuck without a ride. Don Rene found another opening in the traffic and disappeared. It was like sitting in a broken sailboat, watching a rescue ship steam away over the horizon. We were silently aghast.

"At least now we know where he is," Chuck finally said.

A creeping fog only added to the inky darkness as we desperately tried to parry the unseen branches that threatened to scrape us off our perch. At last we lay down and hooked our hands around the rusty, six-inch railing of the rack. The long caterpillar of lights wound its way up the misty mountainside. Two hours later we stiffly untied ourselves and went in search of Don Rene. We found him having a dinner at a roadside eatery. He was beside himself with fury for being made to wait for hours on the side of the road.

We explained about the flat tires. Why, we asked, hadn't he pulled over at the next turnout, like we told him to?

They were all full, he huffed.

But Chuck had walked beyond the traffic jam and found two empty ones, I pointed out.

He began to work himself into another towering, 70-year-old froth. I checked my watch. It was nearly 10:00 p.m. Too late to try to make it to the Inca Road.

"Don Rene," I said. "We're all tired. Let's just go home."

It was an hour before I realized that it wasn't the thick fog that was causing us to swerve dangerously on the highway, but rather Don Rene's even thicker glasses, perched stubbornly on the dashboard. By the time we were safely back in La Paz, my anger had faded into relief. Don Rene was just a tired old man at the end of a long day. And besides, everything had turned out all right. I gave him a big tip, apologized again for the delay, and toppled into bed.

The next day we prepared to hike what was probably the most extraordinary piece of Inca Road still in existence. It began in the Bolivian highlands, two hours out of La Paz. From there it clawed its way still higher, topping out at a 15,000-foot Andean pass. Then down and down and down, from stone to grass to shrub to tree. From gray to brown and then to jungle green. From the bitter, barren highlands to Bolivia's fertile heart—the Amazon. When I started looking for a driver to the trailhead, John suggested that we rehire Don Rene.

"You're kidding," I said. Forgive did not mean forget, and Don Rene wasn't exactly reliable.

John put forth a variety of arguments, all of which led back to the fact that Don Rene's employer—the owner of the jeep—was John's good friend and needed the money. Don Rene knew the Inca Road like the back of his hand, John said, and could find us llamas at the trailhead to carry our gear. By mid-afternoon I was willing to compromise. We would take Don Rene but leave John's heavy Betacam behind. That way if there were no pack animals we still had a chance of making it over the pass ourselves.

Don Rene agreed to go, but arrived two hours late. We dashed off, hoping to make the trailhead by midday. The road gradually deteriorated into a stony track without any sign of life. "Do you know where we might rent a mule or two?" I asked Don Rene carefully. "Farther up," he muttered. It was becoming increasingly apparent that he had never been here. By the time we reached the trailhead, the last farm animal was at least ten miles back.

Chuck wasn't yet acclimatized to the altitude. The 15,000-foot pass towered above us, wreathed in mist. Without pack mules the whole expedition was starting to look downright dangerous. We huddled in the rain. "I'll give it a shot," Chuck said.

We were now dependent on Don Rene to come get us on the other side. I drew him a map of the pickup point. We expected to arrive between 4:00 and 6:00 p.m. the following day. I watched Chuck resolutely shoulder his heavy pack and turned back to Don Rene. This time there was no room for gringo-gets-it mistakes. "Do NOT leave without us," I told him. "Even if you have to spend the night. DO NOT LEAVE until we get there."

We followed the valley until we reached the Inca Road. Even Chuck stopped dead at the sight of it. Twenty-feet wide and made of seamless stone. The rain had polished it to a high sheen. Chiseled aqueducts drained water off the shiny flagstones. It was a work of art, a sculpture, crafted by inhuman human hands; its builders, it seemed, had found a way to melt the stone and pour it into a giant mold. This was what the chroniclers were talking about when they wrote, "Although in many places ruined and destroyed, it still reveals what a splendid undertaking it was, and the power of those Incas who ordered it built.... In the memory of mankind I doubt that there is a record of another highway comparable to this...." It was the answer to my dreams, the vision I'd been chasing ever since I'd first drawn that thin red line on my bedroom map.

The fog enveloped us. The air got thinner, and we had to stop every few steps to breathe. The hours ticked by. At last, the layers of mist parted and we saw a huge cairn of stones and just beyond it, a yellow metal cross. We'd reached the top.

The cairn was a tribute to the Inca gods. Travelers who passed this way knew to toss a rock onto the pile to placate the mountain deities and beg safe passage down the other side. The cross was a vain attempt by the Catholic Church to turn a pagan site into a holy one, after centuries of preaching had failed to wipe out the ancient ways. We dropped our stones and carried on.

Once we'd crested the pass I felt my chest expand, as though the air had suddenly been thickened with oxygen. It was practically all downhill from here, and Chuck was looking good. We hiked a few more hours and then took shelter in a tumbledown hut for the night. I gathered up an armload of llama dung in the futile hope that a thorough treatment with gasoline might dry out the sodden little balls and provide a merry fire. Not a chance. Our combined backgrounds in economics and computer science didn't begin to match a farmer's practiced hand.

We rose early and continued down the ancient road, secure in the knowledge that we were no more than six hours from its end. We even stopped briefly at a small waterfall for a invigorating bath. By 2:00 p.m. we hadn't reached the halfway village, and I was beginning to get concerned. "Who told you it was a 12-hour hike?" I asked John. "Wolfgang," he replied. The owner of the jeep. I'd met him once; he was over 50, and overweight. He had probably never been on this trail before. I increased our pace. By 4:00 p.m. I knew exactly where we were—in trouble. Chuck was starting to flag. "How much faster can you go?" I asked him.

He thought for a moment. "I'm at 97 percent," he said. "I can go to 103."

I showed John the map. "Can you go ahead and try to catch Don Rene before he decides to go home?" I asked. "I'll follow with Chuck."

John shook his head. "I'm tired. Don Rene'll wait."

"Can we at least divvy up Chuck's pack? He's absolutely beat."

John shook his head again. "I've got enough to carry."

I took what I could from Chuck. "I'm going after Don Rene," I told him. "We'll never make it to Challa—the pickup point—by 6:00." I jogged off down the trail.

Two hours later I staggered up a long steep hill. Several children watched me impassively from the doorway of a farmer's hut.

"Is this Challa?" I asked breathlessly.

The little girl shook her head.

"How far?" I asked.

"Two hours," she said, then looked me over and reconsidered. "Three."

That didn't seem possible. I checked my map. That would put us...ouch. I wasn't sure Chuck would even make it up that last hill, let alone two hours beyond that. I stashed my pack and went back for him.

He was deathly white and breathing hard, though still gamely putting one foot in front of the other as he struggled up the hill. Encrusted salt had grayed the roots of his bushy beard. His eyes were guttered. They had that inward look of the very old who live among their memories. He was aging before my eyes.

I waited until we were at the top to break the news to him. "Two more hours," I said. "Bolivian pace. That's at least three for us."

It was already past 6:00. If I kept jogging I could get to Challa before eight. Chuck was concerned about separating with darkness coming. I wasn't too happy about leaving him behind. If John was unwilling to take some of Chuck's pack, then what would happen if he had to stop and camp for the night?

But more than anything, I was ashamed. Chuck had trusted me enough to take a leap of faith into the unknown—a country where he didn't speak the language and a trek into the remote and rugged wilderness. I had promised him pack animals and provided none, dragged him over a pass that he wasn't ready for. I had miscalculated the length of the trail and hired an unreliable driver who might or might not be there to pick us up. This sort of thing had happened to me before, but I'd never had to ask a friend to pay the price. Chuck looked utterly miserable. I wanted more than anything to have a car waiting for him in Challa, to whisk him back to a comfortable bed in La Paz and a hot meal. I wanted to redeem myself.

I argued him into letting me go on ahead. He placed his trust in me—again. This time I wasn't going to let him down.

I slung my pack onto my shoulders and said good-bye. Once out of sight, I settled into a slow trot that was tolerable going downhill, aching on the flats, and needle sharp when gravity got in the way going uphill. Twilight faded as I turned away from the river and began the last long climb up the mountainside to the distant twinkling lights above me. I was in a desperate, slow-motion race against the clock. I was sure that Don Rene wouldn't wait past 8:00 p.m.—and that was just 30 minutes away.

I reached the first row of houses on the dot of eight and was greeted by those tireless sentries of a pre-television age—a ragged knot of kids. I immediately offered a scandalous amount of money to the first child who could find a balding older man in a mustard yellow jeep. They scattered like mice, picking up more searchers as the news spread. Within 15 minutes they were back. Yes, the gray-haired man had been in town earlier that the day. No, he was no longer around. The oldest girl suggested that we visit the local telephone exchange—a single line that ran out to a police control booth some 20 minutes outside of town. They would have a record of both Don Rene's arrival and departure if indeed he had returned to La Paz.

The young man in charge of Challa's only telephone looked down in surprise as I lay flat on my back on his filthy wooden floor while waiting for the call to go through. He politely handed the headset down to me. Yes, Don Rene had come through on his way to Challa at 6:40 p.m. He had clocked out on his return to La Paz about an hour later. Just long enough to buy himself a potatoes-and-sausage dinner and inquire casually if anyone had seen three gringos. Apparently he'd ignored several suggestions that he drive down the same steep hill I had just staggered up. I lay on the floor of the phone exchange, thinking evil thoughts.

But he was gone and wasn't coming back. The next order of business was to find Chuck and John. I spread the word among the village men that I was putting a price on two foreigners—five dollars for anyone who went out to look for them. Twenty for bumping into them. One hundred for carrying their backpacks and guiding them back to Challa. The basketball game came to an abrupt halt. I was immediately surrounded by swarthy young Aymara men, all clamoring for a description of my friends. They sorted themselves into groups of five—two were too few, they said, to protect them against the spirits that preyed on nighttime travelers.

Five teams headed down the mountain. I reserved a couple of rooms at a boarding house, then ordered some food at the local eatery. I had already been in Challa for an hour and a half. Chuck and John couldn't have fallen that far behind me. Surely they would turn the corner any minute and stumble into town.

An hour later the first of the search teams returned empty-handed. Two men fitting their description had been spotted at the bottom of the mountain some 30 minutes ago. They had apparently continued on along the river and disappeared. They're lost, I thought. Wandering around somewhere in the Bolivian jungle. A silent wail rose up and clogged my throat. *What have I done?*

Other teams were coming in. I sat down with the searchers and scratched out maps in the dirt, struggling to understand their mix of broken Spanish and Aymara dialect.

By now it was nearly midnight. I rotated teams along the roads into town and sent another group to scout the river trail. Chuck and John had almost certainly bedded down for the night. The searchers might already have passed them a dozen times without knowing it.

"Call out CHUCK and JOHN while you're walking," I told the men.

"Fuck Anon," one of the men said.

"Forget it. Try NATIONAL GEOGRAPHIC." I repeated it slowly.

"Natunal Jeomaic."

We tossed it back and forth until they more or less got it right. I told them it was a powerful incantation against the spirits, in case they got tired of calling out the words. I could hear them shouting at the top of their lungs as they headed back down the hill.

I bought candy bars at the local dry goods store and, rather hopelessly, a plate of hot fried potatoes at the stand. Then I went to a lookout point over the valley and sat down in the persistent drizzle to wait.

At 2:00 a.m. the last of the search teams straggled back. The consensus was that the two gringos had continued down the river path and were somewhere along the trail.

I sat on my crumbling balcony long after everyone had gone to bed, two candy bars and a bottle of cola on the ground beside me, willing them to appear.

The search resumed with the first light of dawn. Word of the two foreigners and their plight had long since spread throughout the village. When the normally reserved Aymara women passed me on the village stairs, they smiled and said, "Your friends will show up soon."

At last, at 10:00 a.m., the wife of one of the searchers came racing down the steps, her pigtails flying. "They found them!" she cried out, and was greeted with a great bear hug. "They are down by the river. They will be up in less than an hour."

I planted my elbows on the edge of my balcony. Children stared down the path as though watching TV, and even the women found reasons to glance up from their chores. By the time Chuck and John turned the corner, the entire village was waiting for them.

It didn't take long to figure out where they had gone wrong. After missing both turnoffs to Challa, they had wandered into a small power plant and spent the night in one of its storage rooms. The next morning they were already on their way back up the river when the searchers intercepted them and brought them to me. By the time I'd heard all of this Chuck was happily prone on his sleeping bag, sucking down a soda and a candy bar.

"I hate to do this and...no promises anymore but...if you can walk up two flights of stairs, then there's a good chance you'll be in La Paz by 6:00 p.m.," I told him. "There's a bus leaving in an hour."

While they were packing, I made my rounds of the village to thank the searchers and their families. Everyone seemed genuinely pleased that things had turned out all right. The children swarmed around me and grabbed my hands. Old men tipped their hats and grinned toothlessly. The owner of the dry goods store handed me free soft drinks for the weary wanderers, and the police control called through the telephone exchange to make sure they had been found. The entire village had come together to help a stranger in need. I felt a pang of sadness that I would probably never see this place again.

It wasn't until near noon the next day that I inventoried my equipment and realized that my Nikon was missing. I knew instantly where I'd left it—in the ticket office in Challa. I called through the telephone exchange and, when no one answered, hired a driver to take me back to the village. For the last hour of the ride I prepared myself for the expected outcome. The camera was insured. I could make do with an Instamatic for the remainder of the trip. The Nikon was worth five years' income to the average farmer—I couldn't blame them if it disappeared. Still, when we finally reached Challa, I found myself plunging down the steps, hoping desperately....

The woman behind the counter looked at me blankly for a moment. My heart missed a beat. Then her face lit up in recognition. *"Karina!"* she said. "How are the two gringos? Better now? You left this behind." She pointed at my camera bag in the corner. "I put it here to keep it safe until you came back."

I hugged her, long and hard. She smiled.

CHAPTER 21

THE TRAVELER

FIELD NOTES: Once word gets around, I doubt that anyone will ever visit me again.

I t was a misshapen monstrosity, layered with blankets and bloated with flowers. A large plastic Christ child stood on the hood. Twenty stuffed armadillos crawled over the rear window and scuttled down the trunk. The priest seemed not to notice, flicking water here and there with an old shaving brush and muttering prayers under his breath.

We were in Copacabana for the annual blessing of anything on wheels, from trucks to tricycles. Chuck had two days left before boarding his plane for home; I wanted him to know that there was more to Bolivia than remote jungle, narrow roads, and high mountain passes. And this festival—with its Catholic overtones and pagan underpinnings—was a perfect example of how Bolivia had managed to bring its two conflicting worlds into apparent harmony.

An unruly fleet of vehicles groaned under a veritable mountain of flowers and bright paper offerings. Some trucks had come from as far away as Sucre—a 12-hour journey—to get a blessing that would ensure an accident-free year.

All around us dancers swirled, dressed in masks and long pleated skirts, sweeping across the square in rhythm to the mesmerizing beat. We wove gingerly through the wild throng, past stout women doing brisk business in beer despite the early hour, and into the main church. The raucous celebration faded, replaced by the single, solemn voice of a Catholic priest reciting mass. Several hundred faithful packed the pews in reverent silence. Incense floated skyward from the swaying lamp in the priest's hand. Several black-robed women—blood cousins to the beer-drinking dancers outside—knelt near the nave with flowers in their hands. Tears ran down their cheeks. It looked like a thoroughly modern Catholic ceremony—until I glanced toward the back of the church and noticed a fringe of feathers and a skull grinning back at me. Gradually I picked out other costumes—a man in leopard skin and buffalo horns, four young ladies in silver body sheathes and the shortest skirts I'd ever seen. The back three pews were peopled with the kind of crowd guaranteed to make a cleric's heart skip a beat.

The priest seemed not to notice. When he finished the mass, his flock came forward, clutching their skulls and skins. They took the wafer, crossed themselves, and walked backward to the door. Once they were outside, they put on their masks and joined the drunken crowd cavorting in the streets.

I waited until the church had emptied and the priest came out.

Did it bother him, I asked, that some of his parishioners showed up at mass dressed in devil suits?

"Not at all," he said. "We each celebrate the Lord in our own way. There is no conflict. As a matter of fact," he grinned, "I'll be dancing with my troop shortly—the Tinku." A peculiar dance, based on pre-Christian rituals, where the male and female dancers carried whips and flailed each other mercilessly. The priest fingered the end of the rope that cinched his robe. "No conflict at all."

Taking our cue from the easygoing clergyman, we threw ourselves into the revelry. We lit homemade firecrackers, downed bongs of beer to the chanting of the crowds, and followed the inevitable statue that made its way around the central square. I remembered how welcome the people of Latacunga had made me once I joined the Mama Negra festival. If only Chuck could have the chance—just once—to take that step from tourist-spectator to full participant. But then, he'd been in Bolivia for all of a week and spoke only a smattering of Spanish. Perhaps next time.

When night fell we headed back to our tiny hostel. I went straight to bed, pleading a rebellious stomach from too much beer and street-side meat. Chuck hesitated, then pulled out his flute. "I think I'll go back outside for a little while," he said.

"Are you going to play with one of the bands?" I asked. He was a skilled musician and could play variations on a tune he had heard only once.

"No," he said, fingering his instrument wistfully. "I'll probably just listen."

I didn't see him again until late that night. By that time word had already filtered back—he had been spotted piping merrily at the center of a backstreet band, tossing the melody back and forth with other players, sharing a common language in an unfamiliar land. He bounded into my room bubbling over with joy, happier than I had seen him since he first arrived. He described the evening, the company, that feeling of universal comradeship, and laughed at how easy it had been. I saw immediately that he had changed. Perhaps he was standing a little straighter, or was just slightly more at ease. He had opened a door into another world. He would, if not today or tomorrow then someday soon, walk through it. He had become a traveler.

CHAPTER 22

COCAINE

FIELD NOTES: Two shots rang out. "We've been spotted," the lieutenant said.

"Tomorrow morning, six o'clock," I repeated into the phone and said good-bye. A casual comment at the police checkpoint had grown into a possibility which, accompanied by a slew of letters, faxes, and phone calls, had unexpectedly become reality. John and I were going deep into Bolivia's eastern Amazon—the center of the country's huge cocaine-making industry—to join the Bolivian special forces on a drug patrol.

Cocaine. It was the final chapter of a story that began 1,000 years before Columbus set foot in the New World. Evidence of coca leaves have been found in virtually all ancient Indian cultures from Argentina to Colombia. When the Inca first conquered the Andes, they systemized its production and controlled its use. When the chronicler Cieza de León arrived in 1547—14 years after the Spanish conquest—he noted that "All through Peru it was and is the custom to have this coca in the mouth; they keep it in their mouths from morning until they go to sleep. Now all labor in the sierra is geared to it; if it did not exist, Peru would be very different."

The discovery of cocaine and its eventual prohibition forced the Andean governments to face the near impossible task of wiping out the production of cocaine while maintaining intact an ancient custom that forms the very foundation of their indigenous society and identity. And it was in Chaparé, where we were heading, that the battle against "illegal" coca-leaf production was being waged.

There was a certain amount of risk, of course. The narcotics people had been quite clear about that. On the other hand, it was the best—and safest—way to witness a critical step in the production of street cocaine. Chaparé grew enough coca leaves to produce one quarter of the world's cocaine. It was also jam-packed with jungle labs that churned the coca leaves into almost a million pounds of pasty-white cocaine. Although it was impossible to prove, drug enforcement sources estimated that more than two-thirds of Bolivia's informal gross national product was derived from the production of cocaine.

All of which led to the "Dignity Plan"—the Bolivian government's campaign against drug use and trafficking with the declared objective of eliminating illegal coca-leaf production by the year 2002. The plan is to declare war on drug production while introducing substitute crops such as citrus trees, banana, hearts of palm, and pineapple. Thus far their efforts have met with limited success.

The main Inca Road out of La Paz led deep into the heart of the Colla-suyu—the vast southern quarter of the Inca Empire. Once we reached the fertile green bowl of Cochabamba, on the eastern slope of the Andes, we settled down to await the Bolivian military truck that would take us east, into the trackless jungle.

Two days later we pulled into a nameless military base in the middle of the untamed jungle. I sat outside the commandant's office, watching a line of soldiers stretched flat out on the ground, staring down their rifle sites with coins balanced on the muzzles of their M-16s. An instructor walked back and forth behind them. The guns were pointed directly at the camp museum. Once practice was over I slipped inside.

Tables groaned under enough confiscated booty to make the lieutenant on the Death Highway smile for a year. False-bottomed shoes with off-white, gooey soles. Sardine cans and cookie tins and thermoses still sloshing with fake coffee. Irons and televisions and suitcases. There seemed no end to the places one could hide a doughy lump of paste. Several old bicycles sprouted long white salamis in place of inner tubes. An entire wall was lined with a large piece of plywood, painted olive green and creaking under the weight of confiscated guns. Pistols and revolvers, a shotgun or two, and automatic weapons.

A soldier waved me to the door. The patrol was ready to leave. Ten men, all armed to the teeth, stood near a pickup. As we were loading up, several other patrols pulled out, their flatbeds bristling with men and guns like defiant porcupines. A helicopter clawed its way into the air and disappeared behind a wall of jungle canopy.

Our patrol roared out of the central square and turned onto a bumpy single track. Half an hour later we came to an abrupt stop in the middle of nowhere. The soldiers clambered out and checked their weapons, then pointed out a spindly log laid over a small stream and a footpath disappearing into the dense undergrowth. One by one the men were swallowed up by the tangled leaves.

I plunged into instant twilight. Branches and vines wove wormholes through the gloomy tentacles of green. The heat was a grasping, sucking, life-depleting parasite. The bugs formed fuzzy domes around our heads. The soldiers moved at military pace—almost four miles an hour. The sweat left slug trails along my ribs. We slowed only to negotiate the frequent swamps, to wobble over rotting logs and slog through murky water. After an hour of hard going, we broke out into a field with a half dozen straggly coca plants fighting for space amid the rapidly returning jungle growth. The soldiers slowed, milled about, and sat down for a smoke. I waited, slapping at the stinging gnats, wondering what we were doing in this godforsaken place. I asked one of the soldiers.

"We patrol all the paths," he said with a shrug, and took another drag of his cigarette.

An image of Bolivia appeared before my eyes. Chaparé was the enormous green stain on its eastern flank. Thousands of square miles of impenetrable jungle. This is ridiculous, I thought as we began our long trek back. An exercise in futility. I'd be surprised if they found a single wad of well-chewed coca leaf this way. I asked the lieutenant how many labs they burned down a year this way. "About twelve hundred," he said.

After two more unsuccessful forays into the jungle, I began to understand their method. They were still searching for a needle in a haystack, but it was a calculated search. The lead soldiers kept an eye open for footprints, bent leaves—any sign of recent passage. Because the farmers carried heavy sacks of coca leaves, their boots made unusually deep imprints in the mud. A typical jungle lab required several hundred gallons of water and was therefore almost always built near a stream. Firm, flat ground was also at a premium. Sites near established coca fields dramatically reduced the distance needed to haul the leaves—better still if it was also near a road, since the paste-making process used a significant amount of diesel fuel. All this meant that the best sites tended to be used again and again, even after the military knew where they were. It was a calculated game of chance—a few labs sacrificed to the government patrols, allowing the majority to slip through.

The soldiers were neither enthusiastic about their jobs nor averse to the endless jungle treks. They were in it for the long run, like a postman delivering mail. Nobody complained when lunchtime slid by. Nor did they seem bothered by their sodden clothes or the rings of dead bugs that had drowned in the sweat around their necks.

We'd been underway since shortly after dawn. I watch the sun settle on the western horizon with increasing resignation. Just as I'd given up all hope of finding a lab, I heard the lieutenant's radio crackle. For the first time there was urgency in the static-filled voice on the other end of the line. One of the other patrols had struck white gold.

We scrambled back to the truck and drove like fiends along the one-lane road. Another patrol pulled in behind us and again the radio spoke. A second strike. We reached another trailhead and got out, moving quickly along the overgrown footpath. Half an hour later we were still plunging along a narrow trail that wriggled through the jungle, jogging past coca fields and clawing our way up steep ravines. Two shots rang out.

"We've been spotted," the lieutenant said. We redoubled our pace. A mile farther on we stopped abruptly. One of the soldiers hauled a 60-pound bag of coca leaves out of the bushes. A few meters farther we discovered two more, dumped by the drugmakers in their haste to get away. We were getting close.

Somehow I'd been expecting a scene straight out of Hollywood: a high-walled country estate with sophisticated surveillance equipment and an army of stone-faced guards with ammo belts draped across their naked chests. And inside, some pockmarked Mafia boss living in splendor while casually dispensing death and drugs. What I found was a long rectangular pit, ringed in plastic and filled with decomposing coca leaves. The whole thing stank like pig manure.

The lieutenant explained the paste-making process while his men tore down the plastic canopy. The coca leaves were dumped into the pit, along with 900 liters of water and sulfuric acid. The farmers then began to "dance"—stomp back and forth on the leaves—in order to leach the alkaloid into the water. This lab, he said, probably had about 16 sacks of leaves in it, enough to make two kilos of raw cocaine.

"Do they use boots?" I asked. Just standing near the toxic fumes was like rubbing sandpaper across my eyes. He shrugged. "When they have them." From the hasty footprints in the mud, these farmers were not among the lucky few.

The alkaloid-laden water was then siphoned off into a large container. They tossed in cement and stirred vigorously. Eighty liters of diesel fuel went into the toxic brew. Eventually the mixture separated into three layers. The cocaine-laced alkaloid was tested with a drop of potassium permanganate. If it coagulated, then it was ready for its own bucket. A dash of bicarbonate of soda, more whisking, and it was filtered through a piece of cloth. The resulting damp white powder—sulfate of cocaine—was packed up and found its way to the border of Brazil or Argentina, where it was further refined into the cocaine powder that would eventually hit the streets.

We had caught these guys in mid-act. In their haste to get away, they had left behind almost 50 liters of diesel fuel. We poured it over the coca leaves and set them alight. I wondered if their former owners were hiding anywhere nearby.

We watched it burn. "What time of year do you find the most labs?" I asked casually.

"Christmas," the lieutenant said. "And carnival. That's when they need money to buy presents for their kids." It was a bitter-sweet victory.

CHAPTER 23

THE DEVIL'S DANCE

FIELD NOTES: I limped out to the starting line—red paint on my lips, false eyelashes, miniskirt, leather boots, high heels...and horns.

Three hours west of Cochabamba, in the foothills of central Bolivia, lies the city of Oruro. At 12,153 feet, it is higher than La Paz. Oruro began life as a silver mining town in 1606. By the 1800s production had declined and the city was virtually abandoned. It got its second chance in the early 20th century with the increasing world demand for tin and copper. Lately, falling metal prices have laid off droves of miners, many of whom have immigrated to Chaparé to grow illegal coca leaf.

Oruro is the only major city in the southern altiplano. Ninety percent of its inhabitants are pure Indian and refer to themselves as *quirquinchos*—armadillos. They are equally impervious to the biting altiplano winds and the soft and buttery foreigners who gasp for air and shrivel up with cold when nighttime settles like an icy blanket over Oruro's streets.

Except one week a year. In early February Oruro throws open its doors to one and all in an extravagant celebration of Andean folklore, mythology, deities, and tradition.

Carnival was still nine days away and already Oruro was teeming with a rather unusual crowd—mushroom-shaped dancers with wobbly, eight-foot umbrella hats; tar-faced men with fake fruit hanging from their necks and ears; and rubber-lipped trombone players wrapped in python loops of brass tubes. Hotel prices doubled, then doubled again. Receptionists became surly and vague. Shop owners secretly stockpiled balloons and shaving cream.

Oruro boasts the second-largest dance festival in all of South America. But it is far more than just a celebration—it is a re-creation of historic mythology, a living, moving lesson in Bolivia's past. In the age-old oral tradition of an Andean society that never developed a written language, it is a way to remember one's roots.

And what a tale it told. The entire history of Bolivia was stitched into the fabric of the Oruro parade. The Morenada dancers represented the forced marches of the African slaves who were put to work in the mines. The Caporrales were their Spanish slave drivers. Amazon warriors drew a big crowd. Aymara weavers had their own troops, as did the Inca. Sikuri dancers gyrated beneath enormous hats decked out with rhea feathers. Bears and condors shuffled past at intervals, and there were even a few of the despised colonial lawyers and their secretaries. And there were the Diablada. Wrapped in elaborate masks that writhed with everything from snake's-head dragons to bat-eared tarantulas, the thousand-strong Diablada troops represented hell's invasion of Earth. Once they reached the central square, they performed a skit derived from a 16th-century Spanish sacramental play—the battle of St. Michael the archangel against the devil and his seven deadly sins. With the predictable victory of good over evil, the dancers shed their masks and shuffled into the Church of the Virgin of Sovacon to hear mass.

The vast pageantry of Oruro's yearly festival did not come cheap. Twenty-five thousand dancers joined troupes and practiced for an entire year. The more elaborate costumes cost more than $1,500 dollars each in a country that has one of the lowest per capita incomes in the Western Hemisphere. What made people invest such vast amounts of time and money into a one-day spectacle?

"The dances are designed to harmonize the mind and the body," an old man watching the preparations told me. He was grizzled and gray haired and had come to the Oruro festival for the past 20 years. He spoke Spanish and English and Aymara. He believed in God and Mother Earth and had read Plato and Joseph Campbell. "The dancers are participating in the balance of power between the indigenous deities and the Christian God," he continued. "That is why, at the end of the parade, they remove their pagan facades and repledge their allegiance to the Catholic faith."

I didn't realize that the entire festival was so carefully choreographed—an elaborate folktale to revalidate the existing social order. Just like the Inca had forced everyone to celebrate their sun god Inti.

The old man shook his head. "The folk story is for entertainment. The reenactment of the myth is for spiritual instruction. Those who participate in the festival die to their flesh and are born to their spirit." He paused and looked at me. "You must dance to understand."

I found the man in charge sitting behind his desk, utterly unruffled despite a huge crowd of supplicants with a hundred last-minute needs. The festivities began at 7:00 a.m. on Saturday morning and ran through Sunday night, he told me. Spectator stands were being erected along the path of the parade and windows boarded up. A monumental effort, it seemed. I felt ashamed just asking to participate in such a grand event.

"No problem," he said, and wrote a message to the chief of police, who headed up one of the lesser-known devil troupes.

I flew down the stairs with the precious note in my hand. A long shot, but you never knew....

"It would be our pleasure," the police chief said. "You'll need a costume." He personally escorted me to a mask-maker's shop.

The masks were magnificent—dozens of them, marching across the floor in orderly rows of twisted horns and bulging, dinner-plate eyes. I tried on the biggest one of all, with layered dragons and a tarantula clinging to each ear. It weighed 14 pounds and rested almost entirely on the bridge of my nose. After two minutes I felt like I'd run headfirst into a street pole. The owner took me by the elbow and led me gently away. That kind of mask, he said, was worn only by the men. I would need a female mask, much more delicate and petite.

Next we hightailed it to the costume maker. I had hoped to sew the dress myself over the ensuing week, but one look at the bevy of young girls laboriously stitching thousands of pieces of glitter onto yards of cloth quickly disabused me of the idea. Angelina, the owner of the shop, was also the chief outfitter for our troupe. "Red or yellow hair?" she said, measuring me from the hips to the collarbone. She held up a ridiculously short skirt and flourished a pair of knee-high stiletto boots. "You're kidding," I said. I hadn't worn heels like that since...well, ever. We started trying on boots. Nothing fit. My feet, it seemed were anything but petite. She promised me a proper pair by the following week, told me to show up promptly for practice, and shooed me out the door. I was in the festival.

By dawn the next morning I was already on the street, wreaking havoc among my beleaguered troupe. I had exactly one week to learn a year's worth of steps. Angelina arrived with a whistle already clenched between her teeth and ran me through my paces. One-two-three left, one-two-three right. At odd moments the two lines of dancers would loop back on themselves and skip around in a wide circle, kicking up their heels. One-two-three, one-two-three. A man with angel wings stopped briefly to crank up my elbows and elevate my chin. One-two-three, one-two-three. We bumped up against the musicians in front of us and did our steps in place. We were sandwiched between two brass bands—held hostage to the tuba players, who were engaged in an epic struggle to blow air through narrow pipes while hauling their heavy instruments across town at 12,000 feet.

Within an hour I was little better off myself. The thin air left me gasping like a landed fish. I barely managed to kick up my heels whenever the whistle blew to do those intermittent prancing steps. The man with angel wings kept a finger under my elbows and Angelina watched my feet.

It could have been worse. The Morenada dancers were dancing in what looked like layers of oversize lampshades. They were so constricted that they couldn't reach their own faces to wipe off the sweat. The Tobas women all looked like Pocahantas and their men wore nose plugs. The Negritos really had it tough, each dressed in a huge sombrero, orange pantaloons—and a ball and chain.

I slipped away just before the mass and limped back to my room. Four and a half hours at 12,000 feet in full costume. What had I gotten myself into?

John had been unusually pensive all afternoon, impervious to the vibrant costumes of the dancers during their practice parade. It took most of the evening before he would tell me why.

"My mother's about to have surgery—for stomach cancer," he said.

I was surprised he'd stayed around long enough to tell me face-to-face. I would have been on a plane the minute I heard the news. "When are you leaving?"

He thought about it for a moment. "It's not going to happen for a couple of weeks. I'll keep calling and see how it goes."

His mother must be nearly 70 years old. I started to say something, then held my tongue. I looked at his familiar gray eyebrows and aquiline nose and realized suddenly that I didn't know this man at all.

As the week went by Oruro looked more and more like a children's fairy tale—men wandering around in wooly bear suits and flocks of women dressed like glittering disco balls. I went in search of Angelina to make sure my king-size boots had come through.

"Panty hose," she said. "And lipstick. Be here tomorrow morning at 6:00 a.m."

In theory I had nothing against panty hose. In fact, I used them all the time—to filter dryer lint, prop up tomato vines, strain gasoline, and catch bugs. I just couldn't see the point of enclosing the lower half of my body in them. But then, who knew what eagle-eyed Angelina might do if I showed up hose-free. I bought a pair.

Five-thirty in the morning and the streets were a nightmare of shadowy devils with bulbous, bloodshot eyes and shuffling transvestites with brightly rouged faces and whips. I dressed quickly at Angelina's shop: an absurdly short black skirt, layers of glittery breastplates, El Zorro's cape, cascading locks of flame-red hair—and boots. Pointy monstrosities, with heels narrow enough to pick a lock. I tried them on. My toes converged in the downhill end. They screamed when I tried to force the rest of my foot into the negligible space that was left behind. Two sizes too small. I tried—unsuccessfully—to stand.

Years of worshiping the Virgin had worn down the inside of each stiletto heel until it angled at 45 degrees. My ankles hadn't sagged like this since my first pair of ice skates. I winced my way over to Angelina.

"Got anything a tad larger?"

She shook her head. She correctly pointed out that this was a dance of penance for the Virgin, and handed me my mask. It was dark purple, with spiral horns and tiny eye slits. I slipped it on. It sat on the bridge of my nose, cutting off what little oxygen was making it through to my lungs, and made me feel like I was trying to see through a slot machine. "Benance," I snuffled, and wobbled to the door.

Not even the miraculous Virgin could make this dance start on time. I shifted my weight from one foot to the other, trying to remember those martial arts films where young men would train for hours standing on some fence post pretending to be a crane. A whistle blew. I limped over to the starting post and we were off.

Spectators lined the road in stands two stories tall. Our troupe was sandwiched between two bands, each playing to an entirely different beat. Every few minutes we would wash up against the musicians in front and either have to dance in place or, at the blast of a whistle, skip snake-like to the back of the line. One-two-three, one-two-three. I counted loudly under my mask as we entered the sphere of influence of the competing band.

An hour later I could still see a candy wrapper back at the starting line. Three miles to go. I found myself eyeing a small hole in the stands and wondering if my dance troupe—nearly a thousand strong—would miss one more thick-lashed she-devil with bright red hair. I was beginning to realize the one great disadvantage to being a part of the parade. Twenty-five thousand dancers in exotic costumes and all I could see was the back of the tuba player in front of me and the occasional pudgy angel with a dissatisfied look on his face.

My blisters had popped and glued the panty hose to my feet long before we hit the final hill below the church. The steep gradient compensated for my high heels; I was once again walking on level ground. "Kick up your feet!" Angelina shouted, and the whistle bleated shrilly. We danced up the hill. And down. And up and down and up. We trotted around and around like thoroughbred horses, red hair streaming out behind us. After several loops, I heard the whistle blast again and there, ahead of me, was a great white cross. I'd never been so happy to see a church in my life. I joined the long line of sweat-soaked devils waiting to greet the priest and limped inside.

A mass was going on. A line of bear's heads filled a pew and a young man clutched a tiny infant who had, it seemed, slept through the entire dance. A row of fancy young ladies could have been at a wedding but for the shiny scorpions stitched to their dresses. I looked around and noticed a host of other creepy-crawly creatures—vestiges of the original myth that inspired Oruro's festival.

According to the legend, the Virgin of the Socavon descended from heaven to convert the local Indians. All went well until her newly catholicized flock ceased making sacrifices to their former deities. The spurned gods grew jealous and sent a tide of giant lizards, ants, and scorpions against the hapless Indians. The Virgin came to their rescue. In the epic battle that followed, she cut the heads off the evil mob, turning them to stone. Almost every costume in the procession displayed some memento—a spider, dragon, or snake—of the Virgin's struggle.

When the priest was done, everyone shuffled forward toward the painting of the Virgin. In groups of three and four they crawled slowly past her image. All around me women sobbed softly. Even the men let slip a silent tear or two. They stood and backed away, still crying, clutching crosses at their necks. It wasn't until that moment that I understood. They hadn't been dancing for the spectators, or to show off for their friends. They were dancing for the Virgin, to show their faith. The entire procession was really just a moving act of penance to please her as she gazed down on them. I looked back on the next troupe, just arriving, encased from head to foot in wide round tubes and colored feathers.

Today they'd done her proud.

The dancing went on throughout the afternoon and late into the night. When the last dancers shuffled wearily into the church, a sudden surge of spectators swept me toward the central square. The stands were lined with sodden, bubble-cheeked musicians. Every band was doing its level best to outblast its neighbors. "The battle of the bands!" a young man shouted and handed me a beer. The square was packed with partyers—dancing, drinking, impervious to the blare-off going on around them. Thick-waisted matrons did brisk business in boiled goat's heads and the only drink for sale was beer.

I downed my drink, ate an eye, and then snuck away to prepare myself for the second half of Oruro's carnival—a weeklong, no-holds-barred water fight. I quietly purchased a plastic raincoat, a dozen water balloons, and two cans of shaving cream. I felt confident I could defend myself no matter what should come my way. I stepped out onto the plaza....

And got nailed by 20 water balloons. I tossed one back. Twenty more came hurtling my way. I experimented with the shaving cream, got similar results, and decided that escalation wasn't going to work today.

It took three cans of shaving cream to figure out the rules: 1. Take no prisoners: 2. Hold no grudges: 3. Nail the foreigners. Since there were at least 5,000 Bolivians in the stands around me, it looked like they were following rules 1 and 3 and I was left with rule 2.

But I wasn't the only target in the crowd. Not far ahead of me I saw what looked like a walking advertisement for Ready Whip. I caught up and introduced myself.

"It's just not very British, is it?" The blob of shaving cream replied and rearranged itself into a smile. He offered me an arm. "Shall we go for a stroll?"

"Head high, shoulders straight," he said—and whenever I felt the urge to retaliate, a gentle reminder, "with dignity, my dear."

CHAPTER 24

WHEELS

FIELD NOTES: I had given up hope of finding a ride at the curb when two German motorcyclists pulled up within a few feet of me. I jumped up and hugged them. They were quite surprised. I asked for a lift on one of their bikes. They said yes.

South of Oruro lies a bleak and virtually lifeless wilderness of stark peaks, wind-scoured valleys, and shimmering salt deserts. This is Bolivia's altiplano, where the searing midday sun bubbles the skin and icy needles of night air pierce the lungs. It is a gray land. A gray sky. They meet in the seamless distance that recedes like an endless, mind-shattering mirage. The few hardy souls who choose to inhabit this forsaken land are mostly Aymara Indians who still dwell among their ancestral homes. They carry in their blood the same legendary stubbornness that resisted all Inca efforts at assimilation. The Aymara were the only tribe who refused to speak the Inca tongue and survived.

But their very independence still curses them to a precarious life on the edge of human endurance. They live as miners, farmers, and herdsmen, eking out a grim existence against the howling wind, endless drought, thin air, and bitter cold.

The altiplano is in reality a deep valley filled with 15,000 feet of sediment. By rights it should be richly fertile, but the never ending drought and heavily salted soil have put a blight on all efforts at both agriculture and animal husbandry. The stoic Indians, with characteristic ingenuity, have learned to harvest salt.

Set in a remote corner of southern Bolivia, the tiny town of Uyuni lies along the edge of the great salt flats where tons of the white crystals are carved out of the ground, loaded onto caravans of llamas, and marched 300 miles along the Salt Trail to market. I hoped to find one of these caravans and accompany it for a week or two along the ancient route.

By midmorning I had come across a man called Tito, once the head of Uyuni's bureau of tourism. He offered to take us out to the only farmer, he said, who still used llamas to carry salt across the flats. We quickly rounded up a truck and headed out into the desolate countryside.

We found our caravaneer high up in the rolling, windswept hills. Tito immediately stepped out of the car and spoke to the man in Quechua, describing who we were and what we wanted. I wondered why he wasn't speaking Spanish until I heard him tell the farmer to demand no less than $1,000 a day from me. I looked at the old man's torn trousers and fingerless gloves. I wanted very much to go with him but couldn't possibly meet his terms. We drove home in silence.

If it couldn't be a llama caravan, at least I could explore the famous salt flats by motorbike. One-room tourist agencies lined the central square. Large billboards advertised their SuperDeals! across the desert.

"Motorcycle?" the first man said. "Impossible. But I have a group of eight tourists leaving this afternoon in three jeeps...."

I visited the second, third, and fourth. Two-wheeled transport was not in popular demand. I tried stopping random motorcyclists on the street, to ask where I might rent a bike for several weeks. I even begged my way into the local television and radio stations to ask if they might advertise for anyone with a bike for sale.

By late afternoon I was sitting on the sidewalk outside one of the tourist agencies in utter despair. No motorbikes, no llama trains, and not a single truck willing to make the journey south to Chile in the middle of the rains. For the first time since I started my trip, I was at a loss for what to do.

I heard the sound of motorbikes and looked around, hoping that it might be someone I hadn't already spoken to. Two leather-clad riders turned the corner and pulled up against the curb not ten feet away. Their bikes were piled high with gear, all stored in mud-encrusted panniers that looked like they had been to hell and back.

"Hello," I said. "Do you have room for a passenger?"

The guy nearest me didn't skip a beat. "Sure."

I hugged him.

"If you don't have too much luggage," he added.

Just John and all his gear. "Not much," I said.

I took them out to have a beer and celebrate. They were both from Germany. Martin was a 32-year-old occupational therapist with more hair on his face than on his shiny, sunburned head. He had started in Alaska three motorbikes ago and met up with Andi in

San Francisco on his way to Patagonia. This was, he said with a sheepish grin, probably his last trip. His California girlfriend wanted him to settle down and give up his vagabond life.

Andi was a year older and a social worker. He had been on his way to domestic bliss as well, until a letter arrived for him in Guatemala, informing him that he was now a single man. On the bright side, he hadn't had to replace his motorbike—a sturdy 650 BMW—since the trip began.

The two travelers had met five years earlier, when Martin put an ad in the paper asking if anyone was interested in riding from Germany to India for six months. Andi called, they had a beer or two, and off they went. Five years later they were on their third transcontinental trip.

We agreed that it was hard to watch our friends all getting married and having children and that we would soon have to bite the bullet and settle down. Then we finished off our beers and went out for a ride.

The sun was just dipping toward the horizon as we crossed over into the salt flats. An inch of water covered the snow-white crystals, creating a perfect mirror image of the iridescent clouds. Andi was a rock-solid driver, submitting stoically as I stood and leaned this way and that while snapping photos from the back of his bike. The waters parted before us in rippling waves of reflected fire as we raced toward the bloodred, sinking ball. The brilliant colors weren't just on the horizon, they were all around us, and underneath our wheels, and spreading in our wake. It was the first time I'd ever seen a sunset from the inside.

That night I asked John to fly ahead and meet me in Chile. I would travel with Andi and Martin across the salt flats and pick up another motorcycle on the other side. My own wheels! No more waiting for overcrowded buses or unwieldy mules. The freedom of the road....

But it was not to be. "I called home this afternoon," John told me. His mother had just had her cancer surgery. She was in intensive care with tachycardia. His father had asked him to come home. Unfortunately we were no longer within easy access of La Paz. From where we stood, California was several days away. John might not make it back in time.

He packed his bags and I ran to get tickets on the next train heading for the capital. "Sold out," they said. I waylaid every truck that was heading north, trying to hitch a ride. There were no buses until the next day, and drivers coming down the road warned of washed-out sections and a 20-hour delay. I made an appointment with the train station chief and sat down to plead John's case. He promised to speak to the conductors on our behalf. I saw Andi and Martin just long enough for one last beer and a promise to find each other in Santiago. That night I walked into the train station waving a hundred dollar bill and bought a ticket from another passenger. The second ticket appeared only moments before the train left. We'd made it.

We arrived at La Paz late the next afternoon and divided up our gear. To my surprise, John booked a flight to Peru. His mother was doing better, he told me, and he had some things to take care of in Lima before heading back to the States.

"Are you sure that's a good idea?" I asked, and was firmly put into my place. I asked him to wake me up the next morning to say good-bye, but when the early sunlight fell across my bed, I got up to see that he was already gone.

Practically all of the equipment left with John. Suddenly I was alone with nothing more than a backpack and my little video camera. Two days later I had found a motorbike and was heading for the border of Chile. It was a straight shot down to Santiago—a thousand miles along a desert, with nothing in the way. The purring bike ate up the miles and the mesmerizing yellow line slid by beneath my feet. At last, I had time to think.

CHAPTER 25

THE CHRONICLER

FIELD NOTES: Cieza de León left Spain for the New World at the tender age of 13. For the next 11 years he served as a common soldier, exploring and conquering the tribes of Colombia. He was 26 when he entered Peru for the first time. By then his notes were so bulky that he had to walk so that his horse could carry them.

I came to South America to travel the Inca Road. I brought with me a map with a red line already drawn on it and a suitcase full of photocopied 16th-century Spanish texts that described "the longest and grandest road in the world." I had no idea how much of this stupendous engineering achievement— once "paved with flagstones, bordered by fruit trees, and lined with aqueducts"—had suffered at the hands of modern development, indifference, and war.

In reality the road has left behind a much greater legacy than carved stone blocks and crumbling way stations. It encouraged the spread of Inca culture to the farthest reaches of the empire— customs that thrive to this day. In Huanchaco, they build reed boats with designs that have been passed down from father to son for 1,000 years. In the sacred northern mountains, sorcerers brew hallucinogenic herbal remedies to help their patients—lawyers and doctors and perhaps even a president or two—cross into the spirit world. In the remote Andean highlands hundreds of villagers spread out in human chains to capture the priceless Golden Fleece in a yearly celebration older even than the Inca times. And in every festival, even if it's dedicated to the Virgin, there'll be a witch or two.

The history books have it all wrong. The Inca Empire was never really conquered. It's alive and well.

I had once thought that I was embarking on a "hero's journey"— an odyssey into the unknown, filled with obstacles, success and failure, and newfound knowledge. And so it had been—only I wasn't the hero of this story. I was just the chronicler. The true heroes were the people I met along the way—Buso, who once paddled home with cholera because he had a family to feed. And Willerman, who had left the comforts of a modern city to raise his child in a place he wanted him to be. Anselmo, who would one day stand proudly to receive his father's blessing. Federico's patience and his mile-eating trot....Welby's unshakable good humor amid the million-man Milagros crowds.... And the drunken bullfighter who taught me what courage really was. I had learned about the power of faith—whether in the form of a Catholic festival or a sorcerer's pagan ceremony. I had felt the purest kind of magic at the Mama Negra festival on a night where there were no strangers, only friends. I had learned kindness in the middle of a riot. Nambija had taught me about hope. And so had Ricardo, walking three days and nights along the beach until a mango appeared miraculously at his feet.

They had all stopped for a while to lend me a hand. What I had learned from them would carry me through the weeks to come. As long as their memories stayed with me, this journey would never really end.

FIELD NOTES: Saw three movies back-to-back, ate two hot dogs, and slept 26 hours straight.

It's nice to be home.

An expedition is an iceberg. The people in the field do only a fraction of the work that makes this kind of journey a success. The real credit belongs to the unsung heroes who toil tirelessly behind the scenes. Those who drop everything to answer frantic e-mail requests from a place that must seem as distant—and relevant—as Pluto. Long-suffering folk who let me descend upon their homes with a mountain of gear and who are still steadfastly (and inexplicably) available seven months later to sweep the pieces off the airplane and carry me home. And most of all, those who believed in my dream when I had no more proof than a one-page proposal and the light in my eyes. They had more courage than I'll ever have.

These are my heroes.

My parents, of course. I am a kite and they hold the other end of the string. If they ever let go then I will be lost. They provide the emotional center from which I venture forth. And the home I always come back to. Dave and Cathy Staples at Images Group, Inc., who believed in me long before there was any reason to think I deserved it. Their confidence in me has given me enormous strength to weather the hard times. Peggy Keller—my agent, my friend. There is no one I'd rather have on my side. Rebecca Martin and the National Geographic Expedition Council. She makes dreams come true. I'll never forget the phone call that changed my life. Kevin Mulroy, whose comments were a transforming force in this manuscript. Sponsors provide equipment and sometimes cash, but in my case they gave me something far more valuable. They believed in me enough to put their corporate logos on my expedition—something that kept me warmer than a sleeping bag, tent, or adventure clothing during the long months out in the field. Rick Insley, Senior Vice President of Sales, Marketing and Merchandising at Woolrich, Inc., and Lederle Eberhardt, Women's Senior Merchandise Manager, who provided wrinkle-free, dirt resistant, lightweight clothing that did not dissolve in vicuña spit. Danny Richardson, Mountain Projects Manager at Easton Technical Products, and Sally McCoy, President of Sierra Designs, whose tent hosted everyone from unexpected military guests to remote Andean farmers. Walter Gardiner, President of Imperial Schrade Corp., and Jeff Ahearn, Director of Marketing, whose Multitool™ single-handedly fixed my motorbike in the Chilean desert. The only problem with their Switchit™ Knife was getting it back whenever I lent it to a farmer or a fisherman. Jeff Bowman and Malden Mills who gave me not one, but two Polartec™ Performance Challenge Awards. And Wally Smith of REI who offered corporate financing and excellent equipment in both Asia and South America. Nikon, Inc. who lent me the kind of equipment that most photographers can only dream about. Magellan Systems Corp. who not only made sure I always knew where I was (not an easy feat), but also gave me a satellite e-mail system so that I could "phone home." AlpineAire Foods and Clif Bar, Inc. who kept me and the occasional Andean villagers fed and my vegetarian cameraman alive. Omni Resources whose beloved maps now bear the markings of many a soggy mountain pass. Outpac Designs Limited—their extraordinary backpack security system was single-handedly responsible for the fact that nothing was stolen over 3,000 miles and seven months.

"Just doing their job" doesn't begin to cover the extraordinary lengths some people went to in order to get this expedition off the ground. Jenny Apostol and Maryanne Culpepper, my Knights in Shining Armor, who took on the establishment to make my dream come true. John Armstrong who worked late into the night and still got up to shoot the sunrise the next day. Andrea Nix and Carlyn Gray who solved problems with incredible efficiency and graciousness and were therefore asked to do much more than their share. And the Expeditions staff, with Rebecca Martin at their head: Christina Perry, Jennifer Vernon, Julie Rushing, and Laura-Ashley Allen. They make things happen, they make it look easy, and they're a joy to be around. Antonia for her patience. And Chuck Malloch, for not telling everyone how bad it really was.

Then there are those people that you meet on the road. They have no reason to help a stranger but they do anyway, sometimes going to unbelievable lengths for someone they may never see again. Colonel Ivan Borja, Subteniente Duval Arevalo, Capitan Fernando Iácome, and Marcelino Uyunkar of the EjËrcito Ecuatoriano who took incredibly good care of me. Dr. Martinez and the Consejo Nacional de CamËlidos Sudamericanos who offered me the opportunity of a lifetime—a chance to see a vicuña roundup. PromPeru who provided logistical support and a great deal of useful information. The FELCN & UMOPAR of Bolivia who are fighting the war against drugs with determination and integrity. Jose Koechlin, a refined, intelligent, and generous man who has dedicated his life to Peru. Ashton and Kristy Palmer, for their help in Huanchaco and even more so for their friendship. George Fletcher at the Sierra Madre and his gracious staff, for a mountain of information and much appreciated lodgings. Inti Briones, for three days of high-quality camerawork and a never-ending smile. Jory Angulo Alcoveza, for a remarkably steady hand at the camera and what I hope will be a life-long friendship. Johann Welby Leaman, another natural with the camera—unflappable and untiring despite the long hours and a million people. And the Walker—Ricardo Espinosa. Generous to a fault, kind, and charismatic. I am proud to be his friend. Dr. Juan Domingo Jaramillo who made sure our journey started out right. And Marco Antonio Escobar, one of those rare human beings who gives everything and asks for nothing in return.

Karin Muller